The Place of Revelati

in the Practices of

Christ Apostolic Church, Nigeria,

1930-1994

(Creativity and Dynamism in Indigenous Christianity)

Olusegun Ayodeji Alokan

The Place of Revelations and Healings
in the Practices of Christ Apostolic Church, Nigeria,
1930-1994

(Creativity and Dynamism in Indigenous Christianity)

Revised Edition.
Copyright © 2018 Olusegun Ayodeji Alokan
+234 8034741729

ISBN-13: 978-1508445036

ISBN-10: 1508445036

Published by

CreateSpace Independent Publishing Platform
4900 Lacross Rd, North Charleston, SC 29406
United State of America

DEDICATION

This book is dedicated to:

God;

Oluwaseun Temidayo Obaseki, a servant of God who was born on July 21, 1978 and died on April 22, 2014 in a ghastly motor accident. May his gentle soul rest in perfect peace. Amen!

CONTENTS

FOREWORD

The new book by Dr. Olusegun Ayodeji Alokan, "The Place of Revelation and Healings in the Practices of Christ Apostolic Church, Nigeria, 1930-1994: Creativity and Dynamism in Indigenous Christianity", is an authoritative account on some of the core doctrines and practices of the Christ Apostolic Church, which stands as one of the foremost Indigenous - Aladura - Pentecostal Church in Nigeria today. Moreover, the book is the fruit of many years of scholarly study and painstaking research effort.

Some of the revelations in the book is that not only do the Christ Apostolic Church strongly subscribe to Pentecostal doctrines — baptism, gifts, graces, power, authority and manifestations, and in particular, the two that are highlighted in the book, that is, 'Revelations' and 'Healings', her founders are major contributors to the growth of indigenous Pentecostal Churches (recent religious history) both in Nigeria and abroad. According to the author's bold assertion, which I equally affirm, "the uniqueness of the place and practice of prophecy and prophetic activities in the Christ Apostolic Church has sustained the practices of revelations and healings in the Church." Moreover, the premium placed on spiritual baptism gifts and graces as taught in the Scriptures and to the congregants of the CAC over the years, resulting in the rise of numerous people with spiritual, and, or prophetic gifts among whom the Church has recorded the emergence of prophets and prophetesses since its inception, has greatly projected the CAC as an outstanding indigenous Aladura-Pentecostal-Church in this generation.

It is to the credit of Olusegun Alokan to have carefully brought out in this book, in spite of the possible criticism of abuse, or strangeness or peculiarities often attached to prophetic visionary or the doctrine of spiritual people and, or gifts in general, a substantial defence for the CAC's claim on the doctrine of the Holy Spirit, as well as, its strong demonstration of Pentecostal power, gifts and authority. He has done this clearly and profoundly through practical illustrations drawn from participant observant method, personal interviews, library search and statistical analysis coupled with the fact of an insider knowledge as a second/third generation and a Pastor of long years standing.

The author engages in factual discussion of observable facts, and where necessary drawing comparisons with other similar church groups. His literature bears testimony to this scholarly erudition and which greatly advances the contributions to the religious phenomena, or the objective reality of 'Revelation' and 'Healings' in the Christ Apostolic Church.

This new book is a useful material for anyone seeking to have basic understanding of Pentecostal truths, gifts and demonstrations especially in the CAC. It is written in lucid refreshing and sequential manner and leads the reader to probe further.

Given this background, I strongly recommend the book as a must-to-be-read to all interested persons, Christian and non-Christian— believers alike, educational institutions, students of religious studies, churches, research institutes, libraries, Christian Theologians and religious scholars of other religious faith in the hope of promoting inter-religious dialogue that could in turn forge a sustainable co-existence and mutual understanding in the land.

Professor C.O. Oshun, Lagos

May 2018

ACKNOWLEDGMENTS

First, I give glory, honour and majesty to God, who through His infinite mercy has made this book a reality. This book is a product of many years of research and study. In the process, I have received inestimable assistance from many directions. Primarily, I want to place on record the wonderful cooperation I have received from Professor Bunmi Oshun, the pioneer Vice Chancellor of Joseph Ayo Babalola University, for taking time to go through the chapters of the book and as well for writing the forwarding.

Also, I am grateful to Professor M. A. Ojo the Vice Chancellor of Bowen University, Iwo, Nigeria for his cooperation and assistance at all times. I also appreciate Professor David Ogungbile, David Olayiwola and Professor S.A. Owoeye for their efforts in polishing my academic acumen.

I am greatly indebted to the following people: Late Pastor (Dr) Joshua Adeware Alokan *J.P.* and Mrs Lydia Ore Alokan (my biological parents), Professor Bayo Alokan (Federal University of Technology Akure), Elders Tokunbo, Gboyega, Tunde and Pastor Abimbola Alokan for their moral and spiritual supports.

Finally, I want to thank my sweet-heart, Toyin Alokan for her conviviality and also, my children namely: Ebunoluwa, Gideon Olaoluwa and Ifeoluwa Alokan for bearing with me all the times. Others to be appreciated are: Dr Ariri Chidomere (ex-H.O.D., Department of Religious Studies, Joseph Ayo Bablola University), Professor Richard Olaniyan, Mr O.A. Afolabi, Mr. Chuks Metuonu, Pastor S.F. Babalola and Evangelist D.A. Taye Akintoye who assisted in the computer editing. The Lord shall bless you all abundantly. (Amen).

Olusegun Ayodeji Alokan

PREFACE

This book discusses the spiritual practices of one of the foremost indigenous Pentecostal churches in Nigeria- the Christ Apostolic Church (C.A.C). Many religious scholars have written on the growth, development and practices of the *Aladura* Pentecostal churches particularly CAC but on the whole, there are still gaps to be filled. Based on this fact, the book traces the historical background of the Christ Apostolic Church to revelations and healings as religious practices in the Church by analyzing the oral traditions connected with the prophetic activities of pioneer leaders from 1930 to 1994.

The book further discusses the place of charisma and its connections to revelation and healing in the practices of the Christ Apostolic Church. It also explains the impact of revelations and healings arising from 'changes' in the admninstrative structure of the Church due to the emergent style of modernization and globalization. The book further investigates the crises (schism) in the Church from 1990 to 1994 and their links with practices attributed to revelations and healings. The work therefore analyses the impact of the schism on the spiritual practices in the Church.

The study employs primary and secondary sources of data collection. The Primary source includes materials from the National Archives in Ibadan, and also memos like diaries, correspondences, annual books of reports and minutes of annual conventions from the library of Christ Apostolic Church General Secretariat in Ibadan.

Furthermore, interviews were conducted with 51 purposively selected aged people who were eyes witnesses of the events in the early history of the Church. Moreover, the leadership of the Church with 18 Conferences' Secretaries and 37 Chairmen of some District Coordinating Councils, Senior Pastors and Elders that constituted policy making in the south western Nigeria were interviewed.

In addition, 41 purposely selected youths in the Church were interviewed. A questionnaire was also administered randomly among 300 pastors (District and Zonal Superintendents) that attended the re-training programme at Joseph Ayo Babalola University, Ikeji Arakeji, Nigeria. Secondary data include books, journal articles, newspapers, church bulletins and internet. Data collected were analysed using historical and hermeneutical approaches.

The book reveals that the Christ Apostolic Church pioneering leaders are major contributors to the growth of indigenous Pentecostal churches in the twentieth century and thereafter in Nigeria and abroad. The uniqueness in the works and prophetic activities of leaders in the Church, past and present has sustained the practices of revelations and healings in the Christ Apostolic Church up to the twenty-first century.

In addition, the book discovers that the charisma displayed by the prophets has advertised the Church and assisted in its tremendous spread both in Nigeria and abroad. The work finds out that the CAC crises which had started in 1990 and persisted until 1994 and beyond have its root in the spiritualities in the Church. In the contemporary times, the Church leaders claimed that the crises have been resolved.

The book concludes that the Christ Apostolic Church, in spite of crises and schisms, have continued to expand because of its emphasis on prophecies, visions, dreams, speaking in tongues, prayers and faith healings, which provided solutions to the people's problems.

Olusegun Ayodeji Alokan
Akure, 2018.

CHAPTER ONE

INTRODUCTION

1.1 Historical Background

The Christ Apostolic Church (CAC) has undergone some changes since its inception about one hundred years ago. The changes have occurred as a result of, among other factors, developments in the religious practices of the Church over the years. The phenomena of revelations and healings, though fundamental and indeed the moving engine for the progress of the CAC right from its inception, have also experienced these changes.

The Christ Apostolic Church has been closely associated with *Aladura* Churches since the early twentieth century. Churches that sprang up during this period apart from Christ Apostolic Church which was adopted a new name in 1943, include Cherubim and Seraphim Church (C&S) which was founded by Tunolase Orimolade and Abiodun Akinsowon in 1925; the Church of the Lord (*Aladura*) founded by Josiah Oshitelu in 1929 and the Celestial Church of Christ (CCC) under the leadership of Samuel Bilewu Joseph Oshoffa in 1947 (Ayegboyin & Ishola).[1]

The *Aladura* churches were founded by Africans and run under indigenous leaderships (Omoyajowo).[2] They are characterized by praying, fasting, prophecy, vision, dream and healing. Peel succinctly describes this group as one that

---

[1] Deji Ayegboyin and S. Ademola, *African Indigenous Churches: An Historical Perspective* (Lagos: Greater Heights Publications, 1997), p.90

[2] J.A. Omoyajowo, "The Aladura Churches in Nigeria since Independence." In: Fashola-Luke *etal* (ed.), *Christianity in Independent Africa* (London: Rex Collings, 1978), p.96.

1

emphasizes the efficacy of prayers and fasting to change ugly situations for the better.[3]

The *Aladura*, therefore, believe that God answers prayers and nothing is impossible with fervent faithful prayers and with fasting at all times.[4] They also discourage the reliance of some Christians on medicine (whether traditional or western), and favour divine healing through divine leading or revelation.

By the first quarter of the twentieth century, the *Aladura* churches have attracted many people particularly in Yorubaland. The spirituality and the practice of divine healing have played significant roles in the rapid growth of the denomination. Majority of the early converts of the Aladura Churches were from the Mission Churches. Fashole-Luke discusses the issue of statistics relative to the population of the converts from the mainline churches to the Aladura Churches as follows: about 63% of converts into the CAC and about 66% of converts into the C&S were from the Anglican Church.[5]

The underlying factor for the mass conversion was believed to be revivals, which brought about healings and deliverance of the people through the demonstration of the Holy Ghost power by charismatic leaders who emerged in the early twentieth century. Joseph Ayo Babalola of the Christ Apostolic Church was always remembered for the 1930 revival which swept across the South Western parts of Nigeria. Indeed, from available records, it appears the patriarchs who became the leaders of the Christ Apostolic Church seemed to have laid legacies which the succeeding leaders

---

[3]. J.D.Y.Peel, *Aladura: A Religious Movement among the Yoruba* (Oxford: Oxford University Press, 1968), p.119.

[4]. Ibid, p.119.

[5].Luke Fashole, *etal* (eds.), *Christianity in Independent Africa* (London: Rex Collings, 1978.

built upon in the contemporary period.

Based on the foregoing, this study attempts to examine the position of spirituality in the establishment of the Christ Apostolic Church, Nigeria. It is important to mention that many scholars of religion have written on the emergence of Aladura churches and their leaders in Nigeria; their works serve as useful materials and also as motivation to writers and research students. However, this book is designed to complement the work of these scholars as it traces the historical background of the Christ Apostolic Church and the connectivity to revelations and healings as religious practices in the growth of the Church from 1930-1994.

Also, the book sets out to analyze the oral traditions that are associated with the prophetic activities of the pioneering leaders in the Church from 1930 to 1994. It achieves this objective by discussing the place of charisma of the pioneering leaders and its connections to revelations and healings in the practices of the Church.

The book finally investigates the crises and schisms in the Church from 1989 to 1994 and beyond; and their links with practices of revelations and healings. The study achieves this objective by analyzing the impact of the schisms on the practices of revelations and healings in the Church.

The book therefore has filled some gaps. Previous studies on the Christ Apostolic Church have been mainly on its historical background and activities of its leaders in the building and expansion of the Church. Little attention has been paid on the influence of globalization in the spirituality and religious practices of the Church. Also, there is scanty information on the fundamental factors arising from the sudden changes in the institutional and ministerial practices which have positive and negative impacts on the Church in the twenty first century.This book has filled this gap as it reflects on the changes and the effects on the growth and the divisions that have taken place in the Church.

This book covers sixty-four years in the history of Christ Apostolic Church, beginning from 1930 to 1994. The 1930 is important as a starting point for this study because it marks the beginning of different revivals in the history of the Christ Apostolic Church particularly in the western and northern parts of Nigeria. Such revivals were engineered by prophetic leaders like Joseph Ayo Babalola, Daniel Orekoya and J. A. Adelaja.

In the same argument, the 1994 marks the climax of crises which gradually began in 1989. The study of the crises in this book therefore covers five years (1989-1994) out of the twenty nine years of the crises in the Church (1989-2018). Owing to the scope of this study, the field work has been limited to some assemblies in Ilesha, Efon Alaye, Ibadan and Lagos (in Nigeria); these being the revival spots in the 1930s.

Also, the study focuses on assemblies in Akure, Ibadan, Abeokuta and Lagos (in Nigeria); these being the hot spots for the church crises that ranged between 1989 and 1994. These historic periods would enable readers to have insights into the different events in the CAC from inception and up to date.

However, this book has its limitations. Three main hindrances were encountered in the course of the research. The first is that the diaries and many of the correspondences of the early founders of the Church that were initially intended for this study were not found. This is probably because there was poor knowledge of proper record keeping of these important documents at the local level, especially in regions where most activities pertaining to the history of the Church took place. Such regions include Ilesa, Efon Alaye, Ikare Akoko and Ibadan in Nigeria.

Also, some documents relating to the patriarchs of the Church and information on the formulation of the Church doctrines are available in memoranda and monographs kept at the National Archives in Ibadan and the library at the CAC headquarters, Basorun, Ibadan, but they are scantily documented. Also, information about revelations and healings in the newspapers, CAC newsletters, Year Books are not properly kept in the archives and the CAC Library. This is because only few copies were available.

It is not an exaggeration to mention here that, the internal crises within the Church have divided it into at least three camps, namely: the General Executive Council, the Supreme Executive Council, and the Interim Group (as at time) and the situations have made it difficult to freely gather data for the work.

In spite of these shortcomings, the scholarship of this book is essential because of its relevance to scholarship and the *Aladura* Pentecostal churches in Nigeria. Also, the book is significant because it has revealed the uniqueness in the spiritual practices of the Church which has contributed to its rapid growth and expansion in Nigeria. Furthermore, it also serves as an eye-opener to the understanding of how the schism and secessions in the Church are connected with the practices of revelations and healings.

Finally, the study in this book is significant because it has broadened our understanding to know the importance of spiritual gifts in promoting church growth and establishing members of the Church in the faith.

Methodologically, the book adopted the historical research approach to analyse the genesis of revelations and healings in the development of the Church from 1930 to 1994. Data for this study were collected through the archives and also through oral interviews. In addition, relevant materials for bibliography were got from reputable librarie in Ibadan, Akure and Ogbomoso. The processes are as follows: First, archival materials on the Church at the National Archives in Ibadan, and other records such as diaries, correspondences, annual books of reports and minutes of annual conventions in the library of the CAC General Secretariat at Bashorun, Ibadan, CAC Theological Seminary, Ile-Ife and the Christ Apostolic Church headquarters, Akure were consulted to obtain the history of practices attributed to revelations and healings in the Church.

Second, interviews were conducted with purposively selected aged people, fifty one in number (thirty-eight male ministers and thirteen female ministers), who were eye-witnesses to the extant practices in the CAC, many of which also had direct connections with the founding fathers of the Church.

In addition, forty one youths (thirty three males and eight females) were purposively selected and interviewed to know the positions of revelations and healings in the CAC between 1988 and 1994, which marked the climax of schisms and crises in the Church. The age statistics were between 20 and 40 years. Moreover, the present General Executive Council of the Church, with all eighteen conference secretaries and some thirty seven Chairmen of the District Coordinating Councils which included Senior Pastors and Elders that constitute the policy making body in the Church were also interviewed.

Furthermore, structured-interviews were conducted in CAC assemblies in Akure, Ondo State, Omuo and Ado Ekiti in Ekiti State and Warri in Delta State in order to study the numerical strength of prophets and prophetesses between 1989 and 1991, being the background to the beginning and climax of crises in the CAC. Through the structured questions, interviews were conducted with 44 selected pastors from District Coordinating Councils and

Zonal Headquarters in the study areas.

The processes of the interviews were as follows: In Akure, 16 assemblies that are of the status of District Coordinating Councils and Zonal Headquarters were visited and the chairmen and senior pastors in the assemblies were interviewed during their joint prayer meetings. Similarly, in Omuo and Ado Ekiti in Ondo State, 8 assemblies were visited (each from the two towns). These areas are District Coordinating Councils and Zonal Headquarters. The chairmen and most senior pastors on the assemblies were interviewed. In the same process, interviews were conducted individually with some Chairmen and senior pastors in some assemblies of CAC Warri District Coordinating Council and Zonal Councils. Also, secondary sources such as books, articles in learned Journals, newspapers, Internet resources, etc were consulted.

The data collected were analyzed historically and hermeneutically. The historical method gave a clear picture of the numerical strength of prophets and prophetesses in the CAC assemblies over a period of time. The hermeneutical method of research gave an interpretation of the practices of revelations and healings as a factor of growth and schism in the CAC. It also gave an accurate assessment of leaders, particularly their contributions and weaknesses, in the spirituality of CAC.

1.2 Literature Review

Scholars across the globe have written on churches founded by the Western missionaries in different parts of the African continent. In like manner, a good number of seasoned scholars have written on *Aladura* churches, particularly on the Christ Apostolic Church. Some of these writers have also written on the pioneering fathers and subsequent leaders of the Church, with references to their contributions to the spiritual development of indigenous Pentecostal churches in Nigeria.

In an attempt to justify the need for this work, this study reviews the literature of these writers and their works. The book, therefore, focuses on the writings on Apostolic and indigenous Pentecostal Churches in Nigeria, and the schisms and secessions that occurred in them, which necessitated the need for one to examine the history of spirituality in the Church (CAC).

The literature review under this study is sub-divided into the following: Pentecostalism in Africa; classification of Aladura Churches; distinguishing features of Aladura churches; history and development of the Christ Apostolic Church; persons and personalities in the history and leadership of the Christ Apostolic Church; Christ Apostolic Church and leadership in the modern period; and revelation and healing in Nigerian Christianity.

1.2.1   Pentecostalism in Africa

Nigerian Pentecostal Churches adopted a new style of worship from the beginning of 1970 with the name charismatic renewal or neo-Pentecostalism. From the historical background of new Pentecostal movements in Nigeria, Ojo explains that the Charismatic renewal in Nigeria began at the University of Ibadan in January 1970 with the leaders of the Christian Union who formed the Tuesday Group of those who had experienced the baptism of the Holy Spirit.[6]

The Tuesday Group later metamorphosed into the World Action Team for Christ, and through their activities impacted other students to introduce the new Pentecostal ideas into many non-pentecostal denominations in Nigeria.

[6]. M.A. Ojo, "The Contextual Significance of the Charismatic Movement in Independent Nigeria," *Africa*, Vol. 58. No.2 (1988), pp.179-180.

Ojo points out that the Charismatic Movements began as evangelical revival and later became known as Pentecostal movement in Eastern Nigeria through the influence of the Scripture Union traveling secretaries, Mike Oye and Muyiwa Olamijulo in 1971. The author also mentions the features of the Pentecostal campus movement, particularly in the areas of 'holiness' and the demonstration of the spiritual gifts through speaking in tongues, prophecy and deliverance.

Ojo's writing is on Charismatic Movements and not on the Aladura Pentecostals. The main focus of the writer is on the features of the Charismatic in relations to holiness, evangelistic outreaches and emphasis on speaking in tongues. This study fills this gap by establishing the most important features of the *Aladura* churches and their relevance to church growth and spirituality.

Allan Anderson statistically makes an assertion that 11% of Africa's total population (including the predominantly Muslim north) was 'charismatic' in 2000.[7] The writer mentions that the term 'African Pentecostal' refers to African Churches that emphasize the working of the spirit in the church, particularly with ecstatic phenomena like prophecy and speaking in tongues, healing and exorcism.

Anderson also identifies the variety of Christian churches that are named as Pentecostal churches in Africa. Examples of such are '*Zionists*' in Southern Africa and '*Kimbanguists*' in the Congo. Also, 'spiritual', 'prayer healing' or '*Aladura*' (prayer) churches in West Africa and 'spiritual' or 'Holy Spirit' churches in East Africa. The writer further identifies additional two other types of African Pentecostal, particularly those of western 'classical' Pentecostal origin and new independent Pentecostal or Charismatic

---

[7].Anderson Allan, "Pentecostalism in Africa: An Overview." *ORITA*, XXXVI/1-2 (2004), P.38.

churches.

However, it seems there is a mix-up in the typology of the African history from Allan Andersons' writing. The African history is arranged chronologically according to the record of events. Normally, the typology of African history takes this format, namely: (1) The African Independent Churches (Ethiopian churches, Zionist churches and the Prophet Praying Churches) (2) The Charismatic Churches, and (3) The New Pentecostal Churches.

Nevertheless, the work is an insight into the statistics of records of Pentecostal churches in Africa. Historically, Allan Anderson traces the background of Classical Pentecostal which has been operating in Africa since 1907 (i.e. the Assemblies of God) with about four million members estimated throughout Africa in 1994.[8] According to the writer, most African independent churches are of a Pentecostal type that has contextualized Christianity in Africa.

These churches, to Anderson, have an African expression of the worldwide Pentecostalism because of both their characteristics and their origins. Take for instance, in Nigeria; the 'Aladura' churches are increasing daily because of their spiritual practices especially in the area of healing and prophetic manifestations. This study has taken a step further to investigate the place of spirituality in the Aladura phenomenon

In another write-up, Allan Anderson traces the history and beginning of Pentecostalism and Charismatic Movements from America and Britain in the late nineteenth and the early twentieth centuries.[9] The Pentecostal revival, according to the writer, began

[8] Ibid, p.19

[9].Anderson Allan, *An Introduction to Pentecostalism: Global Charismatic Christianity* (Cambridge: University Press, 2004), pp.103-122.

earnestly in Africa with the manifestation of the Spirit, including speaking in tongues, prophecy, visions and other ecstatic phenomena, and with an emphasis on prayers and confession of sins. However, the intention of the writer is to write on Pentecostal Movements with their classifications from the western World to Africa. There has been no trace of discussion on the practices of revelations and healings in the *Aladura* churches, particularly the Christ Apostolic Church of Nigeria.

In another perspective, Joseph Kenny gives a comprehensive analysis of the uniqueness in the phenomenon of Pentecostalism.[10] According to him, Pentecostalism is a particular idea of prophecy which is found in every religion. From this base, the author examines prophecy as it is found in different strands of Judaism, Christianity and Islam, so as to bring to light how Pentecostalism resembles or contrasts with them.

In comparative observations, the author makes it known to his readers that among the gifts of the Holy Spirit, Catholic theology places priority on those that are relevant to the practice of the moral and theological virtues, which are the measure of the holiness of a person. The author further explains that Pentecostal churches on the other hand, emphasize "holiness" and that this seems to give greater prominence to charismatic gifts, which are taken as a measure of spiritual maturity. On this ground, the writer assumes that Pentecostalism focuses on miracles that assure health, wealth, posterity and prosperity, first of all, for the pastor as an example to others.

In spite of this broad analysis, Kenny's focus is on comparative theological perspectives of Pentecostalism and

---

[10].Joseph Kenny, "Authority in Pentecostalism: Comparative Theological Perspective." In: David O. Ogungbile and Akintunde, E. Akinade (eds.) *Creativity and Change in Nigerian Christianity*, (Lagos: Malthouse Press Limited), pp. 75-78.

orthodox churches. He has neither written to discuss Pentecostal styles in Africa nor about the features and practices of Pentecostal gifts among indigenous churches in Africa or elsewhere.

It is on this note that the study points out the religious practices and spirituality of the mainline churches and the Aladura churches (particularly the Christ Apostolic Church) and their contributions to the growth and establishment of indigenous Pentecostalism in Nigeria

Nkwoka traces the history of modern Pentecostalism from the "Baptism in the Holy Ghost" of the Bethel Bible College students of Topeka, Kansas.[11] He also mentions that the assignment was given by the Reverend F. Parham, a teacher of the holiness movement and former Methodist Church Pastor who founded the College in 1900.

He also discusses the association of Pentecostalism and the Anglican Church. The book complements his work by examining the background of the *Aladura* Pentecostals and its influence on the practices of the mainstream churches, particularly the Anglican Communion which is the focus of the writer.

1.2.2   Classification of Aladura Churches

Omoyajowo classifies the Christ Apostolic Church and the Cherubim and Seraphim under the *Aladura*. He traces the historical background of the *Aladura* Churches to 1918 with the emergence of Diamond Society, the commencement of Faith Tabernacle in Nigeria and the revival of Joseph Ayo Babalola in 1930.

---

[11].A. O. Nkwoka, "Interrogating the Form and the Spirit: Pentecostalism and the Anglican Communion in Nigeria." In: David, O. Ogungbile and Akintunde, E. Akinade (eds.), *Creativity and Change in Nigeria Christianity* (Lagos: Malthouse Press Limited, 2010), pp.79-85.

According to Omoyajowo, the Diamond Society of Ijebu-Ode, the first *Aladura* movement in Yoruba land, came into existence through visions and divine healings of leaders like Joseph Shadare (Esinsinade), Sophia Odunlami, David Odubanjo and J.S.F Odusona.[12]

Omoyajowo differentiates further between the Apostolic Churches that were affiliated with the Faith Tabernacle Congregation and the Cherubim and Seraphim Church which had no record of affiliation with western missionaries. He traces the differences between these Churches (Faith Tabernacle associates and Cherubim and Seraphim Church) from historical backgrounds and doctrinal beliefs.

Omoyajowo explains further that the Cherubim and Seraphim Church differs in a number of ways from the Faith Tabernacle. Such differences could be seen in the organization and doctrines of the churches. Also that, the Faith Tabernacle drew much of its inspiration from foreign organizations. On the contrary, the Cherubim and Seraphim Church has maintained a record of non-alliance with foreign missionary bodies.

These, perhaps, according to the writer, constituted the major differences in doctrine between the Faith Tabernacle and the Cherubim and Seraphim Church. The writer concludes that the Cherubim and Seraphim Church is the only *Aladura* Church of note which did not develop from a Faith Tabernacle background.

Omoyajowo, from all indications, made contributions to knowledge through the use of primary sources in his research work as he highlights the background to the emergence of the two Churches within the *Aladura,* as well as, their similarities and

---

[12]. J. A. Omoyajowo, *Cherubim and Seraphim: The History of an Independent Church* (New York: NOK Publisher, 1982), pp. 122-123.

differences.

However, this book makes a difference as it discovers that it is not only the Cherubim and Seraphim Church which did not develop from Faith Tabernacle background as the writer (Omoyajowo) has rightly pointed out in his work. It must be noted that there are other churches like The Church of the Lord Aladura and the Celestial Church of Christ who have no link with the Faith Tabernacle Congregation.

Also, the book has made it clear that the religious practices in the CAC are extremely different from the Cherubim and Seraphim Church and other Aladura churches. Neverthess, each denomination under this category operates individually and with large crowd.

In the same vein, Adewale holds the view that the *Aladura* churches generally include the Cherubim and Seraphim, the Christ Apostolic Church, the Church of the Lord (*Aladura*), the Celestial Church of Christ, etc. The writer comments further that the adherents of these churches believe solely in prayers and discountenanced the use of medicine, be it traditional or orthodox.[13]

Nonetheless, this book explains the differences in the doctrine of the Christ Apostolic Church and other Aladura churches in Nigeria. It explains further that some of the leaders of the Aladura churches do not preach against the use of orthodox medicine unlike the CAC who lays emphasis on divine healing.

The study therefore establishes the fact that there are

---

[13].S. A. Adewale, "African Church Movement and Impact on Socio-Religious Life in Nigeria." In: Emefie Ikenga Metuh (ed.), *The Gods in Retreat: Continuity and Change in African Religion* (Ibadan: Claverianum Press, 1985), p.174.

historical events to support the argument that only CAC among other Aladura preaches divine healing (*cura divina*). Take for instance; Oshitelu of the Church of the Lord Aladura died in a hospital and *so* did Oshoffa of the Celestial Church of Christ.

Olupona makes a submission that *Aladura* Churches are the praying or prophetic Churches that lay great emphasis on divine healing, vision, prophecy, fasting, dream; and the need to worship God through relevant cultural media[14]

Olupona also traces the historical background of the *Aladura* to the 1918 episode of the prayer band. According to the writer, the first *Aladura* Churches were established during the period of the great influenza epidemics, world wars and the disintegration caused by the European occupation of the country. [15]

Olupona also discusses the characteristics of the *Aladura*, which the Christ Apostolic Church seems to possess. He states that the *Aladura* movements today are generally headed by self-proclaimed prophets and charismatic figures. The founder normally acts as the pastor claiming a divine revelation.

However, the book examines further the work of Olupona by assessing the activities of the self-proclaimed prophets and charismatic figures in the leading *Aladura* churches whose history, unfortunately were overwhelmed with crises and schisms.

Following this historical sequence, Ayegboyin and Ishola trace the history of the CAC to the Aladura group which emerged as prayer band in 1918, and which gave recognition to leaders like Moses Orimolade Tunolase/Abiodun Christianah Akinsowon of the Cherubim and Seraphim in 1925; and Joseph Ayo

---

[14] Jacob Olupona, "Contemporary Religious Terrain." In: Jacob, k. Olupona and Toyin Falola (eds.), *Religion and Society in Nigeria: Historical and Sociological Perspectivea* (Ijebu-Ife: Adeyemi Press Limited, 1991), p.36.

[15]. Ibid, p.36

Babalola/Daniel Orekoya of the CAC in 1930.[16] The writers succinctly conclude:

> The period from the nineteenth century to the present has been characterized by the establishment and growth of the African strand of development of Christianity. This phenomenon has given birth to indigenous churches and prayer groups in Africa. These groups have not only taken root but they have proliferated and shown phenomenal growth, particularly in sub-Saharan Africa.[17]

Both writers further discuss the features of *Aladura* churches which the Christ Apostolic Church possesses. This book however takes a step further by narrating critically the typology of the CAC through its spiritual practices with other *Aladura* and new Pentecostal churches in Nigeria.

In line with this thought, Omotoye agrees with the views of Ayegboyin and Ishola that the CAC is a Church to be recognized among the *Aladura* churches in Nigeria.[18] The writer, therefore, identifies CAC as part of the African Independent Churches (*Aladura*) that have historical backgrounds traceable to the 1920s.

Other Churches, apart from the CAC in the group of the *Aladura* include: the Cherubim and Seraphim, Church of the Lord (*Aladura*) and Celestial Church of Christ. Based on this, Omotoye concludes that the *Aladura* churches became noticeable in Nigeria from the 1920s. They include the Christ Apostolic Church (CAC), Cherubim and Seraphim (C&S), Church of the Lord (*Aladura*),

---

[16]. Deji Ayegboyin and Ademola Ishola, *African Indigenous Churches: An Historical Perspective* (Lagos: Greater Heights Publications, 1997), p.11

[17]. Ibid, p.11

[18]. Rotimi Omotoye, "Women Spirituality in an African Independent Church: A Case Study of Captain Abiodun Akinsowon of the Cherubim and Seraphim Church." In: Wellington, O. Wotogbe-Weneka (ed.), *Religion and Spirituality* (Port Harcourt: Emhai Books, 2001), p.111

and Celestial Church of Christ (C.C.C.).[19]

Nevertheless, Omotoye makes a passing reference in his write-up to the Christ Apostolic Church as one of the Churches within the *Aladura*; his focus of writing is basically the role of women in the spirituality of the Cherubim and Seraphim Church. In the same reasoning (of Omotoye), Babalola strongly agrees that the Christ Apostolic Church is within the *Aladura* group in Nigeria. Babalola has been able to convince readers that the beliefs of the other Aladura churches have similar traits with that of the Christ Apostolic Church.[20]

The argument of Babalola is that all these attributes in the *Aladura* are equally seen in the Christ Apostolic Church up till the present times. However, this book highlights the differences in the religious practices of the CAC and other Aladura churches.

It also spells out in detail how the practices of revelation and healing have contributed to the spread of the Church both in Nigeria and abroad. In another work, Fatokun classifies the CAC as one of the Aladura churches that metamorphosed from the Precious Stone Society (1918), to the Faith Tabernacle Congregation (1923), The Apostolic Church (1931) and the Christ Apostolic Church (1943).[21]

Fatokun's work no doubt has given scholars a clue to the accepted standard of the chronology of the Aladura churches in Nigeria. Nevertheless, the focus of the writer is basically on The Apostolic Church and not the Christ Apostolic Church; and most of his arguments are in support of The Apostolic Church being the

---

[19]. Ibid, 111

[20]. E.O. Babalola, " Aladura Churches and the Phenomenon of Spirit Possession," In: Wellington, O. Wotogbe-Weneka (ed.), *Religion and Spirituality* (Port Harcourt: Emhai Printing and Publication co., 2001), p.136

[21]. S. A. Fatokun, "The Apostolic Church Nigeria: The 'Metamorphosis' of an African Indigenous Prophetic-Healing Movement into a Classical Pentecostal Denomination,." *ORITA*, Vol.XXX.VIII, (2006), PP.49-70

first classical Pentecostal Church in Nigeria in early 30s. The book therefore examines the position of the Faith Tabernacle and other Pentecostal churches that had made spiritual impact in Nigeria before The Apostolic Church surfaced in the twentieth century.

In another perspective, Ogungbile sees the CAC as one of the *Aladura* churches in Nigeria. This refference could be seen in the light of belief, worship, practices and teachings. The CAC, like the *Aladura*, believes in praying and fasting to combat spiritual forces. In addition, the writer believes that the unique characteristics of prayers, which CAC possesses, makes it part of the Aladura communion. On this fact, Ogungbile remarks:

> Prayer is the main distinguishing feature for which the CAC is called *Aladura*, 'prayer people'…Prayers are constructed in consequence of the penetrating forces of ubiquitous malevolent and benevolent beings, which struggle to dominate human universe as manifested in Yoruba worldview.[22]

Ogungbile has made contribution to knowledge in his approach to the study of the Aladura through their traits. However, this study makes reference to the uniqueness in the religious practices of the *Aladura* and which have distinguished them from the classical or charismatic churches in Nigeria.

In another article, Ogungbile classifies the CAC under the Nigerian Indigenous Churches, popularly called Nigerian Independent Churches [NICs] or Nigerian Initiated Churches [NICs]. According to Ogungbile:

> Another phase of the change which Christianity in Nigeria witnessed in a very great measure came in the first quarter of the twentieth century with the

---

[22] David, O. Ogungbile, "Faith Withouth Borders: Culture, Identity and Nigerian Immigrant Churches in Multicultural American Community." In: David, O. Ogungbile & Akintunde, E. Akinade (eds.), *Creativity and Change in Nigerian Christianity* (Lagos: Malthouse Press Limited, 2010), p.317

emergence of the group of Churches known as Nigerian Initiated Churches, Nigerian Indigenous Churches or Nigeria Independent Churches (NICs). The Churches that belong to this group are Cherubim and Seraphim Movement (C&S)..., the Christ Apostolic Church (CAC)..., the Church of the Lord, *Aladura* (CLA), and the Celestial Church of Christ (CCC).[23]

Based on the foregoing, the author writes only with the intention to examine the factors that engineered the creativity and change in the *Aladura* Christianity and not on revelation and healing in the practices of CAC in Nigeria.

1.2.3   Distinguishing Features of the Aladura Churches

Peel's book deserves to be received with enthusiasm, as he provides explicit narrations on the features of the Christ Apostolic Church and Cherubim and Seraphim Society in Nigeria.[24] The writer is able to trace the similarities between the two churches in terms of practices and liturgy. In addition, the writer discusses the factors that have contributed to the spiritual growth of the *Aladura* Church namely prophecy, dream and vision.

From the foregoing, this study therefore complements the work of Peel as it discusses the potency in the spiritual gifts of the Aladura churches on healing, deliverance and guidance; particularly in a society where the need for spiritual search-lamp is needed to find lasting solutions to unprecedented problems.

[23].David Ogungbile, Creativity and Change in Nigerian Christianity: Issues and Perspectives." In: David, O. *Creativity and Change in Nigeria Christianity* (Lagos: Malthouse Press Limited, 2010), p.14

[24]. J.D.Y. Peel, *Aladura, a Religious Movement among the Yoruba* (London: Oxford Press, 1968), p.60

Based on this discussion, Ayandele elaborates further the future of the *Aladura* churches, the Christ Apostolic Church being a notable point of reference, and their contributions to the development of orthodox churches in Nigeria.[25] The author also identifies the various ways in which the mainline churches differ from the indigenous churches with reference to their peculiarities, spirituality and organizational settings

It is noteworthy, however, to mention here that the writer's focus has been mainly on the contributions of the Aladura churches to the mainline churches particularly in the area of spirituality. This view may not have very strong historical backing because the mainline churches no doubt played vital roles towards the ministerial and institutional growth and development of the *Aladura* Christianity at its inception in the early twentieth century.This study has filled this gap.

From another perspective, Ndiokwere discusses prophecy in the *Aladura*, which the CAC has imbibed as its practice up till the present time.[26] The writer also differentiates between ecstatic prophecy and supernormal experience so as to know the group to which the CAC belongs. He remarks:

> Prophecy may range from serious warnings and threats against sinful life, to calls to repentance and condemnations of injustice in government circles and in society as a whole. Prophecy includes forecast of wars, famine, outbreak of plagues, and the imminent fall of wicked heads of government and local rulers.[27]

---

[25] E.A. Ayandele, "The Aladura among the Yoruba: A Challenge to the 'Orthodox Churches." In: Kalu, O. (ed.), *Christianity in West Africa: The Nigerian Story* (Ibadan: Daystar Press, 1978), pp.20-25

[26] Nathaniel Ndiokwere, *rophecy and Revolution: The Role of Prophets in the Independent African Churches and in Biblical Tradition* (London: SPCK, 1981), PP.78-80.

[27] Ibid, p.77

Ndiokwere discusses further the role of prophets in the building of morality and its integration into the society. He states:

> There is no monopoly of leadership in the independent churches. The respect and credence given to leaders are due to their ability to manifest charismatic gifts and impact them to others.[28]

In addition, Ndiokwere identifies prayers, fasting and chastity as important pre-requisites for the acquisition of the extraordinary powers in the Independent Churches. He remarks:

> Fasting is particularly underlined as an indispensable exercise in this regard (stimulation to ecstasy)... members who desire visions or hope to be possessed on any occasion engaged in fasting.[29]

From the writings of Ndiokwere, the study further research to discover the uniqueness in the spirituality of the Church and its roles in the rapid spread to many parts of Nigeria and abroad. From another perspective, Obi identifies Holy Spirit as one of the crucial Pentecostal gifts in the CAC.[30]

He believes that this gift has been very important in the ministry of the CAC because of the biblical injunction attached to it (Acts of Apostle, Chapter two) Obi also examines the relevance of spiritual gifts, particularly speaking in tongues and interpretation of tongues as a means for church edification.

Similarly, E.O. Babalola, from a different view, traces the

---

[28] Ibid, 78

[29]. Ibid, P.82.

[30]. Chris Obi, "The Sign Character of Speaking in Tongues in Pentecostal Spiriyuality: A Critique." In: Wellington, O. Wotogbe (ed.), *Religion and Spirituality* (Port Harcourt: Emhai Printing and Publishing Company, 2001), p. 156.

unexpected growth of the Christ Apostolic Church to the emergence of charismatic leaders who possessed the spiritual power of healings, ministrations and revelations in the twentieth century.

According to the writer (E.O. Babalola), adherents of the *Aladura*, especially the CAC, believe in prayers and faith healings to the use of medicine; be it traditional or orthodox. Babalola succinctly describes the *Aladura* Pentecostal thus:

> Prophecy plays a vital role in these churches (Aladura).The churches believe that witches and sorcerers are the sources of man's problems, and that prayers are the solutions to these problems. The leaders of these churches profess to specialize in dealing with problems and ailments which are beyond the domain of the ordinary person...[31]

However, this study harmonizes the work of Babalola as it explains the reasons why people trooped into the Aladura churches and also why their leaders have become the darlings of the indigenous people. Also, Offiong in another work discusses the varieties of Christian spirituality in Nigeria. He explains various Christian spiritualities in the context of Orthodox and Pentecostal Churches.

The writer (Offiong) mentions further that the distinctive characteristics of Pentecostal spiritualities consist of personal convictions, baptism of the Holy Spirit, extemporaneous prayers, emphasis on the Bible as the sole authority of their beliefs and practices, as well as the teachings on eschatology and the second coming of Christ. Offiong comments:

> ...the power of the Holy Spirit in the individual is manifested in the gifts of the Holy Spirit which Paul lists in 1 Corinthians 12:4-12. Those gifts include

---

[31]. E. O. Babalola, " Aladura Churches and the Phenomenon of Spirit Possession," In: Wellington, O. Weneka (ed.), *Religion and Spirituality* (Port Harcourt: Emhai Printing and Publications Company, 2001), p.156

wisdom, knowledge, faith, miracle, healing, prophecy, distinguishing of spirits, speaking in tongues and interpretation of tongues.[32]

Also, Offiong explains further the features of Aladura spirituality within the context of socio-cultural perspectives. According to the writer:

> *Aladura* spirituality is characterized by emphasis on miracles, prayers, visions, prophesies and faith-healing. Added to this is their attachment to sacred sites and sacred objects. Sometimes, the sacred sites are the birth places of their founders or some open space in the natural environment. [33]

However, this book builds on the work of Offiong by examining the relevance of Aladura spiritualities in the area of church proliferation and organizational structure.

Furthermore, Gideon Oshitelu discusses the relevance of the Holy Spirit as engine of growth in the administrative structure of the CAC from its inception. The writer sees that the CAC differs from other *Aladura* churches because leaders and members believe in divine instruction through the Holy Spirit before embarking on any project or any undertaking. Oshitelu remarks:

> The Christ Apostolic Church in particular believes in the baptism of the Holy Ghost with accompanying signs. This in fact makes the Christ Apostolic Church (CAC) different from other *Aladura* Churches.[34]

Oshitelu has made contributions to knowledge by   identifying the

---

[32]. E. A. Offiong, "Varieties of Christian Spirituality in Nigeria." In: Wellington, O. Weneka (ed.), *Religion and Spirituality* (Port Harcourt: Emhai Printing and Publications Company, 2001), p.156

[33] Ibid, p.186.

[34] G. A. Oshitelu, *History of the Aladura Churches, 1918-1940, an Interpretation* (Ibadan: Hope Publications, Ltd, 2007), p.102

uniqueness of the CAC spirituality from among other *Aladura* churches like the Cherubim and Seraphim, The Church of the Lord (*Aladura*) and The Celestial Church of Christ.

However, the book complements the work of Oshitelu by comparing the CAC spirituality at the time of the founding fathers in the twentieth century with the spirituality in the Church in the twenty-first century. This gap that the book fills has enabled researchers to have an insight into the divisions that have engulfed the Church in the contemporary time.

Ruth Marshall elucidates in her writings on the resurgence of modern Pentecostal Movement in Nigeria and its accompanying features of holiness. [35] She remarks:

> The Born-Again revival in Nigeria begins in the 1970s, gathering momentum through the 1990s and continues to grow up until the present. From the outset, the movement self-consciously represents itself as a form of rupture, both individual and collective.[36]

Ruth Marshall discusses further that most modern Pentecostal movements in Nigeria today have adopted styles of the *Aladura* Churches that sprang up in the early twentieth century. This perhaps accounts for the reason why many of the contemporary Pentecostal Churches in Nigeria have their historical background traceable to the Precious Stone Society that emerged in 1918.

The writer therefore makes the submission that the teachings on holiness and being born-again (Yor. *atunbi*) by the patriarchs of this paying group (Precious Stone Society) have been adopted and modernized by the Pentecostal churches that emerged in the 1970s. However, the intention of writing this book is to

---

[35] Ruth Marshall, Political Spiritualities: The Pentecostal Revolution in Nigeria (Chicago: University of Chicago Press, 2009), p.51

[36]. Ibid, p.51

make contribution to knowledge on spirituality in the CAC Pentecostal Church and not on the Classical charismatic and new Pentecostal Churches in Nigeria.

From another perspective, Ogungbile discovers that prayer is one of the noticeable features of the Christ Apostolic Church. The author believes that the CAC directs most of its prayers to combat malevolent spirit and evil powers in the cosmic.[37]

These powers are addressed with local cultural significations. They are collectively called 'ota'.[38] Ogungbile also confirms further that the CAC fast and pray fervently to combat these 'ota' (enemies of progress. See footnotes for detail). The writer concludes that praying to combat enemies is accompanied with choruses and songs, beating of drums, clapping of hands, stamping of feet on the ground, and touching of certain parts of the body.[39]

The writer narrates how cultural symbolic bodily actions are employed in the CAC prayer services. He explains how members are instructed to lay hands on their heads to ward-off evil powers and command divine blessings on themselves.[40]

---

[37] David, O. Ogungbile, "Faith Without Borders:Culture, Identity and Nigerian Immigrant Churches in Multi Cultural American Community." In: D. O. Ogungbile & Akintunde, A. Akinade (eds.), *Creativity and Change in Nigerian Christianity* (Lagos: Malthouse Press Limited, 2010), p. 318

38."Òtá" is known as enemy= adversary (ies) in Yoruba land. It has various forms and are described by their various functions. Ogungbile in his sociological analyses sees 'ota' from four perspectives, namely: *elenini* (enemies of progress); *alaroka* (those who disclose of good plans to enemies);*asenibanidaro* (enemies that harm and still sympathize) and *aye* (spiritual forces that twist good fortune to bad fortune)-See D. O. Ogungbile, "Faith Without Border...," p. 317 for detail.

[39]. See D. O. Ogungbile, "Faith Without Borders...," p.318

[40]. Ibid, p.318

Ogungbile, nevertheless, sees the CAC as having same features of practice, worship, songs, prayers and teachings as those of the affiliated foreign missions abroad. He relates the ritual practices and worship activities in the CAC in America as follows:

> CAC, to immigrants' members and non-members, is 'a place to feel at home' or 'a home away from home'. Several of the CAC use Yoruba language in worship; others are bilingual, Yoruba and English. They employ indigenous music (songs, choruses and drums), sacred water and extemporaneous kind of prayer. Social relationship is expressed in a typically African (Yoruba) setting where respect for elders and greetings are observed, as an expression of cultural values... [41]

Furthermore, the author discusses that the use of materials in naming ritual such as water, honey, sugar and other observation of symbolic numbers in ritual activities such as three, seven and their multiples in prayers confirm the world-view of the CAC in its expression of worship. In addition, the author mentions that during religious and socio-religious occasions as naming, members appear in traditional dressing and local Nigerian (Yoruba) foods are served.[42]

Nevertheless, the focus of this book is not really on the characteristics of immigrant Churches in multicultural American community but on the features and religious practices of *Aladura* Churches in Nigeria with CAC as a reference point.

Ogunrinade holds the view that the issue of *cura divina* (divine healing) has a very special place in the tenets of the CAC. It forms the twelfth of the thirteen tenets of the Church. The writer traces the history of divine healing in the CAC to the divine manifestation of healings during the epidemic of 1918 and Apostle

[41]. Ibid, p.315

[42] Ibid, p.316

Ayo Babalola's prophetic ministry that began in the 1928. According to Ogunrinade:

> ... Pentecostals believe in *cura divina* (divine healing). This forms the twelfth of the thirteen tenets of Christ Apostolic Church. This is traceable to the divine manifestation of healing during the epidemic of 1918, and Apostle Ayo Babalola's healing ministry starting from 1928. They hold that through faith and prayer alone, God can cure all diseases.[43]

Ogunrinade's work has indeed discussed issues related to spirituality in the CAC, but, this book has made further references by comparing spiritualities in the CAC with other Aladura churches in Nigeria.

1.2.4 History and Development of the Christ Apostolic Church

Some writers like Welsh (1976), Oshun (1981), Olayiwola (1986 & 1991), Ayegboyin and Ishola (1997), Engelbert (1997), Oshitelu (2007) and Ogunrinade (2010) are of the opinion that the emergence of the Diamond Society (also known as the Precious Stone Society) in 1918 at Ijebu-Ode served as the starting point for the history of the CAC.

One of the notable scholars who supported this view with primary source materials is Robert Welsh. He believes that the Christ Apostolic Church is a continuation of the Precious Stone Movement under the leadership of Joseph Shadare, popularly known as Esinsinade and Odubanjo. The writer concludes thus:

> The Precious Stone Movement under the leadership of Joseph Shadare blossomed into the so called Faith Tabernacle of Nigeria in 1920, with its headquarters in

---

[43]Adewale, O. Ogunrinade, "Predilection for African Indigenous Practices in the Pentecostal Tradition of African Indigenous Churches with reference to CAC...

Philadelphia, America...Members of the Precious
Stone Movement had contact with this ministry
through one of the Prayer group members named
Odubanjo...This contact greatly influenced the early
preaching and evangelism of the Precious Stone
Movement which was later called Faith Tabernacle
(Fate Tabernacle) and Christ Apostolic Church...[44]

However, the book complements the work of Welsh by
tracing the historical analysis of the Church particularly the
interactions of its patriarchs with the British Apostolic Church up
till the separation that came up in 1939 and which eventually
culminated into the registration of the Church in 1943.

In another write-up, Oshun traces the emergence of the
Christ Apostolic Church to the alliance that came up in 1921
between the Precious Stone Society (P.S.S.) in Ijebu-Ode and the
Nigerian Faith Tabernacle (N.F.T.), which had its base in Lagos.
The writer sees the role of the American Faith Tabernacle as the
source of inspiration in the formation of the future nucleus of the
Christ Apostolic Church. Christopher Oshun remarks:

The emergence of what later became known as the
Christ Apostolic, which can fairly claim to be
considered the doyen of Aladura Pentecostals in
Nigeria, was a gradual process with a somewhat
chequered history. Its origins can first be traced to the
alliance around 1921 between the Precious Stone
Society (P.S.S.) in Ijebu-Ode and the Nigerian Faith
Tabernacle (N.F.T.) which came to have its base in
Lagos.[45]

---

[44] Robert Welsh, *Ecumenism Exercise Iv: The Wesleyan Church, the Christ
Apostolic Church and Mennonites,* Faith and Order paper, No.79 (Geneva:WCC
Publications, 1976), p. 418.

[45]. C. O. Oshun, "Christ Apostolic Church of Nigeria: a Sugested Pentecostal
Consideration of Its Historical, Organizational and Theological Developments,
1918-1975." (An unpublished Doctoral Thesis, University of Exeter, 1981), p.24.

Christopher Oshun further discusses the role of western missionaries, particularly the American Faith Tabernacle, in the building of *Aladura* churches with special reference to the Christ Apostolic Church. He comments further that the work of missionary volunteers (although their employments and circumstances differed), made a considerable impact in the spread of evangelism in Yoruba land.

Christopher Oshun also highlights the factors that contributed to the tremendous growth and development of the church (CAC) in the twentieth century. He also discusses the circumstances that led to the formulation of the doctrine and practices in relation to revelation and healing at the inception of the Church. Furthermore, Oshun agrees that the CAC developed some teachings through the study of the scriptures and memos of sermons from the Faith Tabernacle leaders; which later served as part of the tenets for the church.

Again, Oshun mentions that the CAC revised its doctrinal and ecclesiastical positions in order to embrace both the scriptural and prophetic aspects of its emergent Aladura Pentecostalism and produced a more comprehensive and acceptable doctrinal formula to guide the whole Church.

David Olayiwola also agrees with Oshun that the CAC began as a prayer band known variously as the Precious Stone Society, Diamond Society or The Faith Tabernacle. Beginning from Ijebu-Ode, now in Ogun State; Nigeria, through a series of interconnected events and factors, the Society changed in 1922 into an autonomous Church, The Nigerian Faith Tabernacle.[46] According to the writer, personalities like Joseph Shadare

---

[46] David Olayiwola, "Hermeneutical-Phenomenological Study of the Aladura Spirituality in Ijesa Social History." *Asia Journal of Theology*, Vol.5, No.2, (1991), p. 254.

(Esinsinade of Ijebu-Ode), David Odubanjo (Ijebu-Ode), a nephew of the former; Isaac Akinyele (late Olubadan of Ibadan, 1955-1964), A. Babatope (Ilesha) and Joseph Ayo Babalola (Ilesha) laid a solid foundation for the CAC.

David Olayiwola explains that the Nigerian Faith Tabernacle developed into The Apostolic Church in 1931, having full co-operation with the Bradford Apostolic Church representatives like Pastor D.P. Williams, Jones Williams and Andrew Turnbill in the first instance and later with Pastors George Perfect, C.H. Russell, J.I. Vaughan and S.G. Elton also of the Bradford Apostolic Church in Great Britain.[47] The writer discusses further the doctrinal controversy which caused rifts and schism between the Nigerian-bloc and the British-bloc between 1936 and 1941. He mentions further that the Christ Apostolic Church became officially recognized in 1943.

David Olayiwola therefore concludes that in the contemporary time, the CAC and The Apostolic Church (TAC) will continue to expand in Yoruba land. On this, Olayiwola remarks: "Both the CAC and The Apostolic Church were well entrenched in Ijesa land. The immediate factor that contributed greatly to the development of the CAC/TAC was the great revival of Oke-Ooye, Ilesha in July, 1930.[48]

From the historical chronology of events of the CAC showcased above, Engelbert makes his contribution to the history of the Church by explaining the causal factor for the break-up between the prayer group and the Anglican Church in 1918. He sees the division as a breakthrough to the formation of the prayer group, which culminated into the Faith Tabernacle and later to the Christ Apostolic Church. Engelbert writes:

---

[47]. Ibid, pp. 254-255

[48]. Ibid, p. 255

> In 1923, they separated from the Anglican Church
> because they rejected infant baptism and because of
> their exclusive insistence of faith healings and their
> reliance on visions and dreams for guidance.[49]

Despite the contributions of these writers mentioned above, the book has filled the vacuum of the history of the Church by paying attention to the socio-cultural setting of the Church (CAC) in the twentieth century which perhaps contributed to its rapid growth and global expansion.

1.2.5 Persons and Personalities in the History of the Christ Apostolic Church

Samuel Adegboyega highlights the activities of prominent prophets and prophetesses like D. O. Orekoya, Sophia Odunlami G. Sakpo, and J. B. Esinsinade in the development and growth of The Apostolic Church and Christ Apostolic Church in Nigeria.[50]

Samuel Adegboyega explains further the role of David Odubanjo as a link-man between the Precious Stone Society and the Faith Tabernacle Congregation in Philadelphia ; and between the Faith Tabernacle in Nigeria and the Faith and True Temple Congregation in Canada and finally with the British Apostolic Church in Britain.

Samuel Adegboyega highlights further the development that took place in 1930 through the revival of Joseph Ayo Babalola and its impact on the development of the Church (CAC) and other indigenous Pentecostal churches in Nigeria.

---

[49]. B. Engelbert, *New Christian Movements in West Africa* (Ibadan: Oluseyi Press, 1997), p.14

[50]. S. G. Adegboyega, *Short History of the Apostolic Church in Nigeria* (Ibadan: Rosprint Industrial Press, 1978), pp.1-36.

Nonetheless, the focus of Adegboyega is more on the historical and chronological order of the inception of The Apostolic Church in Nigeria and not on the dynamism in the gifts of the spirit and healing powers of the prophets in the Christ Apostolic Church, Nigeria.

Akinyele Omoyajowo discusses the role of Joseph Ayo Babalola in the establishment of revival in July 1930 in Ilesa. Here, the author enumerates the healing miracles performed through Joseph Babalola and which attracted hundreds of people. The writer declares: "Joseph Babalola, a former staff of P.W.D.(Public Works Department) roller-driver turned prophet... performed healing miracles. According to Odubanjo, within three weeks, he had cured about 100 lepers, 60 blind people and 50 lame persons."[51]

The Akinyele Omoyajowo establishes the fact that Cherubim and Seraphim Movement (C&S) had gained ground in Ilesha before the revival of Babalola in 1930; that, Christianah Abiodun of the C&S also attended the 1930 revival, and that, the Police Chief at that time confused the Cherubim and Seraphim with the famous Babalola revival of 1930 in Ilesha. Based on this, Omoyajowo remarks:

> The police chief was definitely confusing Orimolade of the Cherubim and Seraphim with the famous Babalola Revival of July 1930 in Ilesa. Joseph Babalola, a former P.W.D. roller-driver turned prophet, had accompanied leaders of the Faith Tabernacle, D.O. Odubanjo and Senior Pastor J.B. Esinsinade to Ilesha for a special conference. There, he performed healing miracle. While there seemed to be no direct conflict between Cherubim and Seraphim and the Babalola group at Ilesha, we may conclude that the revival

---

[51] Akinyele Omoyajowo, *Cherubim and Seraphim: The History of an African Independent Church,* (Lagos: NOK Publications, 1982), pp.54-55

32

was in part responsible for the temporary setback the Cherubim and Seraphim Society suffered in Ilesha during these years.[52]

The Omoyajowo also comments that the Assistant District officer at Ife (who also had jurisdiction over Ilesha) made a remark about the revival thus:

> I found a crowd of many hundreds of people including a large contingent of the halt, and lame and blind. The whole affair was orderly.[53]

Okoronkwo makes a research into the advent of the Christ Apostolic Church in Igbo land. He also highlights the role played by church leaders, particularly Godwin Nwoye, in the building of the Christ Apostolic Church in Enugu Zone and Imo State of Nigeria. Okoronkwo, in assessing the work of Godwin, writes:

> Miracles, healings, signs and wonders were the result of our crusade in halls and car parks at Agbani. Many testified of God's healing touch, God's grace in special ways, forgiveness, love from above and real joy of salvation in their hearts. As the lame walked, the dumb spoke; there arose as it has always been great opposition, oppression and suppression. As great were the battles, so great were the victories.[54]

Abi Olowe, on the other hand, traces the history, prophetic life and ministry of Joseph Ayo Babalola from 1904-1959. He highlights the contribution of Babalola to the growth of Pentecostalism in Nigeria and overseas by saying that he (Babalola) was one of the greatest men of his generation. He opines that his

---

[52]. Ibid, p.55

[53]. Ibid, p.55

[54] S. N. Okoronkwo, *Christ Apostolic Church, Igbo land, 1952-2002* (Enugu: El-Demark Publishers, 2003), pp. 1-25

33

work will go on as its influence continues and increases throughout the ages, bringing blessings to many.[55]

In the same line of thought, Abi Olowe identifies the prophetic gifts and words of wisdom possessed by Babalola. The writer succinctly summarizes the scenario as follows:

> Apostle Babalola sometimes received revelations and prophesied while praying alone, for an individual, for a church or for a community. He could also receive revelation while preaching or counseling. ...Babalola prophesied on detraction, length of ministry, war abroad, translation, dreams, visions and revelations.[56]

The quotation above reveals the inputs of one of the founding fathers in the demonstration of prophetic ministry in the establishment and growth of the Christ Apostolic Church in Nigeria. However, the scope of works of the aforementioned writers are limited to the South and Eastern parts of Nigeria and no specific reference is made to CAC leaders in other regions of the Country.

1.2.6   Christ Apostolic Church and Leadership Crises in the Modern Period

Nathaniel Ndiokwere attempts to differentiate between fake and original prophecies among indigenous Pentecostal prophets in Nigeria. According to him:

> It is not denied that there are genuine prophets of God but the question is, how can the cockle be separated from the barley?[57]

---

[55]. A. Olowe, *Great Revivals, Great Revivalist: Joseph Ayo Babalola* (Lagos: Omega Publishers, 2007), pp.281-282.

[56] Ibid, pp. 281-282

[57] Nathaniel Ndiokwere, *Prophecy and Revolution: The Role of Prophets in the*

He explains further the numerous yardsticks for detecting fake prophecies in the *Aladura* setting in Delta-State. The writer also elucidates the various factors responsible for the abuse of spiritual gifts in the modern Pentecostal Churches, but no particular reference is made to the abuse of spiritual practices in the Christ Apostolic Church.

David Olayiwola in his article traces the problems in the Christ Apostolic Church to mal-administration and the abuse of prophetic gifts amongst church leaders.[58] He also highlights the relevance of Holy Spirit as a major factor of unity in the Church. In the same line of thought, Christopher Oshun gives a clear picture of the various factors responsible for the tremendous expansion of the Christ Apostolic Church in the twentieth century.

Christopher Oshun also traces the reasons for the crises in the CAC from the mid twentieth to early twenty-first centuries to poor leadership and organizations. He remarks further that with the developments in the growth and progress of the Church, a number of problems became manifest.

The first problem is that, the Church had seen itself as a revival church and there was the necessity to ordain prophets and evangelists so that they could put on the clerical collar in addition to their cassocks. However, the standard of the Church remains that they could not wear suits as this was reserved as identification for literacy and pastoral authority.[59]

Independent African Churches and in Biblical Tradition (London: SPCK, 1981), p. 77

[58] D. O. Olayiwola, "Hermeneutical-Phenomenological Study of the Aladura Spirituality in Ijesa Social History." *Asia Journal of Theology*, Vol.1, No.2 (1991), pp. 253-261.

[59] C. O. Oshun, "The Experience of Christ Apostolic Church." In: Ademola Ishola & Deji Ayegboyin (eds.)*Rediscovering and Fostering Unity in the Body of Christ: the Nigerian Experience* (Lagos: A.T.F. Publications, 2000), p.159

However, Olayiwola and Oshun have not really discussed the fundamental issues for the schism and secession in the CAC and the effects on the development in the Church. The book filled the gap as it examines the causal factors for the crises and the impacts on the society where CAC has been notably recognized and on other denominations which have been competing with the Church.

Deji Ayegboyin on the other hand discusses the divisions in the early church and in the twentieth century which resulted in the Ecumenical Movements, starting from the International Conference in Edinburgh in 1910.[60]

Ayegboyin believes that the Conference of Missions in Nigeria was organized at the instance of the Scottish Presbyterian Mission at Calabar to discuss missionary matters. In addition, the Church Union Movement flowered into many branches, in 1931. Such branches, he states, include The Christian Council of Nigeria (CCN), Evangelical Church of West Africa (ECWA), the Christian Association of Nigeria, the Christian Pentecostal Fellowship of Nigeria (CPFN), and Organization of African Instituted Churches (OAIC), to which CAC belongs.

Oshitelu from another perspective traces the division in the Christ Apostolic Church to theological, political and cultural reasons.[61] However, he specifically mentions that the fundamental

---

[60]. Deji Ayegboyin, Rediscovering and Fostering in the Body of Christ: The Nigerian Experience." In: Ademola Ishola & Deji Ayegboyin (eds.) *Rediscovering and Fostering Unity in the Body of Christ: the Nigerian Experience* (Lagos: A.T.F. Publications, 2000), pp. 17-36

[61] G. A. Oshitelu, "The Ecumenical Movement: A Historical and Theological Perspective." In: Ademola Ishola & Deji Ayegboyin (eds.) *Rediscovering and Fostering Unity in the Body of Christ: the Nigerian Experience* (Lagos: A.T.F. Publications, 2000), pp. 78-79.

reason for the division and crises in the white garment *Aladura churches* is leadership problem. Nevertheless, Oshitelu did not specifically mention the names of the *Aladura* churches that were seriously involved in the crises.

Joshua Alokan (Snr) writes on the background to the crises in the Christ Apostolic Church, starting from 1980 until it became uncontrollable in 1990. The writer gives various reasons for the division and secession in the CAC and also highlights the problems of prophetiking in the Christ Apostolic Church as a result of egoism, insubordination and flair for acquiring wealth.[62]

And again, Joshua Alokan traces extensively the background of the crises in the Church to 1990 as a result of a controversy between some militant pastors and the Church Authority over certain practices in the Church. He posits that the controversy got out of hand because the leaders of the Church were hasty in deciding to discipline the vocal young militant pastors. On the other hand, the young militant pastors reacted by taking the church authority to the Court of Law to settle scores.

However, this work by Joshua Alokan (Snr) has given us insights into the misunderstanding and schism in the CAC, but it has not expressed the opinion of other groups that have been involved in the crises. This book fills the gap. From another perspective, Fatokun discusses the historical background of rifts in the Christ Apostolic Church (CAC) and The Apostolic Church, Nigeria in the twentieth century. The writer traces the schism within the folds to leadership problems resulting from administrative ineptitude and doctrinal differences.[63]

---

[62] Adeware Alokan, *Cradle and Beyound* (Ile Ife: Timade Ventures, 2005), p.200

[63] S. A. Fatokun, "The Apostolic Church Nigeria: The 'Metamorphosis' of an African Indigenous Prophetic-Healing Movement into a Classical Pentecostal

Furthermore, Samson Fatokun attributed the schism between the leaders to personality clashes as a result of grievances over misappropriation of funds allegedly perpetrated by David Odubanjo.[64] However, this book complements Fatokun's work by tracing the events that characterized the Church from 1990-1994.

1.2.7   Revelation and Healing in Nigerian Christianity

Boer describes Pentecostal gifts as the spiritual and divine endowment for evangelical purpose.[65] The writer also sees Pentecostal gifts as symbols for spiritual empowerment for missionary witnessing. Also, the writer claims that the Pentecostal gifts consist of revelation, faith healing, prophecy and discerning spirit, word of wisdom and word of knowledge.

John Peel also holds the view that the sources of practices in the Aladura Churches, particularly the CAC, could be traced to the Faith Tabernacle of Philadelphia in America.[66] According to him, the CAC drew much of its inspiration from the foreign organization of the American Faith Tabernacle. The writer also discusses the influence of the foreign missions, particularly their spirituality, on the development and growth of indigenous Pentecostal Churches in Nigeria. However, the writer did not mention specifically the practices and beliefs which the CAC has accepted or rejected in recent times and which have implications for the growth of the Church.

In the same vein, Samuel Adegboyega discusses about the progressive divine revelation and healing which The Apostolic

Denomination." *ORITA,* XXXIII/1 & 2, (2006), PP.51-65

[64] . Ibid, pp.63-65

[65] H. Boer, *Pentecost and Missions* (London: Lutterworth Press, 1961), pp.24-28

[66] J. D. Y. Peel, *Aadura: A Religious Movement among the Yoruba* (London: Oxford Press, 1968), pp. 62-95.

Church enjoyed between 1935 and 1940.[67] He remarks:

> As the work was progressing administratively, the
> divine order of the church government was being more
> realistic and practical. The principles and practices of
> The Apostolic Church vision were being taught to us
> by the European missionaries and were eagerly
> assimilated. The Lord through prophetical ministry
> was calling into offices of pastors and overseers,
> presiding elders, deacons, deaconesses, General
> Deacons, as well as, local evangelists. The callings
> were in each case critically examined by the
> Apostleship before they were ordained into the
> respective offices. [68]

Samuel Adegboyega also mentions the relevance of
spiritual gifts in the building of The Apostolic Church in the year
1940. He states that the word of God became more pronounced
through the teachings of the leaders of The Apostolic Church. He
also mentions that the administrative relationship and distinction
between the five gifts of the spirit revealed in Ephesus 4 verse 11
and the nine gifts of the spirit revealed in I Corinthians 12:8-11
was wonderfully propounded because it served as an eye-opener to
the Church. The author finally narrates the essence of the spiritual
gifts in the growth of the Church.[69]

Geerhardus Vos discusses the differences between
'General' and 'Special' revelations. The general revelation is also
called natural revelation while the special revelation is called
supernatural revelation. The author explains that the general
revelation comes to all human beings for the reason that it comes

---

[67] Ibid, pp. 73-74

[68] S. G. Adegboyega, *Short History of the Apostolic Church in Nigeria* (Ibadan:
Rosprint Industrial Press, 1978), pp.73-75

[69] Ibid, pp. 73-74

through nature. Special revelation comes to a limited circle of people for the reason that it springs from the sphere of the supernatural through a specific self-disclosure of God.[70]

Furthermore, Geerhardus Vos also explains the place of prophetism in Old and New Testament revelations. The writer discusses the biblical theology of revelations in the Old Testament from the time of Noah (Noachian revelation), Abraham/others (Patriarchal revelation), Moses (Mosaic revelation) and the prophetic epoch of revelation.

In addition, Geerhardus Vos enumerates the structure of the New Testament revelation right from John the Baptist to the ministry of Jesus Christ and the Apostles of Christ. Indeed, his work has provided some basic understanding for this study, most especially on matters relating to revelation. However, this study complements the work of Geerhardus as it shifts base from examining revelations and healings from the theological approach to a more rigorous scholarly approach.

Babalola analyses the practices of revelations in the Yoruba traditional religion. The writer compares revelations and healings in Yoruba traditions and the Aladura churches, using the Christ Apostolic Church as the thrust of his comparison. Babalola further explains that some practices of the Yoruba traditions have been retained by some Christian faiths, particularly the CAC. Such traditional practices which the Christians retained include harvest anniversary, where the first fruits are brought into the church for God's blessing.[71]

Also, Babalola states that the traditional festival for the

[70] Vos Geerhardus, *Biblical Theologh, Old and New Testament* (Michigan: Eerdmans Publishing Compan, 1991), p.19

[71] E. O. Babalola, *Current Research Studies in Religious Interaction* (Department of Religious Studies, Obafemi Awolowo University, Ile Ife, 2001), p.9

youth (*Ajodun ewe*) has been adopted by the *Aladura* churches as a medium of celebration for children. Here, children are committed into the hands of God for blessings, protection and long life. Through this process, healings usually take place. In the CAC, the leader, during the children/youth anniversary, blesses water for the children to bathe with and drink. The belief is that such sanctified water will clean all sicknesses and infirmities. The practice of prayers, as imbibed since 1930, has its origin traced to the traditions and culture of the Yoruba.

Babalola explains further that most practices in the Church have close interaction with traditions. The writer concludes by saying that the church of God has found a way of continuing the practice of these phenomena even after being converted from traditional religion into Christianity. The writer therefore has only attempted to evaluate the relationship between the practice of CAC and the traditional religion; but not on how the CAC practices were formulated and how it later replaced the practices of the traditional religion.

Steve Ganz writes about the relevance of the prophetic church in the building of Christian community.[72] He traces the background of revelation and healing to the time of Moses, Joshua, Paul and the disciples of Jesus Christ. The writer further sheds light on the abuse of gifts and the ways to correct abnormalities.

Steve Ganz also mentions that the gift of prophecy needs to be reclaimed by the Church as it has fallen on hard times through misunderstanding, misuse and abuse. However, Ganz did not make any particular reference to any church which has been the victim of abuse of spiritual gifts and crises.

In another work, S. A.Owoeye (2003) discusses the place

---

[72] See http://www.opensourcetheology.net/node/1368. Accessed on 1/4/2002

of music in healing processes among prophet- healers in Yoruba land.[73] The author mentions that it is a unique practice in the CAC to see revivalists serving as singers. Due to the inseparable relationship of music from Pentecostal revival activities, CAC revivalists sing a great deal as they lead the congregation in a bid to inspire and encourage the congregation.

Owoeye also comments on the performance practices of music among Christian prophet-healers in Yoruba land. Take for example, in the CAC, the leaders encourage congregational hymns. In the liturgy, hymns and lyrics are predominant. Also, songs are rendered during prayers.

Most times, the songs are sung to perform healings, breakthroughs and deliverance for the concerned. Nevertheless, Owoeye' s paper is an inspiration to this book because it takes a step further to study spirituality in the Church from a larger perspective in Nigeria rather than Yoruba land. .

Harvey Cox traces the origin of Pentecostal power and spiritual gifts to the untiring efforts of the founding fathers of the *Aladura* Churches, particularly in the twentieth and twenty-first centuries.[74] The writer discusses the display of spiritual gifts by these spiritual leaders as from 1918 to 1930, and up till the time when The Apostolic Church arrived in Nigeria in 1931. He also mentions in his discussion the events which resulted into the separation between The Apostolic Church and the Christ Apostolic Church in 1939 which emerged from the former.

---

[73].S. A. Owoeye, "The Place of Music in Healing Processes among Contemporary Christian Prophet-Healers in Yoruba land, *"Nigerian Music Review,* No.3 (2003), pp.33-46.

[74]. Cox Harvey, *Fire From Heaven: The Rise of Pentecostal Spirituality and the Reshaping of Religion in the Twenty-First Century* (London: Oxford University Press, 2008), p. 263

Ogbu Kalu also reasons with the argument of Harvey as he traces the history of the African Independent Churches to the beginning of indigenous Pentecostalism in Nigeria. He states thus:

> In the nineteenth century, prophetic figures emerged in one place after another..... The movement could be regarded as the first response by Africans. It challenged the white monopoly of the cultic and decision-making powers within the church, and the monopoly of the interpretation of the canon and the cultural symbols of worship.[75]

However, the arguments of these writers have provoked this study into deep research of spiritual phenomenon of the indigenous churches in Nigeria.

Femi Adedeji discusses the place of music in the healing processes of the Christ Apostolic Church, Nigeria.[76] According to the author, music plays vital role in evangelism and spread of the Church. Here, the writer states further that music dominates all sacraments and activities of the Church. It also performs several functions and plays diverse roles in the Church, and by so doing, has helped in transforming uncountable number of lives.

Femi Adedeji explains further that music is used in the CAC as part of the liturgy to praise, thank, worship, teach, admonish, comfort, entertain, pray, fight spiritual wars, evangelise, preserve history, heal and deliver the sick and the oppressed, receive Holy Spirit baptism, inspire faithfuls during crusades and for general breakthroughs.

Not only that, Femi Adedeji further discusses the

---

[75]. Ogbu Kalu, *African Pentecostalism: an Introduction* (New York: Oxford University Press, 2008), pp.23-24

[76] S.O. Adedeji, "The Theology and Practice of Music Therapy in Nigerian Indigenous Churches: Christ Apostolic Church as a Case Study." In: *Asia Journal of Theology*, India, 22 (1), 2008, pp.142-154

theologies and philosophies in the CAC which have made the religious practices in the Church unique. In the first place, songs rendered in the Church must be given by the inspiration of the Holy Spirit. Also, songs must be conformed to biblical standards and must be tuned in the sacred form to bring spiritual meanings particularly on eschatological events. In spite of the fact that the writer has shed light on the relevance of music in the spirituality of CAC, he has not related the position of music in the religious practices of revelations in the Church. In addition, the writer has not explained the influence of secular music on the sacred songs in the CAC; and also on how it (secular music) has undermined the religious practices of revelations and healings in the contemporary times.

From another perspective, Glen gives a comprehensive view of different scholars on revelation.[77] He also compares the biblical ideas of revelation with the modern theory on revelation as proposed by Gerald Downing. He (Downing) argued that the biblical ideas of revelation are wholly inconsistent with the contemporary doctrines of revelation which comprise of theological propositions or existential experience. Based on this argument, Glen explains that the act of revelation is simply an unmasking or making known of that which was previously unknown.

Revelation therefore should be seen as a proposition based on religious experience and personal piety. The idea of applying knowledge into critical issues in the scripture should be discontinued. The expression of revelation therefore should not be based on rationalism and empiricism.

To round off this section, the literature review has given us hint about the objectives and interest of this book. The book has

[77]Harris Glen, *Revelation in Christian Theology…* (For detail of this publication, see www.churchsociety.org/churchman/documents/cman-120-1-Harris.pdf.

filled the gap which notable scholars in the field of religion have not covered particularly in the areas of the practices of revelations and healings in the CAC and other *Aladura* Churches. This book therefore has also created avenues for other researchers to further researches on the phenomena of revelations and healings in other denominations. Based on the foregoing, the theoretical framework for this study is Max Weber (1864-1920).

Max Weber, a German scholar proposes that there is a correlation between religious beliefs and practical ethics of the society particularly the economic activity. Max Weber examines the structure of the society through meanings. The German scholar believes that under certain conditions, religious beliefs can have a major influence on the social and economic behaviour. He then examines three main themes: the effect of religious ideas on economic and social activities, the relationship between social stratification and religious ideas and the distinctive characteristics of western civilization.[78]

Weber studies Methodism, Calvinism, Baptistism and Pietism to provide a code of ethics on economic impetus. One of his leading doctrines which he has taught many people is that "a person was called to be a carrier by God. So then a carrier was not just a secular job, but a divine calling which he was urged to pursue in a committed and single-minded manner". The reference above implies that a carrier is a religious responsibility.[79]

Also, that God has commanded the individual to work hard, efficiently and productively for the honour and glory of God. Lastly, Weber believes that when one succeeded in one's calling, it meant that the individual has received a blessing from God.

---

[78] Akpenpuun Dzurgba...*The Sociology of Religion,* (Ibadan: Wemilore Press (Nig) Ltd, 1991), p.29

[79]. Ibid, p.29

Success, therefore, is an evidence of God's grace upon such a person. The application of Weber's theory to this study is that human beings must discover their divine gifts and must be handled profitably for the glory of God. Therefore, those who manage the gifts endowed them profitably are successful in their callings and carriers in life.

CHAPTER TWO

CONCEPTUAL ISSUES OF REVELATIONS AND HEALINGS

2.1   The concept of Revelation

Revelatory manifestation is the most dramatic and intimate means by which devotees maintain contact with the Supreme Being. Definitely, the Supreme Being operates at higher levels to unfold secrets or mysteries that have been hidden for a long time to his devotees. Such secrets may be revealed in form of warnings against dangers or with the intention to give directions about futuristic events. At times, the revelatory manifestation may come in the form of an eye opener for devotees to have more knowledge of their Supreme Being.

Revelation, therefore, simply refers to the act of unfolding secrets hidden or futuristic things. It is also an act of making people aware of something that is considered to be unknown. The unknown may be hidden facts, scientific inquiry and archeological findings. However, from the theological perspective, revelation can be considered to be a sign or message from God (Trembath, 2002).[80]   This form of spiritual message is known as divine revelation.

In the course of this study, divine revelation will be

---

[80] Kern Robert Trembath, "Revelation." In: Nicholas Lossky, Jose Mignez Bonino etal (eds.) *Dictionary of the Ecumenical Movement* (Geneva: WCC Publications, 2002), p.983

discussed from two perspectives, namely: (i) progressive revelation and (ii) prediction. Progressive revelation deals with the disclosure of God to human beings. Geerhardus Vos sees progressive revelation as a process between God and human beings. From the biblical view, God gradually makes Himself known to people through the course of history. According to Geerhardus Vos:

> The process of revelation is not only concomitant with history, but it becomes incarnate in history. The facts of history themselves acquire a revealing significance.[81]

Progressive revelation is centered on 'God' because it is believed that through Him, human beings and other creatures were created and He is the only channel through which pure and true visions, trance and other revelations are communicated to human beings. God reveales Himself through appearance. At times, it may be through audible voice, and He also reveals Himself through His angels. God reveals Himself through His creation. This implies that some truths or revelations about God can be learned by studying nature, physics, cosmology, etc. Natural enquiries about divine revelation find support in biblical verses such as "The heavens declare the glory of God" (Psalm 19:1-4).[82]

Prediction as a form of revelation, on the other hand, complements the progressive form of revelation. The gifted ministers of God claimed to have special experience of Him (God) through the spiritual gifts of prophecy, discerning spirit, dreams, visions and divine healing so as to meet the spiritual needs of people in the society.

---

[81] Geerhardus Vos, *Biblical Theology, Old and New Testament* (Grand Rapids: Eerdmans Publishing Company, 1991), p.6

[82] The psalmist shows the greatness and power of God as the skies proclaim the work of His hands (verse 1b) and the day and night display his knowledge and supremacy as the creator (verse 2)

This form of revelation comes directly from God as a result of power encounters with human beings. Such messages therefore unfold secrets about upcoming or futuristic events, disclosed source of human problems and remedy to different problems.

Most often, prediction tells about the future or futuristic events. It foretells about the blessings ahead, warning against dangers, issues related to marital and family problems, poverty and the like. The Aladura feature very well in this aspect. Christ Apostolic Church recognizes and reverses the manifestations of the Spirit to speak the mind of God on sensitive issues like marital, job opportunities, chosen careers and the like (Olupona, 1991 & Olupona, 1987). [83]

This aspect of revelation (prediction) was left untended by the western mission churches when Christianity was brought to Africa and Nigeria. However, one cannot dispute the fact that the preachings and other ministrations offered by the mainstream churches did go a long way in the transformation of lives, healing and spiritual comforts of the people in the society.

Nevertheless, scholars of religion agree that the western mission churches created a vacuum in the spiritual yearnings of African Christians. The Aladura churches have contributed appreciable efforts towards filling this space. Christ Apostolic Church acknowledges the nine gifts of the Spirit namely: word of wisdom, word of knowledge, faith, the gift of healing and working of miracles. Others are prophecy; discernment of spirit, divers' kind of tongues and interpretation of tongues (1st Corinthians 12:4-

---

[83] Jacob K. Olupona,"Contemporary Religious Terrain," In: Jacob K. Olupona (ed.), *Religion and Society in Nigeria: Historical Perspectives* (Ibadan: Spectrum Books Limited, 1991), p.36. Also see Jacob, K. Olupona, "The Celestial Church of Christ in Ondo: a Phenomenological Perspective." In Rosalind, I.J. Hackett (ed.), *New Religious Movements* (New York: Edwin Mellen Press, 1987), pp.45-73.

11)

In spite of these categorizations of revelations, scholars of religion agree that the Bible is the source of revelations which prophets and prophetesses should emulate. Take for instance, Prophet Isaiah in the Old Testament claimed to receive his message through visions, where he saw Yahweh the God of Israel, and the Seraphims adoring Him saying: 'Holy, holy, holy, is the LORD of hosts: the whole earth is full of his glory' (Isaiah 6:3). This form of revelation, or prophecy constitutes the bulk of the text of the Book of Isaiah and other texts attributed to the prophets (example is found in 1 Kings 22:19-22).

2.2 The concept of Healing

It is generally observed that life is one of the most treasured possessions of men and women. In many cases, it is terminated by sickness, disease or accident. The primary concern of every human being is to ensure good health and preserve life. In the pragmatic study of human existence, healing is paramount. In every community, when life is threatened or exposed to any form of tarnishment by an ailment, healing is uppermost in thought and action. Healing, as a universal phenomenon, is achievable through two major means- the procedure of medical sciences or religio-therapeutic techniques (Nkwoka, 1992).[84] Sometimes, the two methods are combined before a total healing is achieved.

Healing as a phenomenon is an important issue of discussion among medical practitioners, traditional worshippers, Aladura/Pentecostal worshippers and Islamic adherents in Nigeria. Human beings seek various means for healing when they have health problems. In the Nigerian context, the phenomenon of healing could be discussed in the light of western medicine,

---

[84] A. O. Nkwoka "Healing: The Biblical Perspective." *NABIS*, Vol.1 (1967), p.20

Traditional religion, Christianity and Islamic. In the real sense, healing as offered by modern science is, more or less, universally accepted.

The Health Organizations in the advanced world have played significant roles in providing health facilities for under developed countries and developing countries in the world. In the advanced countries, medical science has created awareness among the citizenry on health matters. In fact, there are some countries in the advanced world that have made health facilities free so that at least every citizen could benefit from the services. Some of the health organizations include United Nations Children's Education Fund (UNICEF), World Health Organisation (WHO) and the International Red Cross Society (IRCS).

The UNICEF provides for the emergency needs of children in devastated areas. It also improves the nutrition of under-nourished children. Also, it provides medications, clothing and other needs for the children. The WHO on the other hand is a specialized division of the United Nation Organisation (UNO) established in 1948 with headquarters in Geneva, Switzerland. Its major aim is to improve the health of the people in all countries of the world. This organization has been able to address some incurable ailments such as heart diseases, AIDS, blood shortage, cancer, ebola, etc. (Nkwoka, 1992).[85]

Not only that, the International Red Cross Society plays important roles in two major ways; (a) in time of war, it provides emergency aid to those in distress and also takes proper care of the injured. Also, it provides welfare and health services for the prisoners of war. (b) in time of peace, it provides the general first-aid to patients. It assists in the training of nursing aides. Red Cross

---

[85] Ibid, p.21

Society maintains maternal and child welfare clinics and finally, it provides help to victims of natural disasters such as earthquakes, flood and fire (Michael, 2008).[86]

From this background, it is obvious that there is a stong link between healing, religion and society. The kind of healing one seeks in the face of ill health may, therefore, be influenced by that person's religion within his or her immediate environment. For a complete healing of any disease which has the spiritual or supernatural dimension, the root cause of the sickness has to be removed and the disrupted relationship restored into normal position.

Against this background, there will be an extensive discussion of revelations and healings from the global perspectives through the contexts of the biblical, traditional, Mission, the *Aladura* and the New Pentecostal Churches.

2. 3. Revelation and Healing from the Biblical Contexts
Geerhardus Vos groups divine revelations in the Old Testament into parts, namely: (a) The Mosaic epoch of revelation and (b) The prophetic epoch of revelation. (a) The Mosaic epoch of revelation covers the time of Noah (Noachina revelation) and the great patriarchs (Patriarchal Revelation). The patriachial in this context covers the time of Abraham, Isaac and Jacob (Gen 26:2); Here, revelations were confined to definite localities, all of which lay within the borders of the land of promise (Geerhardus, 1991:61-62). On this, Geerhardus Vos remarks:

There is here a beginning of the attachment of

---

[86] M.C. Michael, *Essential Biology* (Lagos: Tonad Publishers LTD, 2008), pp.148-149

Jehovah's redemptive presence to the land of Canaan.[87]

Furthermore, Geerhardus Vos also discovered that there were specific times for revelation during the patriarchal period. It is observed that Jehovah (God) appeared to the patriarchs at night mostly through dreams.The reason may be because in the night, the environment is always calm and therefore it is easier for the soul to withdraw into itself, away from the experiences and scenes of the day to commune with the divine.

This same principle is applicable to vision. The difference is that vision deals with sight. The word 'vision' has both a specific and a generalized one. The original meaning is that of receiving revelation by sight instead of by hearing; although, within the frame of the vision, hearing of an inner kind is included (Geerhardus, 1991).[88]

Based on the foregoing, the Old Testament text in Gen 12:1-2 gives a clear picture of how God revealed Himself as all-knowing, omniscient and giver of blessings to the human race. Here, God instructed Abram to leave his father's house into a land that He will show him. Another portion of that scripture in Gen 12:7 reads: "And the Lord appeared unto Abram and said, unto thy seed will I give this land; and there he built an altar unto the Lord, who appeared unto him". All these directives are indications that God reveals himself to human beings through dreams, visions and trance.

Not only that, God also revealed Himself to Isaac, Jacob, Joseph etc (Gen 26: 2-3). This revelation makes us understand that God spoke to Isaac when he was passing through a difficult time,

---

[87] See Geerhardus Vos, *Biblical Theology...*, (1991), p.51-52.

[88] Ibid, p.70

due to the severe famine in his land. The text reads: "And the Lord appeared unto him and said Go not down into Egypt; dwell in the land which I shall tell thee of: Sojourn in this land, and I will be with thee, and will bless thee; for unto thee, and unto thy seed, I will give all these countries, and I will perform the oath which I swore unto Abraham thy father. And I will make thy seed to multiply as the stars of heaven." This text (Gen 26, 2-4), shows that God finds solution to human's needs during hard times through audible voices, dreams, visions or trance.

(b) In addition, revelation is interwoven with prophecy in the Old Testament. In Numbers 11:24-30, Moses chose seventy men and appointed them as leaders. The Lord empowered them with the spirit that had been given to Moses. Their immediate reaction was to prophesy. Numbers 11:25 reads: "And the Lord came down in a cloud and spoke unto him, and took of the spirit that was upon him, and gave it unto the seventy elders; and it came to pass, that, when the spirit rested upon them, they prophesied, and did not cease."

From the biblical texts quoted above, it is discovered that for revelation to be actualized, the prophets play a prominent role. As earlier mentioned, the prophets are often referred to as the link between human beings and God. Prophecy is found in many religions, but it has occurred mostly in religions such as Judaism, Islam and Christianity.

These religions take it as a matter of faith that God exists, and in some ways can reveal His will to people. Members of these faiths employ some yardsticks to distinguish between true and false prophecies. Those that meet the prophetic requirements are regarded as genuine prophets and they are given due recognition and respect in the society.

In the biblical tradition, prophets are messengers of God; they are spokesmen of God on earth because they possess the spiritual gifts of making known things which are hidden from people (Ayegboyin & Ishola).[89] The word prophet or 'rabi' is found 309 times in the Old Testament, out of which 92 instances are found in Jeremiah alone. In the New Testament scripture, the word prophets appear 144 times, and could be understood as the proclamation of the divine word of God. The word in the plural form signifies historical books and groups of prophets; while in the singular form in early texts, it shows one who speaks on behalf of Yahweh (Brown, 1976:74)[90]

Based on the foregoing, it is glaring that the prophets are seen as servants of God. They receive messages on protection, safety, blessings and success and then pass them to people. In the Old Testament, God used prophets to establish and enforce law (Torah) among the Israelites. In addition to the written Torah, God also revealed to Moses a set of oral teachings, called the Oral Torah, to promote peace, love and unity in the society. The oral teachings were made compulsory for parents and children and for elders or leaders and people in their communities. An example of the Oral Torah could be found in Deuteronomy 11:18-20:

> Therefore shall ye lay up these my words in your heart and in your soul and bind them for a sign upon your hand that they may be as frontlets between your eyes. And ye shall teach them your children, speaking of them when thou sittest in thine house...And thou shall write them upon the door posts of thine house and upon Thy gates (K.J.V.)

Also, the divine blessings for keeping the oral Torah were revealed to the Israelites. Deuteronomy 11:22-25 spells it out that: "For if ye shall keep all these commandments....Then will the Lord drive out all these nations from before you, and you shall

---

[89] Read Ayegboyin & Ishola, *African Indigenous Churches...* (1997), 94

[90].Colin Brown (ed.) *Dictionary of New Testament Theology*, Vol. 3 (London:Paternoster Press, 1976), p.74

possess greater nations... Every place wherein the sole of your feet shall tread shall be yours.There shall be no man who will be able to stand before you, for the Lord your God shall lay the fear of you and the dread of you upon all the land that ye shall tread upon, as he hath said unto you." (K J.V.)

The *Nevi'im*, the books of the Prophets, is considered divine and true. This does not imply that the books of the prophets are always read literally. Jewish tradition holds the view that the books of the prophets should consist of metaphors and analogies. Biblical scholars have confirmed the existence of wide range of commentaries, explaining and elucidating those verses consisting of metaphors in the books of the prophets. Rabbinic Judaism regards Moses as the greatest of the prophets, and this view is one of the Thirteen Principles of Faith of traditional Judaism.

In the same reasoning, the accounts of revelation in the Nevi'im were not always as literal as in the Torah and that some prophetic accounts reflect allegories rather than literal commands or predictions. The directness in the revelation of the Torah could be seen in Deuteronomy 28:1-6 that says:

> And it shall come to pass, if thou shall hearken diligently unto the voice of the Lord the God, to observe and to do all his commandments.... That the Lord shall set thee on high above all nations of the earth....

The Bible reference above also reads further:

> And all these blessings shall come on thee.... Blessed shall thou be in the city... Blessed shall be the fruit of thy body. Blessed shall be thy basket and thy store....

The prophetic epoch of revelations, on the other hand, highlights the place of prophetism in Old Testament revelation. Here, there was connectivity between God and His messengers in order to carry out the messages of reforms in the society.

Geerhardus Vos comments on the position of prophets during this period thus:

> The prophets were guardians of the unfolding theocracy, and the guardianship was exercised as its centre, the kingdom. The purpose was to keep it a true representation of the kingdom of Jehovah. It sometimes almost appears as if the prophets were sent to the kings instead of the people.[91]

From the discussion above, we can explain better the peculiar circumstances under which prophecy arose at the time of Samuel, especially with the establishment of the school of prophets. The prophetic ministry in the Old Testament became more pronounced in the book of Samuel with the establishment of schools of prophets who had the language style of "Thus says the Lord" at the beginning of their prophetic ministrations.

The word "Thus says the Lord" stands for the genuineness of such prophecies. Also, some of the Prophets in the Old Testament scripture had to undergo thorough training for certain periods before graduating from the school of prophets and thereafter commissioned for the prophetic assignment.

The Prophets who were in the School of Prophets were prepared to speak forth the minds of God against corrupt nations and leaders in the society. They were also trained to attend to the socio-political needs of their citizens by campaigning against oppression and human injustice in the society. They also engaged in fasting and praying for peace, unity and divine protection for their citizens and leaders as well.

---

[91]. Read Geerhardus Vos, *Biblical Theology*...p.186. Also see E. D. Adelowo, "A Comparative Study of the Phenomenon of Prophecy in the Bible and the Quran." *Ife Journal of Religions*, Vol 11, (1982), pp.38-41.

From the foregoing, it is clear that prophets at the time of Samuel had influence on the government, the wealthy people in the society and the entire populace as they prophesied against immoralities and social injustice. This divine duty perhaps placed the Old Testament prophets on a very high level in the society. On these bases, Sundkler comments on the qualities attached to the prophetic office thus:

> A person who adequately qualifies to be called a prophet must have been divinely called and commissioned.... Prophets are not self-made but must have received the charisma of the divine call for their new roles through inspiration and revelation.[92]

Also, the prophets during the time of Samuel served as intermediaries between the people and God, just as in the Yoruba Traditional Religions where the *Ifa* priests serve as intermediaries between the people and God (Idowu, 1962: 19). The Old Testament prophets were also known as "Seers" or "*Ishaloh*", meaning anointed people of God. In the life history of great personalities in the Old Testament scripture, it is discovered that people such as kings, warriors and other dignitaries contacted seers (or *Ishaloh*) to know the mind of God, particularly on important occasions or issues. An example was the case of a man of God called Gad who revealed the mind of God to David. 1 Chronicles 21:9 states "And the Lord spoke unto Gad, David's seer, saying..." This text shows that in spite of the relationship between God and David, he (David) had his own seer to help him receive messages more clearly from God.

In the Old Testament text, God was referred to as the great healer. God (Yahweh) was also regarded as the only One who could exercise sovereign authority over creation. From the

---

[92]. Bengt Sundkler, *Zulu, Zion and Some Swazi Zionist* (London: Oxford University Press, 1976), p.68.

declaration of Yahweh in Exodus 15:26, "I am the Lord who heals you", the Hebrews saw healing as a spiritual matter within the domains of Yahweh and his appointed agents like priests and prophets.

This belief was so firmly accepted that no real Hebrew of old arrogated to himself the title of "healer". Treatment of sickness or infirmity was solely based, on prayers to, and faith in *Yahweh Raphael.* Yahweh frowned when they consulted gods of surrounding nations (2 Kings 1:33ff) or depended on human physicians (2 Chronicles 16:12) who are believed by scholars to be non-Israelites.

The major contribution of Ancient Israel to health economy is in the field of prophylactic medicine. It stemmed from the observance of the Mosaic regulations. In this regard, Igenoza comments that out of the 513 commandments in the scriptures, 213 are of a medical nature. Such commandments relating to health include the following: prevention of epidemics, frequent washing of the body and clothes, care for the skin, strict, dietic and sanitary regulations, rules for sexual life and the observation for period of resting (Igenoza,1986).[93]

It is well-attested to in modern medicine that hygiene is very important for human existence. This is because if germs have no chance of entry into one's system, there will be no opportunity for diseases to spread and multiply in human system and in the communities as well. In line with this view, Harrison is prompted to give comprehensive remarks on the nature of pentateuchical sanitary regulations which qualifies Moses to be called "the father of preventive medicine" (Harrison, 1976).[94]

[93]. A.O. Igenoza, "Medicine and Healing in Nigerian Christianity: A Biblical Critique." A paper read at the First Annual Religious Studies Conference of the Department of Religious Studies, O.A.U., Ile-Ife (1986), p.11

[94] R. K. Harrison, "Healing and Health." In R. Harrison (ed.),*The Interpreter's Dictionary of the Bible*, Vol.11, (Nashville: Abingdon Press, 1976), p.542

Two healing cases recorded in the Old Testament are here relevant. The first was Naaman, the Syrian Army Commander, who was healed of leprosy (II Kings 5). The second was that of King Hezekiah of Judah, healed of deadly boil (II Kings 20).

Elisha instructed Naaman to go to Jordan and wash his body seven times for healing. The end result was perfect healing. Also, King Hezekiah suffered from a terminal boil disease when Isaiah delivered a divine message to him that he should prepare to die. His passionate prayer and weeping earned him extra fifteen years.

The Hebrews, therefore, saw ill-health and healing as spiritual, manifested in physiological, psychological or social dimensions. Abney explains further about this phenomenon thus:

> It has been mentioned that demons were ubiquitous and caused, among other things, specific illnesses such as fever, wasting conditions, leprosy, blindness, asthma, and headache. What could be done to protect one from them...Jewish literature recommends sacred texts, especially Aaronic blessing, hung near entrances. Prayer and recitation of certain sacred scriptures like the Shema possess magical efficacy to ban evil spirits.[95]

In the New Testament, healing, as it appears in the ministry of Jesus and the apostles, seems to be an integral part of the gospel and the proclamation of the kingdom of God. The ministration of Jesus could be summarized as preaching, teaching, and healing.

Jesus had so much interest in the healing ministry because he was able to prove to the entire world through his gift of healing that he was the Anointed One of Yahweh (Mat 4:13). Also, his healing ministry signifies the dawn of the kingdom of God. As

---

[95] L.L.Abney, "Demons in the First Century," Ogbomosho Journal of Theology, No.2 (1987), p.42

diseases are healed and demons are routed, the robbers and thieves of the spiritual world are driven out to usher in the reign of peace of the kingdom.[96]

The healings of Jesus can be classified into three main types, namely: healing of diseases, exorcism and raising the dead. Scholars of religions have critically analyzed the healing of Jesus in a systematic pattern; the necessity for healing, the process of healing, and the result of healing. The necessity for healing can be seen when Jesus said that those who are well have no need for a physician but those who are sick (Luke 5:31, Mark 2:17 and Matthew 9:12).

The Disciples of Christ highlighted the relevance of spiritual gifts and also encouraged believers to possess them for spiritual edification. They also admonished believers that the gifts of prophecy, healing and working of miracles through the knowledge and wisdom of God will enhance one's relationship with God and with one another.

Paul, an Apostle of Christ, emphasized the importance of spiritual gifts in Ephesians 1:17-18 that: "the God of our Lord Jesus Christ, the Father of glory, may give unto you the spirit of wisdom and revelation in the knowledge of Him. That, the eyes of your understanding being enlightened, that ye may know what the hope is of his calling, and what the riches of the glory of His inheritance in the saint.".

Here, it is discovered that spiritual blessing is an inheritance, which every believer must possess. Apostle Paul makes it clearer in Ephesians 1:3, that: "praise is to God, father of our Lord Jesus Christ, who has blessed us in the heavenly realms with every spiritual blessing in Christ".

---

[96] See A .O. Nkwoka, p.27

2.4 Revelation and Healing through Traditional Practices

African Traditional Religion has long been in existence in Nigeria before the introduction of Christianity. Traditionally, the peoples of Nigeria believed that the malevolent forces existed and that they had power to influence decisions, change fortunes and destinies. They also believed that the only way to suppress evil forces was through consulting higher powers and mediums. This could result in a struggle in the spiritual realm, between traditional healers and unforeseen forces. The more powerful side would carry the day.

A traditional doctor might be employed to cure someone that witches/wizards or elderly persons have cursed for one reason or another. To cure a curse is one of the most difficult tasks in traditional medicine. It may take months or years for the curse to be finally destroyed. It all depends on the gravity of the offence committed.[97]   At times, the oracle has to be consulted through *Ifa* (Yoruba traditional practice of divination) so as to have full revelation about the causes of the calamity and possible solutions.

The herberlists through the process of consultation with divinities may trace the causes of the calamity to his or her sinful acts or past evil deeds. Any sin committed in the Yoruba society is not merely seen as an offence but as a sin which has both physical and spiritual disciplinary measures. The sin is physical in the sense that the person would have to be punished, either by public ridicule, or flogging etc., and the spiritual aspect is that he or she has to go through one of the various exercises which are considered useful and effective in removing sin and its attendant evil. Some of the exercises include purification, ritual shaving,

---

[97] See Ogunrinade Adeware, "Prediction for African Indigenous Practices in the Pentecostal Tradition of African Indigenous churches with Reference to Christ Apostolic Church, Abala –Itura." *Cyber Journal for Pentecostal Charismatic Research*, p.16

ritual bathing, open confession and propitiatory sacrifice (Labeodan, 2004:31 & Idowu, 1962:149).[98]

Furthermore, in the traditional setting, revelations are linked with the sacred to predict the future. In the Yoruba setting, a new born baby will be taken to the herbalist so as to know the future of the baby (*esentaye*) may be he/she will be the hero/heroine of the family, or may be he/she will be wealthy or poor. A similar thing happens when a woman or a man proposes to marry. The herbalist, through the Ifa divination, will reveal the future of the marriage; may be, it is going to be long-lasting or it will break half-way.

Also, in a situation where there are signs of a bad omen, like the untimely death of youths in a community, the *Ifa* divination reveals the possible solutions. Revelations in traditional settings, no doubt, cover all aspects of human life. This is why Bolaji Idowu said:

> Before a betrothal, before a marriage, before a child is born, at the birth of a child, at successive stages in a man's life, before a king is appointed, before a chief is made, before anyone is appointed to a civic office, before a journey is made, in times of crisis, in times of sickness, and at all times, Ifa is consulted for guidance and assurance[99] (Idowu, 1962:77-78).

Perhaps, the major reason why traditional worshippers fall back on Ifa divination is to know the causes of the problems and possibly find solutions. Such problems include: ill-health, spiritual

---

[98]. Helen Adekunbi Labeodan, "Moral Responsibility and Punishment in the Yoruba Society, *ORITA*, XXXVI/1-2 (2004), P.31. Also see, E.B. Idowu, *Olodumare: God in Yoruba Belief* (London: Longmans, 1962), p. 149

[99] E.B. Idowu, *Olodumare: God in Yoruba Belief* (London: Longmans, 1962), pp. 77-78.

sickness and sundries. The indigenous people believe that wicked powers exist but that through divine revelation and power of God, indigenous healers (herbalists) can suppress such wicked powers and also inflicted ailments (Baeta, 1967:51).[100]

From the above, it is clear that the herbalists (*babalawo*) consult gods to diagnose the ailments and probably carry out the spiritual surgery according to the dictates of the gods. On this issue, Olayiwola remarks:

> The elements of prophecy, vision, dreams and healing used as strategy for mission and conversion by the Aladura are not strange in traditional Yoruba milieu. The *babalawo*, a religious specialist with keen knowledge of Ifa divination system plays a prominent role in traditional divination and healing in Yoruba land.[101]

On this ground, it may be argued that one of the reasons why the *Aladura* at inception were firmly rooted is as a result of the way they met the needs of the indigenous people. The indigenes prefer the *Aladura* because healing is free, whereas the herbalists charge huge sums for sacrifices and healings. The *Aladura* also meet the needs of the people in areas of praying against witches, wizards and wicked people in the society.

Nevertheless, the role of herbalists in traditional settings cannot be over-emphasized. They are known as specialist doctors in the healing of certain diseases that affect the body and spirit (Simpson, 2004).[102] Some scholars argue that the *Aladura's* praxis

[100]. C.G. Baeta, "Christianity and Healing, *ORITA*, ½ (1967), p.51

[101] D. O. Olayiwola, "The Aladura: Its Strategies for Mission and Conversion in Yoruba land, Nigeria." *ORITA*, XIX/1 (1987), P.48.

[102]. G. E. Simpson, *Yoruba, Religion and Medicine in Ibadan* (Ibadan: University Press, 2004), pp.93-108.

of healing, visioning and prophesying has its parallel in traditional religion.

Three specialists are involved in the healing process of the indigenous setting – the medicine-man, the diviner and the priest. Although a person may combine all these roles, the patient cannot escape payment. The medicine-man, who diagnoses the physical and spiritual causes of the illness and treats it, would charge for his services. Nkwoka discusses further that in complicated cases, where the diviner consults the divinities for authoritative diagnosis, he collects some tokens. The writer believes that a typical African does not consult gods with nothing. The reason being, if the priest has to propitiate his gods, sacrificial items must be provided or paid for by the patient.[103]

In a nutshell, from the indigenous perspective, the traditional doctors give a clear picture of the world-view of the Africans as they relate with the supreme beings. This world-view is succinctly summarized by Ogungbile:

> The vertical dimension concerns the influence of the transcendental world which consists of the Supreme Being; the Divinities (primordial divinities), spiritual forces and ancestors.... The second major aspect of the vertical dimension of Yoruba spirituality is the Yoruba belief in ori (inner head) and malevolent spirits. The concept of ori lies behind the operation of Ifa divination. The horizontal dimension of Yoruba spirituality denotes the sociological analysis of the Yoruba world-view; his or her interactions with the sacred cosmos..., sacred nature, sacred space or place and sacred time constitute the major classifications of Yoruba world-view.[104]

---

[103]. A. O. Nwoka, "Healing: The Biblical Perspective." *NABIS*, Vol. Viii, No.1, (1992), p.34

[104] D.O. Ogungbile, "Prognosticism, Explanation and Control: The Interaction of

In the Yoruba traditional setting of prediction, explanation and control of events, Ifa divination plays very significant roles. Other systems of divination employed by the Yoruba include *dida Obi* (casting of kolanut), *wiwo owo* (palmist), *wiwo oju* (gazing at the eyes). The *babalawo* uses the *Eerindinlogun* (sixteen cowries) or *Opele* (divine chain or rosary) in *Ifa* divination technique.[105] The *Opele* (divining chain or rosary) is cast and read at a glance from the right hand side which presents the principal *odu* (which are sixteen in number), while the left presents the minor (which are two hundred and fifty in number)- (Ogungbile, 2001:86).

The *babalawo* invokes Ifa spirit and touches each side of the tray with the *Opele* reading the signature of the *odu* that appears on the chain that he spreads on the floor. Through this, he (babalawo) interprets the *odu* sign by narrating a primordial story connected with the *odu*. The *babalawo* uses this story, which may be in prose or verse form, to explain the message for the understanding of his client (Ogungbile, 2001).[106]

Thus the Aladura spirituality has its offshoot in the religiosity of the Yoruba traditional belief. Ogungbile believes that the profound religiosity of the Yoruba which forms the basis for Aladura healing operation centers on a traditional belief in the multiplicities of spiritual beings. Such spiritual beings include benevolent and malevolent spirits. Thus, at every conceivable occasion, the Yoruba embarks on nothing except he/she consults the *babalawo* who inquires through his *Opele* (divination board)

Ifa Divination Process and the Aladura Churches." In: Lawrence Olufemi Adewole (ed.) *Ifa and Related Genres*, Casas Book Series, No.13 (Cape Town: Creda Communications, 2001), p.85

[105]. Ibid, p.86

[106]. Ibid, p.88

and proffers solutions to his client's problem (Ogungbile, 1997).[107]

Also, at the local level, the adherents of indigenous curative system attach so much to revelations of dreams and visions. The issue of dream is a sensitive phenomenon among the adherents of indigenous worshippers. On this issue, Olaiya in an address on March 7, 2004 states:

> Dream as a means of revelation among indigenous Africans before the advent of the missionaries was less popular than divination. Yoruba people believe that a dead person can appear in dreams to counsel or terrorize the living. If a Yoruba man dreams, he may wish to determine the wishes of the dead person he saw in his dreams by consulting a diviner.[108]

In other words, a diviner could also foretell what may happen in the future. He/she may also be of assistance in interpreting dreams. If it is a dream that may involve life, the diviner or interpreter of the dream may proffer solutions for the person suffering the affliction. At times, some spirits may be consulted to ascertain what the (benevolent or malevolent spirits) want as sacrifice or ransom for either blessing their victims with good things or delivering them from spiritual bondage.

Healing in the traditional setting encompasses healing of the body, mind and soul. Healing means *Iwosan, Alafia,* etc. To the people, "health is wealth" (Yor: *ilera loro)*. The Yoruba particularly believe that if somebody is sick, it has two implications, depending on the existing circumstances. It connotes bodily sickness and at the same time, it can imply spiritual sickness.

If somebody is sick, the people will say *ara re ni ko da*

---

[107] D. O. Ogungbile "Meeting Point of Culture and Health…, p.100

[108] D. A. Olaiya, "True Prophecy." A sermon delivered at the CAC Agbala-Itura, Ibadan, along old Ife Road Assembly on March 7th, 2004.

67

(he/she is not well). *Ara re ni ko da* can also be used to describe a man that is mentally sick apart from physical sickness. To the Yoruba, for example, if somebody is physically well and yet mentally sick, he/she could also be described as a sick person. Therefore, healing is a phenomenon that comprises the well-being of the body, soul and the spirit. (Adeniyi & Babalola, 2001),[109] or what Idowu (1962, 1968) calls total well-being which is comparable to shallom in the Hebrew or wellschataung in German.

Healing, therefore, is strongly interwoven with religion. Here, healing, as a religious phenomenon has some connections with the Supreme Being, deities and the ancestors. It is believed that God who created the world also created the medicine men. God approves the continuity of life and creation through medicine and healing.

Deities, among the Yoruba, have a role to play in healing the people. The deity in charge of medicine is Osanyin. It is this deity that is in charge of all healing proceedings. The ancestral phenomenon in healing is also very important. The names of ancestors that have earlier on practised the profession are to be invoked before the medicine would be efficacious. Here is an example:

> Olodumare ebo mi ree o, Eje o jemi se. Eyin orisa baba mi, Mo juba, Ki iba o se o. Iba baba mi o, eniti o jogun oogun fun mi, Ki iba o se o, Iba Orunmila baba Ifa, Iba Osanyin, Orisa Oogun, sugbon ase dowo Eledumare.

Meaning:

> God, here is my sacrifice, May it be effective for me. You, the tutelary deities of my father, I acknowledge you, may you accept my acknowledgement. I

---

[109] M.O. Adeniyi & E. O. Babalola, *Yoruba Musslim-Christian Understanding in Nigeria* (Lgos:Eternal Communications Ltd, 2001), p.52

acknowledge you, my father, from whom I inherited the medicine, I acknowledge you Osanyin, The god of medicine, but may it be sanctioned by Eledumare (Adeniyi & Babalola, 2001).[110]

The submission above concerns the role of the Supreme Being, that of the ancestors and deities in the efficacy of medicine.

2.5 Revelation and Healing in the Contexts of Protestant and Catholic Christianity

The 20th century has witnessed the slow re-construction of the doctrine of divine revelation in the aftermath of the Enlightenment. In particular, it has been realized again that God is not simply another being in the universe whose existence, essence and self-expression may be assessed on purely naturalistc grounds (Trembath, 2002).[111]

The Protestant sees revelation as the disclosure of divine transcendence to humans through the self disclosing acts of the preached word, the biblical word and the living word (Christ)-(Baillie, 1956).[112] Furthermore, the Protestant believes that through the special revelations of Jesus Christ, human beings have had encounters and solid relationship with God through His grace and redemption (Dulles, 1985)[113]

In the same perspective, Roman Catholic theories of revelation during the 20th century tended to focus more on the corporate encounter with God than on the individual one. The

---

[110] Ibid, pp.52-58.

[111] Kern Robert Trembath, "Revelation." In: Nicholas Lossky, Jose Miguez Bonino et.al (eds.), *Dictionary of the Ecumenical Movement* (Geneva: WCC Publications, 2002), p.983

[112] J. Baillie, *The Idea of Revelation* (New York: Columbia, UP, 1956), p.38

[113] A. Dulles, *Models of Revelation* (New York: Image Press, 1985), p.46

corporate encounter with God has led to the reduction of revelation to salvation only.

Thus, this was the position of the Church until the evolution from Vatican I's *Dei Filius* (1870) to Vatican II's *Dei verbum (1965)*.[114] Between 1965 and 1970, the theories on revelations have been modified by the Church (Catholics) as transcendental as well as immanent.

However, the difference between the two theories is that in the former, the Roman Catholic Church saw itself as the sole and terminal sign of revelation in that it alone bears the verifiable marks of unity, holiness, catholicity and apostolicity in their concrete entirety.

But, the latter insisted that revelation is transcendental as well as immanent, that it proceeds from miraculous divine intervention, that it has a predominant doctrinal or intellectual aspect and that it is gracious and hence not naturally present within the human person.

In the aspect of healing, the Protestant and Catholic have contributed immensely to humanity. They have made significant impact, following the periods of agricultural and industrial revolutions in Europe, in the areas of medicine, education and the establishment of infrastructures like electricity, water and other social amenities for the use of local people. This development was extended to Africa particularly Nigeria. On this, Owoeye remarks that the missionaries introduced western education and established hospitals in various parts of the country and in Yoruba land, in

---

[114] Joint Commission between the Roman Catholic Church and the World Methodist Council, *the Word of Life: A Statement on Revelation and Faith,* Lake Junaluska NC, World Methodist Council, 1996.

particular. For a long time, these hospitals and dispensaries were run by various Christian missions before the government established its own health care delivery system.

It must be noted that it was not that the Protestant and the Catholic churches do not totally believe in faith healing of the apostolic era before they took upon themselves the responsibility of establishing hospitals and health clinics. But more importantly, the establishment of hospitals and building of schools were used as strategies of conversion.

Thus, the established churches through this process have contributed positively in the areas of health services to humanity in Nigeria. In Yorubaland, for instance, the various Missionary societies have affected lives positively through the establishment of the Catholic Sacred Heart Hospital in Abeokuta, Wesley Guild Hospital in Ilesa, the Seventh-Day Adventist Church Hospital in Ile-Ife and the Baptist Hospital in Ogbomosho. These hospitals have become models for other hospitals that came up in Nigeria in the late twentieth and twenty-first centuries.

2.6 Revelation and Healing in Other Aladura Churches

The leading *Aladura* churches, apart from the CAC, comprise the Cherubim and Seraphim, the Church of the Lord (*Aladura*) and the Celestial Church of God. These churches share some peculiar characteristics. They (*Aladura*) engage in fasting and praying for spiritual growth. Spiritual power is much valued and sought mostly after through prayers and fasting (Oshitelu, 2007).[115]

It is through these practices of fasting and praying that the Aladura churches receive divine revelations either through

---

[115]. G. A. Oshitelu, History of the Aladura (Independent) Churches, 1918-1940: An Interpretation (Ibadan: Hope Publications, 2007), p.102.

visions, dreams or inward witnessing. Indeed, the Holy Spirit is believed to feature prominently in their worship as it manifests through visions, interpretation of dreams, ecstatic behaviour and prophetic utterances. It is for this reason that in some of these churches, members are enjoined to wear white gowns. They indulge in this habit because thay claim that the spirit likes white apparel which is the sign of the spirit – purity or holiness (Ayegboyin & Ishola, 1997).[116]

With revelations, the *Aladura* churches provide solutions, through spiritual interpretation, to happenings, especially misfortunes and failures in life. They make prediction to people who want to choose marriage partners, and also predict about the safety of the road to intending travellers etc. The *Aladura* therefore give spiritual interpretation to virtually all happenings especially misfortunes and failures in life such as barrenness, poverty, illness, unemployment, prolonged pregnancy, disappointment and so on. This underlying belief in spiritual causation explains why spirit-induced services, faith healing, and exorcism are prominent in their deliverance services (Ayegboyin & Ishola, 1997).[117]

In addition, women are given recognition in the order of worship of the *Aladura* Churches. Many of the women perform the role of prophetesses and leaders in charge of visions. The involvement of women in church activities perhaps have greatly contributed to the rapid spread of the *Aladura*, as societies, associations of different kinds and welfare unions are

[116] For detail, see Deji Ayegboyin and Ademola Ishola, African Indegenous Churches, An Historical Perspective (Lagos: Greater Height Publications, 1997), p.29

[117].Ibid, p.28

established.[118]

Based on the foregoing, the Aladura, operate a brand of Christianity that is deeply rooted in African traditional culture. The world-view of the *Aladura* adherents is taken into consideration, particularly in their beliefs towards the operation of the malevolent spirits and forces of evil. The *Aladura* therefore, engage in interpretation of dreams, trances and visions. Their prescriptions of solutions to problems are varied, such as rituals, exorcism, prayer, fasting, bathing in flowing streams or rivers.

The *Aladura* therefore contextualize the gospel in such a way to bring closeness between the worshippers and God. The gap between human beings and the Supreme is made known through revelation. Revelation to the *Aladura* therefore is seen as a medium through which God unveils the future.

God is seen as All-knowing and All-wise. His knowledge of things to come is the strongest proof of its divine inspiration. Ability to read the future is not normal for human beings because they are liable to make mistakes. But God is seen as supreme and not liable to mistakes. He knows the future as perfectly as the past. Hence, people that are curious to discover the mystery of God in their lives seek for prophets who have the potentials of the spirit (Oshun, 1983).[119]

As earlier briefly mentioned, spiritual development takes place among indigenous Pentecostals through two ways, namely; (a) visionary/prophetic manifestations and (b) ministerial manifestations. The visionary/prophetic manifestations are the spiritual manifestations that relate to prophecies, visions, dreams

---

[118] Ibid, p.30

[119] C.O. Oshun, "Nigeria's Pentencostalism: Dynamics and Adaptability...," p.47

and trances.

Also, the ministerial manifestations relate to the performance of sacrosanct functions in the church as well as ministering to the sick and the depressed. The *Aladura* often perform these functions through prophets and prophetesses. They see their prophets and prophetesses as gifted church workers who are known for fortune-telling through prophecies, visions or dreams.

In the *Aladura* churches, members believe that prophets are endowed with diverse gifts as ordained by God. The prophets/prophetesses may prophesy on issues affecting individuals, or churches, or on pending dangers (i.e war, pestilence, famine etc) that may affect citizens in a country. Some renowned prophets among the indigenous Pentecostal churches extend their religious activities to the social and political lives of their communities.

Prophecy is not limited to special occasions in the *Aladura* churches. It may take place at any service, particularly during prayer-meetings and Sunday services. Messages through such prophecies could cover a wide range of matters, such as revealing to the people the divine will of God in their pursuit of entering God's Kingdom, offering spiritual guidance in matters affecting members' human problems and allaying fears concerning evil happenings.

According to an interview conducted with Adio, he was of the opinion that the *Aladura* uses prophetic uterances as means to meet the needs of the people and thereby shut the door of consultation with witches, wizards, sorcerers and herbalists. Also, through prophetic gifts, church members are edified in the way of

God. [120] The *Aladura* also encourages gifted ministers within the fold to be conversant with the studying of the Bible and other religious materials.

The *Aladura* also believe that illness or disaster which befalls a man or woman may be the handiwork of witches, wizards and enemies. This accounts for the reason why most *Aladura* churches pray against unforeseen forces which may slow down man's progress.

2.7 Revelation and Healing in the Pentecostal Context

Pentecostal churches believe strongly in speaking in tongues during praying, with the aim of reaching a spiritual climax and also to have direct contact with God. The Pentecostal churches hold the view that divine revelations give excellent results of prophecy, visions, dreams and trance. The Pentecostals see speaking in tongues as the manifestation of the power of God, as stated in the Acts of Apostles Chapter Two.

In the New Testament scripture, there are only three instances where speaking in tongues symbolized the attaining of spiritual powers through the power of Holy Spirit. The first instance is the Pentecost experience (Acts 2). The second is the Cornelius conversion (Acts 10) and the third is Paul's encounter with the Disciples of Christ at Ephesus (Acts 19:6-7). Of these three, the Pentecost account in Acts 2 occupies a central place. Acts 1:4-8 sets the stage while Acts 2 recounts its fulfillment.

Based on this, the Pentecostals believe that the Holy Spirit makes revelation through God to His anointed. Peter was

---

[120] Oral interview conducted with S. I. Adio, a church member of the CAC Agbala Itura, Ibadan, on 9-10-2010. Age-72 years

connected with the Holy Spirit in a trance to receive Cornelius'
messengers and thereby transformed the lives of the family as they
were blessed with diverse gifts through the baptism of the Holy
Spirit. Offiong remarks on the issue of Holy Spirit baptism, thus:

> Baptism in the Holy Spirit is believed to follow
> conversion and is evidenced by speaking in tongues.
> The power of God in the individual is manifested in
> the gifts of the Holy Spirit which Paul lists in
> Corinthians 12:4-12. These gifts include wisdom,
> knowledge faith, miracle, healing, prophecy,
> distinguishing of spirits, speaking in tongues and
> interpretation of tongues (Offiong, 2001).[121]

It has been observed that the spiritual lifestyles of
Pentecostal churches in Nigeria share some features with the
Aladura. Both are pragmatic in their world-view. They lay
emphasis on prayers, miracles, healings and visions. They teach
that believers will be rewarded spiritually and materially both on
earth and in eternity.

However, Pentecostal spirituality differs from the Aladura
spirituality in that the latter tends to be ritualistic and promotes
traditional religion. Such traditional beliefs include the use of ritual
objects and the performance of ritual assignment.[122] Offiong
comments further on this:

> Pentecostal spirituality frowns at the use of candles,
> incense, holy water and other ritual objects. The Bible
> is the sole authority in matters of faith and practice

---

[121] E. A. Offiong, "Varieties of Christians Spritually Nigeria, '' in Wellington O.
Wotogbe- Weneka (ed.), *Religion and Sprituality* (Port Harcourt: Emhai Books,
2001), p.188.

[122] Ibid, p.189

(Offiong, 2001).[123]

From the perspective of healing, the Pentecostals believe that faith healing is an integral function of the church as it happened in the apostolic times. They also see faith healings as a legacy which every living church must embrace. Idamarhare is profuse about this Pentecostal belief:

> Admittedly, there is a general consensus both in the teaching and attitudes of the Pentecostals, which shows that the healing ministry of our Lord is an integral function of the church, not only in the apostolic times but also ours. It is viewed as legacy; the church is to carry on the practice. This was the factor responsible for the rapid growth of the Pentecostal movement and which drew members from the 'historic churches' in the early formative period and especially in the 1970s and 1980s. Several methods of healing can be identified among the churches which constituted the Pentecostals.[124]

The methods of healing in Pentecostal churches in Nigeria differ from one another. In the Winners' Chapel, emphases are placed on anointing oil, aprons and handkerchiefs. Bishop Oyedepo, the General Overseer of the Winners Chapel, is noted to heal poverty through anointing oil.[125] Oyedepo sees oil as representing the Holy Spirit. Owoeye expatiates this belief:

---

[123]. Ibid, p.190

[124] A. O. Idamarhare, "Therapeutic Technique in acts Apostle in the Context of Healing in Selected Pentecostal Churches in Nigeria," NABIS, (2004), p.236.

[125] For detail, read S. A. Owoeye, "African Healer Prophets in Selected Independent Churches in Yorubaland 1963-1993." *PhD Thesis* submitted to the Faculty of Arts, Obafemi Awolowo University, Ile Ife, 2000, p.204.

Oil is regarded in the Pentecostal churches as representing the Holy Spirit. The Holy Spirit, according to popular belief, enables members to be rich once they are sprinkled with it... The oil heals physical disease of people whenever administered to the ailing part of the body. The oil performs other multifarious works; such works include assisting its users to secure jobs (Owoeye, 2000).[126]

In addition, Oyedepo uses aprons or handkerchiefs that he has prayed over to perform miracles of blessings or healing. On this issue, Owoeye reflects:

What probably informs the use of 'mantles' by Bishop Oyedepo and many other Pentecostals was the healing of the woman with the issue of blood during the earthly ministry of Christ. The general craze for the use of handkerchiefs may also be due to special miracles which Paul was performing through the use of aprons and handkerchiefs (Owoeye, 2000).[127]

In the Church of God Mission, one of the therapeutic methods is the use of words in form of prayers to heal the sick or cast out evil spirits from the possessed, or pronounce healing on the sick through the word of authority. The leaders of the Church see prayers as the mother of all blessings, including healing. In every service and meeting, there are usually prayers for the sick. Prayer band groups are established in all branches of the Church. Idamarhare writes:

Several times, healing has been procured as fellow

---

[126]. S. A.Owoeye, "African Healers Prophets in Selected Independent Churches in Yourbaland, 1963-1993." *PhD* Thesis submitted to the Faculty of Arts, Obafemi Awolowo University, Ile-Ife, 2000, pp.202-203.

[127] See Owoeye, (unpublished Doctoral Thesis,2000), p. 203

> Christians hold their hands together and form a circle
> around the patient who is prayed for or it could be
> through the prayer of the pastor... (Idamarhare,
> 2004).[128]

In the Deeper Life Christian Church, healing comes mostly during ministration of songs and preaching. On many occasions, the leader of the church, W.F. Kumuyi prays for the sick directly or might instruct them to pray themselves. Kumuyi, during his healing ministration, usually pronounces thus:

> If you could just beg for alms from God... if you are
> blind, tell God, I want you to heal me, give me healing;
> if you are lame, God I want to be able to walk, make
> me walk. If this man at the beautiful gate asking for
> alms could receive from God, if you ask... you are
> going to receive from God (Idamarhare, 2004).[129]

To sum up this section, Pentecostalism appears to be a unique phenomenon standing apart from other religions or religious movements. Revelation in the *Aladura* is expressed as a form of prediction which deals with the spiritual gifts of prophecy, dreams, visions, discerning spirit and trance. The Aladura also expresses its uniqueness through the use of faith healing. Based on the uniqueness in the practices of African Pentecostal Christianity, this section has therefore critically examined revelations and healings from the scriptural and traditional backgrounds through the operations of various Christian faiths and traditional religions inNigeria

---

[128] A. O. Idamarhare, "Therapeutic Technique in Acts of the Apostles...," (2004), p. 247.

[129] Ibid, p. 247

CHAPTER THREE

CHRIST APOSTOLIC CHURCH: HISTORY AND PRACTICES

3.1 Historical Antecedents to the CAC

The history of the Christ Apostolic Church has been a controversial issue particularly in African ecclesiastical discourse. The preliminary stage in the formation of the Church started in 1918 with the emergence of the Precious Stone Society which was also known as the Prayer Group (*Egbe Aladura*).[130] (Oshun, 1981: 24).

Prior to the activities of Precious Stone Society, a deadly form of epidemic [small pox] struck in several parts of the world towards the closing months of the First World War in 1918. Ayegboyin and Ishola estimated that over ten million people died from the plague and that Nigeria had its share of the calamity.[131]

Not only that, several parts of the world also experienced economic depression coupled with the outbreak of the epidemic. The situations therefore had adverse effects on churches, schools, hospitals, clinics as well as offices because the Colonial administrators closed many of them. It was at the height of this confusion that a few committed Christians through divine instruction devoted themselves to prayers and family worship.

---

[130] See C.O.Oshun, (unpublished Doctoral Thesis…, 1981), p.24.

[131] Deji Ayegboyin and Ademola Ishola, *African Indegenous Churches*…p. 65.

3.1.1   The Prophet Prayer Movements

Historically, the 1918 Prayer Group was born out of a series of divine revelation by one Daddy Ali, the sexton of the Saint Saviour's Anglican Church, Ijebu-Ode which he interpreted to mean the call of God to him to prepare the anointed group for spiritual development and growth. According to Odufowote, Daddy Ali claimed to have seen Saint Saviour's Church divided into two parts: The large part in darkness and the small part in light.[132]

Thus, Daddy Ali had to organise a prayer fellowship because of the divine experience. A five-man prayer group emerged with the combined efforts of some lay members of Saint Saviour's Church. The group was at first headed by Daddy Ali and supported by Messrs J.B. Shadare (the Parish People's Warden), E. O. Onabanjo, D. C. Oduga and E. O. W. Olukoya.

As the group was growing and taking shape, one Mr Shadare popularly known as Esinsinade, the people's warden of St. Saviour's Church and a member of the Lagos Synod for Ijebu-ode became the leader (Ayegboyin and Ishola, 67).[133] Another gifted leader in the group was Miss Sophia Odunlami.

Sophia Odunlami became more prominent in this group because of her prophetic message concerning the use of rain water for healing and deliverance. According to Ayegboyin and Ishola, Sophia Odunlami had a spiritual experience during her five day

---

[132].The large part was in darkness because it gave little thoughts to prayer; whereas the other part, though small was in light because it prayed constantly. For more detail, see G. O. Odufowote, "The Adoption Church as a Denominational Name in Nigeria," B.A. Long Essay, Dept. of Religious Studies, University of Ibadan, 1984, p. 13.

[133] Deji Ayegboyin and S. A. Ishola, *African Indegenous Churches...*, p. 67

illness in which God revealed in a vision to her that rain water and prayer would be the most effectual remedy for the influenza victims (Ayegboyin and Ishola,1997).[134]

Adeniran also confirms that Sophia Odunlami also had another revelation from God: that members of the Christian church had been involved in unholy alliance with medicine both native and orthodox medicine, as it relates to eating of kola nuts, wearing charms and drinking too much palm wine (Adeniran, 1984).[135]

However, the Prayer Group encountered series of challenges through the colonial government and leaders of the mainstream churches, especially the Anglican priests who believed that the idea of organizing a separate group within the Anglican Church was strange and against the Anglican orientation (Oludare, 1999 & Olowe, 2007).[136]

Consequently, the Anglican Priests eventually ejected leaders of the Prayer Group from the Anglican Church because they disobeyed the canon (Fatokun, 2006).[137] The Prayer Group popularly known as Precious Stone Society became a separate group.

[134] Deji Ayegboyin and S. A. Ishola, p. 67.

[135] See F.O. Adeniran, " A Breif History of the Origin and Growth of Christ Apostolic Church in Ibadan (1930-1980)," B.A. Long Essay (Dept. of Religious Studies, University of Ibadan, 1984), p.18

[136] S. E. A. Oudare, "The Trio of Christ apostolic Church Founding Fathers: Odubanjo, Akinseye, and Babalola," (unpublished Master's Thesis, University of Ibadan, 1999), p.18. Also, see Abi Olowe, Great Revivals, *Great Revivalist: Joseph Ayo Babalola* (Texas: Omega Publishers Houston, 2007), p.68.

[137] S. A. Fatokun, "The Apostolic Church Nigeria: The 'Metamorphosis' of an African Indigenous Prophetic-Healing Movement into a Classical Pentecostal Denomination, '' *ORITA,* Vol. XXXVII (2006), P.53.

The members of the Movement initially met regularly for prayers and spiritual instructions at scheduled places. Later, they held Bible studies in different homes of members and devoted more time for prayers. The Precious Stone Society however had imparted many people with teaching in line with the scripture. It also developed through its involvement in a body of doctrines according to which it disapproved infant baptism, thereby regarding the scriptures as final and infallible, recognized healing without medicine, and spiritual gifts as means of divine grace and guidance for members.

Concisely, the emergence of Precious Stone Society characteristically marked in Southwestern Nigeria, the beginning of a pragmatic Christianity rooted in Pentecostal revival. It was with a view to transforming Nigerian Christianity from an intellectual one to a power-demonstrating one through faith healing, visions, discerning spirit and dreams. On this, Oshun remarks, "The Precious Stone Society recognized divine healing without medicine and reliance on dreams and vision as means of divine grace and guidance, and enjoined its members to put total trust in God for their daily needs and personal problems" (Oshun, 1981:25-26)

3.1.2 The Faith Tabernacle Congregation

The Precious Stone Society gradually became the Faith Tabernacle Congregation with its headquarters in Philadelphia, U.S.A. in 1922. The links-man was one Mr. Odubanjo, a strong member of the Precious Stone Society. The Society through Odubanjo initiated contact and ultimate affiliation of the Precious Stone Society with American Faith Tabernacle Congregation through the reading of a Christian magazine called *The Sword of the Spirit*. The article titled "The Seven Principles of Prevailing Prayers", which he read in the magazine, became one of the recommendations to the members of the Precious Stone Society.

All members of the Precious Stone Society, however, accepted this recommendation believing that the two of them shared the same doctrine on issues regarding divine healing, consecration, fullness of the Holy Spirit and the pre-millennium coming of Christ. Within a short time, the Faith Tabernacle in Nigeria expanded to many areas such as Oyo (1924), Minna (1924), Zaria and Makurdi (1920), Ibadan (1923), Oyan (1924), Benin (1925), Ile-Ife (1927) and Calabar (1930).

However, the association did not last more than four years before division set in. One of the factors responsible for the set back was the issue on the teaching of Pentecostal gifts that deals with speaking in tongues, visions, prophecy and dreams. The information on this issue of spiritual gifts from the American Faith Tabernacle played down the doctrine of the Holy Ghost Baptism.

Further, the Nigerian Faith Tabernacle Congregation were disappointed that the American congregation never bothered to attend to their immediate needs of sending missionaries to Africa, especially during times of difficulties and persecutions from mainstream churches,[138] but only related with them by means of correspondence. Lastly, the allegation against the presiding pastor, Clarke for committing serial adultery and his inability to yield to discipline served as the final break up between the Nigerians and Americans Faith Tabernacle in 1929 (Adegboyega, 1978: 9).

3.1.3. The British Apostolic Church and the Emergence of the Christ Apostolic Church

Thereafter, David Odubanjo and his group finally left the Faith Tabernacle and were searching for another foreign mission in order to be free from the persecution of the mainline churches and

---

[138] See appendix one, "The Faith-Healer Babalola and Faith Tabernacle," in *National Archives*, File No. 662, and Class Mark: Oyo Prof. 1, Specimens 2 & 3.

the colonial officers (See appendix one).[139] The mentality of the founding fathers of indigenous movements at that time was that having an affiliation with foreign missions would bail them out of various challenges, particularly on issues related to court allegations and sundries.

Coupled with this fact, some writers are of the opinion that Odubanjo was in search of foreign affiliation for two reasons, namely: (i) the need for spiritual satisfaction that would trigger a nation-wide revival (ii) the need for protection against colonial victimization and persecution from Orthodox churches. In addition, he received confidential report from Government circles to work for a foreign evangelical sponsor.

However, Fatokun was of the opinion that Odubanjo was desperate for foreign affiliation because of spiritual reasons. According to Fatokun "For almost a period of seven years, the Nigerian Faith Tabernacle had been reportedly fasting and praying to God for the ignition of revival flame that would cut through the country" (Fatokun, 2006:49).[140]

This long prayer according to Fatokun received its answer in 1928 with the emergence of Joseph Ayo Babalola. His ministry became known with the outstanding miracle of bringing a dead corpse to life. The unexpected miracle changed the course of Faith Tabernacle history and lifted it into the limelight.[141]

---

[139] See appendix I for more detail. Also, A. Olowe, *A Great Revival...*, p. 180, commented that Joseph Ayo Babalola and twenty-five other Aladura members were detained in jail and charged to court on August 14, 1931. Thirteen of them were sentenced to six months imprisonment.

[140] S.A. Fatokun "The Apostolic Church Nigeria: The 'Metamorphosis'...", p.49

[141] For detail, see file No-1146 as attached in appendix 11

Thus, from this report, it is obvious that Babalola and other Faith Tabernacle leaders agreed to search for a foreign affiliation that would bail them out of victimization and series of persecutions of the older churches, yielding to the advice of the colonial with the colonial government.[142]   Based on this discussion, Olowe remarks that on many occasions, Odubanjo and Esinsinade travelled to Ilesha to plead on behalf of the Faith Tabernacle with the King *(Oba)* and District Officer without any success. This was a move to disorganize, or at least divide the Aladura Movement.[143]

Thus, because of this and other persecutions suffered by the Aladura Movement, Odubanjo decided to write a letter to Daniel Powell Williams, the President of The Apostolic Church in Bradford, United Kingdom, on May 4, 1931.[144]   However, Vaughan in reference to the write ups of Ademakinwa and Oshun confirms that Odubanjo before embarking on writing The British Apostolic Church had earlier made further investigations about its teachings and doctrine through its monthly Publication-*Riches of Grace*-if it tallied with the Nigerians teachings on Holy Ghost Baptism and the signs that followed (Vaughan, 1991)..[145]

---

[142]   For more detail, see appendix II. Also in relation to the involvement of Babalola with the Faith Tabernacle, more Information received from Pastor M. Oyebanji through oral interview at Efon Alaaye on 2-6-2011. He is the current Chairman of Efon D.C.C. He is 70 years.

[143] Olowe commented that Babalola and twenty-five other *Aladura* members were detained in jail and charged to court on August 14, 1931, thirteen of them were sentenced to six months imprisonment. See A.Olowe, *A Great Revival...*, p. 180 Also see appendix I as evidence

[144] Historically, the news of The British Apostolic Church in Nigeria came through a young Briton who was a hair stylist in one of the hotels in Lagos. He gave a copy of the British Apostolic Publication named *Riches of Grace*, to a Nigerian. This in turn came into the hands of David Odubanjo

[145] See I. J. Vaughan, *The Origin of Apostolic Church Pentecostalism...*, pp.16-17

Odubanjo had to make this inquiry about The British Apostolic Church because of the new spiritual experience the Group was passing through. Adegboyega confirms that Odubanjo's Group during this period had been having series of power encounter during prayer meetings. Such demonstration of power included speaking in tongues, prophesying and faith healing. Adegboyega, a member of the Odubanjo Group summarized the scenario at that time thus:

> We decided to hold revival tarrying meeting for the baptism of the Holy Ghost. Accordingly, a series of combined meetings were held at the Lagos and Ebute-Metta assemblies. It was at these meetings in 1930 that two brothers in person of I.G. Sakpo and Silas Ogunlaja received the baptism to the Holy Ghost in a wonderful way, speaking in tongues and prophesying (Adegboyega, 1978).[146]

The above quotation reveals that the Odubanjo group had earlier received the baptism of the Holy Ghost with its evidences before the arrival of The British Apostolic Church in 1931. However, based on this development, Odubanjo wrote a letter of invitation and sent it to the church leaders of The British Apostolic in Britain. In the letter, he explained the situation and sought for their assistance by sending delegates to Nigeria.

Vaughan reports that when the other Aladura leaders (from Odubanjo's Group) in Nigeria heard of this invitation, they felt it was a wrong move because the revival of Babalola had reached its peak as it touched every sphere of human life. In an attempt to cancel this invitation, Odubanjo wrote another letter to Daniel Williams and requested them to defer their coming to Nigeria.

However, the decision of the Nigerians to defer the trip of

---

[146] S. G. Adegboyega, *Short History of the Apostolic Church in Nigeria...*, p.39

The British Apostolic was already too late because Daniel Williams had already made adequate preparations for the delegates coming to Nigeria.[147] On September 23, 1931, the British Apostolic leaders arrived in Nigeria (Daniel Powell Williams, Andrew Turnbull and Jones Williams) to finalize agreement on how The Apostolic Church would take off.

Anim Peter in his historical record confirmed that the Nigerians gave them (British Apostolic) warm reception. The relationship lasted for ten years before divisions set in.[148] Meanwhile, the delegates from the British Apostolic Church and

---

[147] This issue of Babalola's revival on ground before the arrival of The British Apostolic had been a controversial debate particularly on the parts of CAC writers like Adeware Alokan, Abi Olowe etc. Their argument was that CAC had been on ground through the revival of Joseph Ayo Babalola before the arrival of The British Apostolic. Nevertheless, historically, it seems the position of these writers may be questionable.. The issue of concern here is not about 'revival' but about the dates of establishments of the two denominations. The British Apostolic had borne this name in Britain before its extension to Nigeria in 1931. However, the Christ Apostolic Church surfaced as a recognized religious institution in Nigeria in 1943.

[148] The debate on the separation between the Nigerian and British Apostolic Church has been a controversial issue for a longtime in the history of the church. First, some CAC Writers like Elijah Olusheye, Adeware Alokan were of the opinion that the British Apostolic seceded from the Nigerians who later formed the present CAC. This debate had no strong historical backing. Second, Ayegboyin and Ishola were of the opinion that the separation was mainly on the use of quinine by the resident missionaries and which was against the agreement on divine healing (see Ayegboyin and Ishola, *African indigenous and churches*, p.77) However, it has been discovered that the reason for the separation was more than the issue of medication. Fatokun traced the problem to the reaction to a change of misappropation of funds leveled against Odubanjo by the resident British missionary (Pastor George prefect) of T.A.C., Nigeria. (For detail, see Fatokun, "The Apostolic Church Nigeria…", p.2006., pp.63-64. Also see S. G. Adegboyega, *A Short History of The Apostolic Church…*, pp.87-97

the principal leaders of the Nigerian Faith Tabernacle Congregation had deliberations for two weeks. [149](Anim, 4-5).

They discussed issues on divine healing, the position of the Church on offices of the Apostles, Prophets, Evangelists, Pastors and Teachers, the baptism of the Holy Ghost with signs following, nine gifts of the spirit, polygamy, marriage and divorce.[150]

As earlier mentioned, The British Apostolic church leaders impacted life and contributed to the building of the Christian community known as The Apostolic Church in Nigeria before misunderstanding sprang up.[151]

The separation between the Odubanjo Group and The British Apostolic Church prompted the Nigerians' assembly to realize the need for a name for their Group. The name Christ Apostolic Church was finally adopted in 1943. It should be noted that the need for a name was not considered important until after the separation with The British Apostolic Church.

The CAC historians confirmed that Joseph Ayo Babalola was asked to seek the face of the Lord on what the name of the Movement should be called. It was, thereafter, in his vision, that he saw an envelope in which the name Christ Apostolic Church was

---

[149] This record shows that Peter Anim and two other Ghanaians (God Fried Asare and Alex Ankana from Ghana accompanied the British delegates to Nigeria. Anim confirms in his writing that the British delegates first had a stop over in Ghana before arriving in Nigeria

[150] An interview conducted with Apostle I. Gama from Ghana in Nigeria during his arrival for an international conference in JABU. The conference was later postponed till August 2012. Gama is 61 years and the interview was at Joseph Ayo Babalola University (JABU) on 10/1/2012.

[151] The letter of agreement on these numbers of issue raised was published in *Riches of Grace* Magazine on May 1931. See page 215 for detail

boldly inscribed. At last, the Church finally adopted the name the Christ Apostolic Church in May 1943. The Church develops its practices from the experience it had with The British Apostolic Church. For instance, the Christ Apostolic Church formulates doctrines on faith healing after rejecting prophylactic use of medicine.[152]

The practice of faith healing and other practices have formed the basis of beliefs and tenets in the Church. There have been practices in the Christ Apostolic Church, which have been so controversial right from its inception up to the present time. There are practices, which leaders have adopted but ignored by some members. Such practices have created rifts and divisions after many years of the church establishment.

3. 2 Practices of Revelations in the Christ Apostolic Church

The CAC is popularly known as a spiritual church (*Ijo Emi*) because of its emphasis on spiritual gifts of revelations and healings as spiritual weapons to overcome fears, evil attacks and uncertainty about the future. Olayiwola sees the *Ijo Emi* (spiritual Church) as a Church founded by spiritual and prophetic figures to see to the welfare of the people (Olayiwola, 1991).[153] The CAC, therefore, holds the view that for human beings to overcome fears of life, they must reject traditional magic and medicines, and rely solely on divine healing through the directives of the Holy Spirit.

In addition, the CAC also believes that for a servant of God to have good relationship with God as well as receive constant

---

[152] *Ibid*, , p.420

[153] David Olayiwola, "Hermeneutical- Phenomenological Study of the Aladura Sprituality in Ijesa Social History," *Asia Journal of Theology*, Vol. 5, No. 2, (1991), p.256

revelations (as stated in the Bible) from Him, he/she must always seek the face of God in constant prayers and fasting. This may account for the reason why gifted members of the CAC always withdraw to secluded places to pray and fast for spiritual empowerment. At times, the secluded places serve the purpose for church members and leaders to have good time with God and to avoid distractions in their devotions.

Most of the time, as they claim, people withdraw to secluded sacred places like mountains (*ori oke*) and prayer houses (*Ile adura*) under divine instructions such as prophecy, vision and dream, to seek God's face through fasting and prayers. The solitary period is what Olayiwola referred to as the time of incubation, when people withdraw to sacred places for safety, prayers, deliverance and spiritual guidance (Olayiwola, 1991).[154]

Very central to the CAC spirituality is the great emphasis on the Holy Spirit. The CAC shares the Pauline theology generally on the Holy Spirit baptism. Apostle Paul, in the New Testament scripture was the most prolific on this subject. Holding strictly to the biblical injunctions, the CAC holds the view that the propelling force for the manifestation of those gifts (revelation and faith healings) is the Holy Spirit.

Fesojaiye explained that in the CAC, The Holy Spirit is the basis of believers' faith and all members and ministers must possess Him.[155] The use of "Him" here in reference to the Holy Spirit is relevant because the Holy Spirit is not an ordinary force,

---

[154] *Ibid*, p. 260

[155] An interview conducted with Fesojaiye Adedeji on 25-11-2011 (now late) at Erio in Ekiti State. He confirmed that the Holy Spirit is the engine of Mission in the CAC. The founding fathers sustained the practices and heritage of the Church through the power of Holy Spirit.(Fesojaiye Adedeji (Snr) was 76 years when the interviewed was conducted)

but rather, a personality.

The emphasis of the Church on the relevance of the Holy Spirit and gifts has contributed immensely to the expansion and growth of the Church right from its inception. The report from CAC Year Book in 1975 showed that there were series of developments in relation to spiritual and numerical growth in the Church.

The record shows that CAC worshippers were about 1,000,000 (one million) in Nigeria.[156] However, in 2001, Olusumbola arrived at a figure that showed that CAC local assemblies were about ten thousand within the country with about ten million worshippers (Olusumbola, 2001)[157]

Also, the focus of the Church on the gifts of the Spirit particularly on speaking in tongues, protracted fasting, visions, prayers, prophecies and visions is to provide solutions to people's problems. The report from the 1985 *CAC Year Book* confirms that at CAC Agbala Itura Assembly, Ibadan founded by S. K. Abiara, 107 mentally ill people were divinely healed.

The report shows further that 300 people were converted and baptized within a year. It also revealed that the records of attendance increased from 9,409 on 29/1/84 to 13, 062 on 29/1/85. All these records showed the outpouring power of miracles

---

[156] There are few records of events on healing in the CAC Library, Ibadan. However, reliable informations are got from the CAC Year Book. For detail, see *Christ Apostolic Church Year Book* (Lagos: CAC Printing Press Limited, 1975), p. 7 and *Christ Apostolic Church Year Book* (Lagos: CAC Printing Press Limited, 1985), pp. 306-309

[157] O. Olusumbola, *The Growth of Christ Apostolic Church in Erin-Ijesa* (Ibadan: Ayo Press Publishing Company, 2001), p.35

through the Holy Spirit in the Church (CAC Year Book, 1975).[158]

The CAC, therefore, believes that once a person receives the Holy Spirit, the first thing he/she experiences is speaking in tongues. It deals with communication in an unknown spiritual language for the edification of the church. The history of speaking in tongues in the scripture has its roots in the Acts of Apostle during the feast of Pentecost. Obi in one of his articles comments on the background to speaking in tongues as follows: "The teaching of the Apostolic Church concerning speaking in tongues has its roots in the Acts of the Apostles, Chapter Two. That the episode of tongues is as a result of the promise made by Jesus before his death in Luke 24:47 and John 14:26; 15:26".

Another important aspect of discussion is on how the Holy Spirit is received. The CAC lays emphasis on the fact that the Holy Spirit may possess one during tarrying meetings, laying of hands and, or personal devotion. The 1968 CAC *Guidance and Teachings* say:

> *Ona meta pataki ni a n gba ri emi mimo ninu ijo yii. Ikinni, nipa adura agbapo ninu ile isin tabi ni ile idakeje ti o lowo fun adura gbigba. Ikeji, nipa adura, gbigbe owo le ni lori ati iketa nipa adura adagba tabi anikangba pelu itara, yala ninu ile tabi ninu ile isin* (*Iwe Ilana,*, 1968: 53-54)[159]

> There are three major means of receiving Holy Spirit in the Christ Apostolic Church. First, through corporate prayer during worship or in a quiet place reserved for praying. The second major means is through laying of hands and third, through individual

---

[158]   See *Christ Apostolic Church Year Book* (Lagos: CAC Printing Press Limited, 1985), pp.306-309

[159] See *Iwe Ilana ati Eko ti Ijo Aposteli Kristi Nibi Gbogbo* (Lagos: Ilesanmi Press, 1968), pp.53-54

devotion and fervent prayer at home or in the Church.

The tarrying meeting is the coming together of the Church to pray for the manifestation of the power of God in the Holy Spirit. At times, the tarrying meeting may also involve long praying and fasting as declared by the organizers.[160] The second major means is through laying of hands through a third party, especially an anointed minister of God. The personal devotion, on the other hand, deals with the individual through personal fellowship with God

3.2.1   The Place of Revelations in the Christ Apostolic Church

In CAC, revelation has become an important issue in the building of the Church. However, the CAC has a standing order on the use of revelation. Prophecy and other gifts will enable the church to expand but introducing members to the word of God through Bible study, Sunday school and seminars will make church members to know their positions and relationship with God. The position of the Church on this is that when church members are rooted in the word of God, then the Church will be stable and matured both spiritually and numerically.

The stand of the Church on the handling of spiritual gifts perhaps account for the reason whereby a prophet or prophetess must have deep knowledge of the word of God before he or she is inducted into the assembly, so that he or she does not lead his/her members astray in the use of gifts. On this, the CAC regulations say:

---

[160] The CAC believes in the impartation of the Holy Spirit and that the Spirit would be the source of power and fuel to transport them to heaven at the close of the age. This state is only attainable after the recipient might have achieved a sincere conversion and a great deal of closeness to Christ and His atoning grace. Pentecostals also believe that the impartation of Pentecostal power should translate into speaking in tongues other than one's own

Ki a to le pe eniyan ni woli, yio ni iye odun ti o tin lo ebun isotele, ati iriran otito ti o ba si ba oro Olorun se dede. Bi o ba si ni ebun ise Iyanu, ki o je ati owo Emi Mimo wa, ti ki se afogbon ori se, tabi ajeji emi, nitori ajeji emi ati emi alupayida ti wonu aye. Leyin eyi ni a le ya si oto nipa ita ororo si lori lati owo Alase Ijo (*Iwe Ilana*, 1968)[161]

Before a person is ascribed the title "Prophet" or "Prophetess," he or she must have spent a sizeable number of years manifesting the use of the gifts of prophecy and visions in line with the scripture. If he or she is gifted in the healing ministration, it must be directed by the Holy Spirit and not through human wisdom, or strength and spirit. This is because it is difficult in the contemporary times to discern fake from real prophecy. It is after this that he or she can be separated or anointed by the church authority.

The practice of scrutinizing prophets or prophetesses before induction into the CAC assemblies is to ensure that they have better understanding of the word and the wisdom to handle spiritual gifts in their various assemblies. According to the practice and teachings of the Church, the gifts of prophecy, visions and dreams help to reveal mystery or hidden things that are beyond human reasoning. Through these gifts, the Church receives comfort, courage and notes of warning against danger during church services or revivals (*Iwe Ilana (CAC Guidelines and Teachings)*, 1968)[162]

In addition, the CAC believes that all prophecies and visions should be confirmed as genuine through the word of God before they are released to the congregation. Thus, the CAC guidelines stipulate that gifted people must not reveal their visions

---

[161] See *Iwe Ilana ati Eko…*, p.54

[162] See *Iwe Ilana ati Eko…*, p. 54

and dreams to the church or church members without permission from leaders (*Iwe Ilana* (*CAC Guidelines and Teachings*), 1968)[163]

However, the CAC opposes those who have absolute trust in the revelations of the prophets and prophetesses without searching for the truth from the scripture. The Christian lives according to the CAC laid down rules, and this must be on faith in God's word, not solely on prophecies and visions (*Iwe Ilana* (*CAC Guidelines and Teachings*), 1968)[164]

3.2.2 The Roles of Prophets and Prophetesses in Promoting Revelations in the CAC

In the CAC, there are two categories of prophets, namely: the ordained and non-ordained prophets. The ordained prophets are to wear clerical collars during programmes while the non- ordained prophets are recognized as prophets because of their spiritual gifts. Most times, they are called evangelists. Both classes of ptophets usually wear white cassocks.

Ordained prophets are posted out to big assemblies to assist the pastors. Most times, senior ordained prophets are posted only to big assemblies or newly founded assemblies for stability and growth. Prophets posted to assemblies are to possess some qualities. These qualities are mentioned as follows: Prophets are expected to possess and demonstrate genuine and true spiritual qualities. One of the qualities of a prophet is holiness. He must be born again and be godly in character. Prophets, therefore, are seen as leaders who should lay good examples and live by them. They are exhorted to eschew all unnecessary material and carnal

---

[163] See *Iwe Ilana ati Eko…*, p.55

[164] *Ibid*, p. 55

pleasures (Ojo, 1988).[165]

The renewal of the spirit is one of the yardsticks of ascertaining a prophet in the CAC setting. The renewal of the spirit (*atunbi*) is commonly called 'born again'. The idea of being 'born-again' in CAC simply means turning over a new leaf by abandoning an unclean life for a new, purified and unsinful one. A prophet in CAC is to reject worldly things and yield totally to God.

Another characteristic of a prophet is the ability to pray and receive necessary revelations from God in order to meet the needs of church members. He must be able to offer prayers on various issues affecting the lives of church members or visitors who have come for counseling.

The CAC constitution enumerates the functions of an ordained prophet/pastor in an assembly as follows: (i) He is to be responsible for the supervision of the Assembly or Assemblies and workers within his jurisdiction. (ii)He is to administer the spiritual life of members and counsel them according to the Scripture. (iii) He is to organize revivals both at the local and district levels at least quarterly in a year. (iv) He is to preside over the meetings of the Assembly Board of Elders/ Deacons and other committees as the need arises (v) Lastly, he is to conduct Baptism by immersion for church members, administer Holy Communion, solemnize Holy Matrimony and report periodically the progress of his ministry to the District Superintendent.[166]

The prophetess on the other hand shares the same functions with the prophet. She too must receive training for the same period

[165] See detail of the features of the Charismatic renewals on holiness in M. A. Ojo, "The Contextual Significance of the Charismatic Movement in Idependent Nigeria," *Africa…*, Vol.58, No2,(1988), pp.176-179

[166] See CAC Constitution, pp. 41-52

at the church's Women Bible College. The only difference between the prophet and prophetess in CAC is that the prophet is ordained while the prophetess is not ordained. Nevertheless, both function effectively in the Church; the prophet sits at the altar while the prophetess sits at the front row facing the congregation.[167] However, a prophetess because she is a woman and therefore not ordained cannot perform certain formal or sacerdotal functions ascribed to the pastor who is a male. Take for instance, a prophetess in the CAC context, cannot soleminise marriage nor conduct Holy Communion or Baptismal or funeral services.

G. A. Adio explained that the CAC regulations do not allow women ordination and the right of women to run the administration of the Church. However, the situation has changed in modern times as prophetesses in the Church are now mostly Church planters. They often employ Pastors and Evangelists as workers under them. Not only that, these pastors and evangelists also preach on Sundays, organize revivals periodically and perform other religious services like naming, child dedication etc.[168]

The prophetess (according to the constitution) acts in an advisory capacity to the pastor/prophet or the church teacher. She also participates in the decision making process of the Board of Elders/Deacons or any other organ of the church. She is also saddled with the responsibility of assisting the pastor(s)/prophet(s) or church teacher(s) to conduct prayers and service. Finally, she is to perform any other functions as may be assigned by the Assembly council, the pastor/prophet, or the church teacher.[169]

[167] An interview with G. A. Adio, a CAC Pastor on 15-5-2010 at his residence in Ile- Ife. Age-78

[168] This information was confirmed by M. O. Eluyeni, a CAC Pastor on 29-11-2010, Aged-79

[169] CAC Constitution, p. 45

3.2.3   Modes and Operation of Revelation

The modes and operations of revelations by the prophets and prophetesses in the Christ Apostolic Church are similar to the Old Testament. In the Old Testament, Yahweh's instructions were presented with the oracular formula '*ko amar Yahweh*', 'thus says the Lord' and the messages continue with 'I am thy Lord', I change not...' This will be followed by the direct message 'I will...' The messages may be related to issues affecting individuals, or the church or in impending dangers including war, pestilence and famine among the people of a country.[170]

In another way, messages through prophecy are presented in form of parables and allegories. In CAC, the prophets and prophetesses work in line with the scriptures as laid down by the church's founding fathers. These forms of delivering messages are to confirm the genuineness of the prophecy. Some prophets and prophetesses in the CAC present messages through "acted oracles". Such messages are exemplified through vision.

The visionary often rise in the service to narrate his vision, either through trance or through dream. The scope of issues that are covered by visions is as wide and various as that of prophecy. At times, the prophet in the CAC may share what God has revealed to him in

---

[170] In the Nigerian context, the manifestation of the Spirit through prophecy has really replaced the indigenous practices of conjuration, sorcery and enquiry from diviners. Witches that are consulted by the indigenous people are humans who are thought to own intermediating ability; they are called the "owners of the world' because their power to intercede transcends that of the progenitor or the divinities. From the above, it could be said with some degree of confidence that the Church through prophecy has effectively substituted the indigenous practice of consulting diviners, witches and sorcerers to reveal secrets and mysteries.

dream with the congregation. Such vision may refer to a person who is near or far from a church assembly or on a national issue.

As earlier mentioned, it is a common practice that a visionary should hold the Bible, beginning with 'Niwaju Oluwa ati Eniyan' (before the Lord and human beings) before he or she relates the vision. This is to ensure the veracity or otherwise of the vision.

In an assembly where there are senior and experienced pastors-the most senior pastors-checkmate the excesses of prophecies and visions by screening the messages before they are passed down to the congregation. Isaac Olutimehin confirms that senior and experienced prophets/pastors in the CAC generally screen visions before they are passed to the affected individuals or the congregation.

Dreams in CAC are taken with seriousness, the reason being that some dreamers are so gifted that they possess the gift of interpreting such dreams. Dreams that materialize through gifted dreamers always do come true. At times, the congregations go into fasting and praying, as directed by God, to negate bad dreams. Fashina confirms that CAC attached so much to dreams. No wonder, dreaming is a spiritual gift recognized in the Bible.

The visionary gets his or her revelation in an unconscious (sleeping) state. The gift of dream is a way of revealing spiritual secrets to an individual or the church at large. The Church normally teaches its members to be careful of dreams so as not to make members be under the oppression of terror. They teach that when a person has a frightening dream, such a person should pray to God rather than live in fear. [171]

---

[171] The CAC teaches that God reveals event in the future through dreams. At times, the dreams may be positive and negative. If such dream is negative, then there may be needs for intercessory prayers. In addition, the CAC believes when a Christian dreams of acquiring wealth, such a person should rather be more

In the CAC, a matured visionary could disclose his or her revelation particularly from a dream to the persons concerned. However, the CAC regulation disallows this habit but most leaders in the Church overlook this procedure because they recognize the prophetic revelations of some gifted ministers in the Church as real and genuine.

In 1980, two great personalities (T. O. Obadare and S. O. Akande) emerged as prophets in the CAC Supreme Executive Council, even though their positions were not statutory. The leaders of the Church accorded them the respect of being called prophets as they consulted them for divine decisions that might affect the entire Church. In addition, they attended meetings of the General Supreme Council and were given prominence in decision-making.

In lieu of this development, recognized visioners are allowed to relate their revelations to the congregation when it involves the Church. Other young visioners are to be screened before they are allowed to communicate their messages to the congregation. However, the Church leaders may choose to reveal the dreams to the congregation by themselves.[172]

Another vital aspect of revelatory manifestation in the CAC is the gift of word of knowledge and wisdom. It is commonly referred to as divinely inspired knowledge and wisdom expressed in words

---

prayerful and hardworking so that poverty would not set in. This moral lesson is important to teach members who are lazy that the only means for acquiring wealth is through reliance on Jesus, hardworking and honesty

[172] The issue of dream has a long history with the indigenous Africans. Prior to the advent of the missionaries, the Nigerians used to consult diviner and find out the meanings of their dreams. In the Yoruba experience, he/she believes that a dead person can appear in dreams to counsel or terrorize the living. Unlike what is happening in the CAC when such dreams will be interpreted by gifted ministers, the diviner play the role of foretelling what will happen in future and also providing solutions to critical situations. See http://www.pctii.org

(Fatokun, 2005).[173]   Late Pastor Folahan referred to the word of knowledge as revelation that reveals secrecy about an impending danger or goodness and the precautions to take to achieve the desired results.

The CAC therefore being a prophetic Church believes in divine messages as means of guiding members about how to avoid evil and how they could survive without many difficulties. This perhaps shows the reason why members of the Church are careful not to disobey the voice of God through this means of communication. The gift of word of knowledge and wisdom, therefore, is a special gift that serves as a guide and security of the Church. Underlying the use of this gift is the necessity for obedience among members (Ogunrinade, 2009).[174]

3.2.4   Methods of Revelation

The first method often used by the prophet is a liturgical method. This method takes the normal mode of worship in which songs – chorus and hymns- are sung during services. The normal bible reading and exhortation from the Bible would take place. There, the prophet of the assembly would lead the congregational prayer, which is otherwise known as breakthrough prayers (*adura aluyo*). People are asked to stand up to pray so as to disallow members from sleeping off in the course of rigorous prayers. At times, the congregation may be requested to pray the liberty prayer (*adura ominira*).

In the course of the vigorous prayer sessions, people may burst into tongue speaking or ecstasy. Prophecies often come about through the prophets. Directives concerning the people awaiting healing might come and the prophet would then follow the

[173] S. A. Fatokun, "Pentecostal in South Western Nigeria with Emphasis on The Apostolic Church, 1931-2001"'(unpublished Doctoral Thesis…2005), p. 238

[174] See Adewale O. Ogunrinade, "Predilection for African Indigenous Pratices…," p. 13

directives. At times, if there are no specific directives concerning the patients waiting for healing, the prophet, after the congregational prayers, would pray on the ailments in the name of Jesus Christ after which divine healing usually follows.

In addition, prophecy is never limited to special occasions in the Church. It may take place during worship services, particularly during prayer meetings and Sunday services. Messages through such prophecies could cover a wide range of matters, to wit, revealing to the people the divine will of God in their pursuit of entering His kingdom and offering spiritual guidance in matters affecting members' human problems.

At times, prophetic messages may allay the fears of people concerning evil happenings and thus warding off demonic activities witches, wizards, sorcerers and traditionalists, and thereby edifying and encouraging members in the way of God. This explains why at least a prophet/prophetess is needed in each CAC's viable assembly; where such worker provides the needed spiritual guidance for that assembly.

Besides, the role of prophets go beyond church worship. There are occasions when prophets organize revivals, particularly Pentecostal meetings (popularly known as tarrying nights), for those who are eager to receive the Baptism of the Holy Spirit. In a situation like this, the church leaders may go into a special healing session in which members would be singing to glorify God. This singing, at times, would be with vigorous hand clapping and dancing. A song like 'Anointing fall on me' would be rendered. The song runs thus:

> Anointing fall on me,
> let the fire of the Holy Ghost,
> fall on me,
> Anointing fall on me.[175]

---

[175] This is one of the songs rendered in CAC during revivals, particularly at the tarry meetings when interested members are prepared to receive the Holy Spirit.

The prophets therefore listen to God's instruction on how to conduct healing and deliverance for their members. They achieve these missions through fasting and prayer. From the foregoing, it is glaring that the vision of Max Weber about the society with its meaning has become a reality in the setting of the Christ Apostolic Church. Members of the Church see the prophets/prophetesses in the Church as next to God and as people who are gifted to project through spiritual microscope into their future and probably find solutions to their existential problems.

3.3 Practices of Healings in the Christ Apostolic Church

The CAC generally regards illness or disaster, which befalls a man/woman, as the handiwork of witches, wizards and enemies. This reason is in line with other Aladura churches and the African traditional belief. The African traditional adherents do believe that the divinities or witches must be appeased to avert disaster and misfortunes in order to seek special favours. Based on this belief, the CAC practices faith healing through praying and fasting. The CAC carries out healing from three perspectives, namely: physical healing, spiritual healing and ecological healing i.e. land, forest, cities etc.[176]

The CAC gifted leaders are usually involved in these series of deliverances, but basically on divine instructions. Spiritual

---

[176] Healing has continued to occupy a central position in the life of the CAC. The gifted ministers in the Church have extended healing to every sphere of lives-i.e. physical healing, spiritual healing (healing of demonic forces and cultural impediments called deliverance), healing of land, which is conceived as healing in the context of the national socio-economic problems; and healing of social economic difficulties of life often termed 'Success and Prosperity'. For more detail on 'Healing', see the abstract of Matthews A. Ojo "Definitions of Health and Illness within Nigerian Charismatic Movements" in *African Association for the Study of Religions (AASR)*, 4TH International Conference on Religion, Environment and Sustainable Development in Africa, at Obafemi Awolowo University, Ile-Ife (2010), p. 39

power (agbara) is much valued and sought after thorough prayers and fasting.[177] On this, Oshun remarks:

> Within this spectrum of spiritual powers in the CAC, it is possible to speak of prayer-power (*agbara ase adura*) that leads to spiritual healing (Oshun, 1981).[178]

The CAC believes that through prayers and fasting, members would overcome their challenges. In an interview with Pastor Amure, the camp commander of CAC camp ground at Ikeji Arakeji, he comments that the CAC is unique and different from other Aladura churches in respect of divine healing, which emanates from prayer and fasting. Oshun further remarks about prayers resulting in spiritual healings thus:

> As prayer is regarded as multi-dimensional, so it is multi-functional. There are many aspects of praying and so its results are many and varied. Praying in the Pentecostal tradition, is a conversation with God, fired by inspiration, sharpened by fasting and embellished by songs to bring out the result of healing.[179]

---

[177] Power manifestations in the CAC are the demonstration of the power of the Holy Spirit through faith healing and working of miracles. There have been many incidences of miracles that had taken place in the Church which range from healing of land, divine provision to human healings. Through prayers, a lot of ailments of mysterious origins had been got rid of and this increased the membership of the Church such that some people from other religious inclinations became members of the Church Many people from the local surroundings were availing themselves of the opportunity of accessibility and instant answers to prayer through faith. Here, power is portrayed as having the ability to travel through any medium with prayers. Prayer played a great role in healing the sick and working signs and miracles

[178] See C.O.Oshun (unpublished Doctoral Thesis..., 1981), p.49

[179]. Ibid, p.49 & 50.

From the foregoing, the CAC largely forbids the use of medicine in any form.[180] The Church believes that sickness is recognized as a result of sin or satanic attack. Thus, healing and deliverance occur if church members confess their sins and abstain from them. Also, the Church believes that divine healing comes from faith and trust in the atoning Blood of Jesus Christ. The idea is that healing is spiritual and becomes a reality through obedience in God's instruction and holiness with faith in the atoning Blood of Jesus Christ.[181] On this note, it is important to mention here that the doctrine of CAC on faith healing, holiness, obedience and trust in God were formulated through the experience of the Church in its formative years, 1918-1930s.

3.3.1 The Subject of Divine Healing – Prophets and Prophetesses

There are several ways by which gifted ministers in the Church facilitate healing and deliverance. The idea is that sick people are weak, vulnerable and should be handled with care and therefore, give measures on caring for them. These measures include abstinence from prolonged fasting or complete abstinence where necessary.

In addition, the sick should be encouraged only by positive revelations and should not be scared of any revelations that may affect their spiritual lives and faith.[182] The CAC constitution makes

---

[180] From the discussion so far, it is glaring that CAC does not work in isolation. The Church took after the Faith Tabernacle and other Pentecostal churches around her. The Pentecostal churches believe in *Cura Divina*, (Divine Healing). However, due to modernization, this practice has been modified. In the contemporary times, many CAC leaders now visit hospitals to augment their weak faith and health states.

[181] The Bible references on the doctrine dealing with healing of the body and the soul are found in Exodus 15:26; Psalm 107:20; John 5:14; Psalm 91:16, etc.

[182] See *Iwe Eto Ilana ati Eko…*, p. 53-54

it clear that Prophets and Prophetesses in the Church should rely solely on trust in God through fasting and praying for healing of any form. Based on this laid down rules, prophets and prophetesses most often carry out their healing process by praying on water for their members to drink and bath.

Members of the Church are therefore encouraged to bring bottled water, satchet water and olive oil to their church assemblies during revivals, crusade and meetings for prayers and healings (see Plate 1: picture below)

Plate 1: The CAC's practices of praying on water and olive oil for divine healing

Source: CAC Oke Anu, Erio, Ekiti State, 23-11-2011

In some assemblies in the CAC, the prophets and prophetesses would dig wells, sanctify them and separate them for the use of the people with ailments. At times some prophets/prophetesses construct separate buildings for wells. In such buildings, there will be different apartments where members could bath, drink and pray. Such wells are seen as sacred because of the healing powers inherent in them.

Also at Erio in Ekiti State of Nigeria, before climbing the CAC Oke Aanu (mountain from which God's mercy can be felt), a well has been erected for the use of people for drinking and bathing. Many, according to Pastor Adedeji, have given testimonies of healings and breakthrough as a result of the use of the Erio water.[183] (See picture on plate 4)

Plate 2: The front view of the building containing a well

Source: Photograph taken by the author in Akure on 11-08-2011

---

[183] Pastor (Dr.) Femi Adedeji was interviewed on 25-10-2011 at Obafemi Awolowo University, Ile Ife. Dr. Adedeji is 50 years

Plate 3: The sacred well (internal view)

Source: Photograph taken by the author in Akure on 11-08-2011

Plate 4: Front view of the entrance to the prayer water

Source: Photograph taken by the author at Erio Ekiti on 23-11-2011

Plate 5: Full view of the sanctified water.

Source: Photograph taken by the author at Erio Ekiti on 23-11-2011

Plate 6: View of the bathing rooms on the mountain

Source: Photograph taken by the author at Erio Ekiti on 23-11-2011

The CAC believes that such waters are also used for victory and God's special favour. Because of the CAC's belief in the conquering power of God over all evil forces of witches and the devil, the prophets and prophetesses direct their clients having problems to bath with the sanctified water for healing. Another subject of divine healing for the prophets and prophetesses in the CAC is the use of Psalms. All chapters and lines in the Psalms have their significance as far as faith healing is concerned. The use of Psalms was one of the legacies left by Joseph Ayo Babalola before his death in 1959.

The uses of Psalms and the word of God are of strength in the CAC healing system in the contemporary times. Some of the scriptures references and their daily uses by the prophets and prophetesses are as follows:

(a) Problems of overdue pregnancy – Psalms 1, 2, 9, 51, 25, 86 and 87 will be read on water. The clients will drink and bath with it, accompanied by a three day praying and fasting

(b) For headache, eyes, pains, or defect and earache – Psalms 11, 117, 119, lines 161 – 168 will be read into oil and water. The client will bath, drink the water and then the oil will be applied to the affected places with one day praying and fasting (6am – 6pm)- (Abioye, 2000).[184]

(c) For the cure of malaria, ulcer, sore or wound – Psalms 46, 65, 147, 66, 38, 35 and 146 are to be read on water and oil for bathing and drinking.[185]

(d) Dreams and its interpretation – Read Psalms 22, 61, 51, 32, 42, 138 and 112 lines 8-24 into water, drink and bath with it. The client should make one day fasting and praying

(e) Snake and scorpion bite – Read Psalms 146, 148, 147 and 124 into oil with one day fasting and praying and rub into the affected

[184] N. O. Abioye, *Uses of Psalms and the words of God Inspired from Apostle J.A. Babalola* (1904-1959) (Ilesha: Hope Publications, 2000), pp.7-8

[185] This information was revealed during interviews with pastors S. F. Babalola (47 years) and John Fabelurin (34 years) at CAC camp, Ikeji Arakeji on 17-11-2011

parts.[186]

Another subject of divine healing is the use of staff, olive oil (anointing oil) and handkerchief. It must be stated here that those who suffered from sicknesses, diseases and infirmities received healing through a number of ways as mentioned above. The laying of hands is taken from Mark 16:18. Here, the Bible mentions the significance of laying of hands as follows:

> They shall take up serpents, and if they drink any deadly thing, it shall not hurt them; shall lay hands on the sick, and they shall recover.

From another perspective, the prophets and prophetesses strongly believe that the mountains and hills are another subject of healings. One of the obvious contributions of CAC to the spiritual and socio-economic improvements of Nigerians and non-Nigerians alike is the establishment and consistent use of prayer mountains both in Nigeria and overseas.

It is the usual practice in the CAC for prophetesses and prophets to go on mountains and hills to commune personally with God and also to pray for sick people. Such mountains are referred to as sacred because of their nature and God's power attached to them. Examples of sacred mountains and venues of prayers in CAC are: CAC Oke Idanre in Akure, popularly known as *Oluwa sekun mi derin* (God turns my sorrow to joy), CAC Ikoyi Mountain along Ikire in Oyo-State, CAC Mountains in Efon-Alaaye and Ido-Ajinarere, now Ido-Ile.

.   There are other recognized hills like Akinkemi in Ibadan

---

[186] All these Psalms according to Abioye were parts of the revelations of the Lord to Joseph Ayo Babalola in his house at Ipetu Ijesa in 1928, during his seven days praying and fasting. The leaders of the CAC in the contemporary times have adopted the uses of Psalms are part of the tools for healings in the Church.

founded by Oba Isaac Akinyele, Ede hill founded by S.O. Akande (*Baba Abiye*).

Plate 7a: Path to CAC Prayer Mountain, Idanre Road, Akure

Path to CAC Prayer mountain, Idanre road, Akure

Plate 7b: A View of Welcoming Signpost with Instruction

CAC Prayer mountain-top, Idanre road, Akure

Source: Photograph taken by the author in Akure on 29-8-2011

Plate 8: Different views of CAC prayer mountain-top, Idanre Road, Akure

CAC Prayer mountain-top, Idanre road, Akure

A view of CAC Prayer mountain, Idanre road, Akure

Source: Photograph taken by the author at Oke- Idanre Akure on 29-8-2011

Plate 9: Path and top views to CAC Oba Ile Prayer Mountain in Ondo State[187]

Gentle slopes leading to CAC prayer mountain at Oba - Ile

Source: Photograph taken by the author at the site on 29-8-2011

Plate 10: Overall Top view of CAC Oba-Ile Mountain, Ondo State

Churches and buildings of abode on CAC prayer mountain

Source: Photograph taken by the author at Oba Ile, Akure on 29-8-2011

---

[187] The photograph was taken during the author's visitation to the mountain on 29th August, 2011

Plate 11: Sign post and path to CAC, Erio Ekiti

Source: Photograph taken by the author at Erio Ekiti on 23-11-2011

Plate 12: Top view of the CAC prayer mountain, Erio Ekiti

Source: Photograph taken by the author at Erio,Ekiti State, 23-11-2011

3.3.2 Modes and Operations of Healing

In CAC, the prophets and prophetesses use the hydrotherapeutic method to heal their patients. This method demands the patients (sick) to fetch water from the stream, tap or rain and put inside different containers like plastics, bottles and jerry cans. This water will be placed before the prophets/prophetesses for prayers. In most cases, such prayers are always prophetic, direct with the intention to combat the enemies or unforeseen forces. Thereafter, the patients (sick) would drink the water for therapeutic purposes. The sanctified water is also used for women who are barren and those whose wombs have remained closed since they first gave birth or what is medically referred to as secondary infertility.

Another method of healing in the CAC is the laying of hands. Some prophets in the Church are fond of laying hands on patients for prayers and deliverances. Through this method, on many occasions the patients (sick) fall down and receive instantaneous

117

healing. At times, the Prophets may have to re-assure their patients that they should exercise faith after laying of hands and that their problems are not beyond what God can solve.

Another method of healing is jingling of hand bell on the sick during prayers. The prophets/prophetesses will jingle bell at the commencement of the prayer. The same process of prayers continues with jingling of bell believing that there is power of healing and breakthrough in the bell. The prophets/prophetesses will call the name of Jesus three times and say or pronounce as follows: In the name of Jesus, the living God *(Loruko Jesu, Olorun Alaaye)* lose and receive healing *(Tu sile, gba idande ati iwosan)*; and the bell will be jingled.

The background to the use of hand bell in CAC began with the divine instruction to Joseph Ayo Babalola in 1930. God instructed him to jingle the bell to ward off evil spirits within his vicinity and also for healings and deliverances.[188] At times, when a sickness is getting complex, the Prophets/Prophetesses pray on water, pour it inside the hand bell and give to the sick person to drink. The belief is that once such water is drunk, the sickness will disappear immediately. This to some extent has worked for those who believe in it.

Another method is the use of iron-rod (staff) for shattering evil forces and loosing those ones under the bondage of devil. The use of iron-rod is fading off in the practices of the CAC. It has been discovered that some ministers who now cherished the use of iron-rod the followers or lovers of Joseph Ayo Babalola during his time. Such ministers who are living witnesses of miracles through

---

[188] This information was confirmed by the following people in the course of my interview, namely; M. O. Olatunji District Superintendent of CAC Oke Alaafia, Ado Ekiti at Ado Ekiti on 9-10-2010. Aged, 62 years; O. Ojo, the Co-ordinator of Erio Mount on 4-8-2010. Aged, 58 years and O. Alo assistance coordinator, Erio Mount, Ekiti State on 4-8-2010. Aged, 48 years

the use of iron rod are: David Babajide, Abraham Ade Olutimehin, Joshua Adewale Alokan, John Dada Obafemi, Elijah Howard Olusheye, Samuel Kayode Abiara and Daniel Olorunfemi Oloye.[189]

3.4 Other Practices of the Church

Apart from these aforementioned doctrines, it is important to note some of the Church's other practices, namely:

3.4.1. Worship

Worship in the CAC is more informal than what obtains in older established denominations like the Methodist and Anglican churches. Prayers and sermons, for instance, are said extemporaneously. The present CAC by 1946 published its constitution and put in place the order of programme for Sunday worship.

Later, in 1965, the Church published the order of service for morning and evening worship and for other important services, such as Sunday school, Lord's Supper, and induction service (for pastors and workers of the Church). The morning Sunday service normally starts at 9.00am. People arrive half an hour before, and spend the time praying and singing choruses. Many of these choruses are spontaneously rendered by the congregation. Also, church members and leaders sing and dance with clapping of hands and make use of local musical instruments like drums, bells etc.

A lot of songs are rendered by the choir in the Church. This is because songs are believed to supply the sort of inspiration and

---

[189] The following people confirmed this afore mentioned fact; Prophet S. K. Abiara, CAC General Evangelist on 7-3-2008.Age- 66 years. Also, Jacob Alokan, the former CAC General Evangelist on 14-01-2010 at Efon Alaaye, Ekiti State. Aged, 79 years; and Pastor B. Folaju at Oka Akoko on 12-7-2010. Pastor Folaju is 63 years.

captivation needed for soul conversion and make the service lively. Also, songs do help to inspire members during revivals and crusade [190] (See plate 13).

Some of the interesting features noticeable in most of the CAC services, which are in a sense unique to the Aladura churches, include the following: Prayers are not read from a book but extemporized by the elders or the congregation, either quietly or loudly. Nearly all prayers start with the favourite expression *"L'oruko Jesu"* (In the name of Jesus), three times, and also end with a somewhat similar expression, *"L'oruko Jesu Kristi, Oluwa wa, Amin"* (In the name of Jesus Christ Our Lord, Amen). The Amen is said within prayers and at the end of prayers. [191]

Plate 13: Worship in CAC Assembly

Source: Photograph taken by the author at CAC Pisgah, Akure on 13-2-2010

---

[190] An interview conducted with Pastor C. O. Oshun on 17-11-2011 at Ikeji-Arakeji. Age-62 years.

[191] An Interview conducted with Pastor Jacob Akinjare at CAC, Oke-Aanu mount on 26-06-2011. Aged- 71 years

In addition, every member of the Church is expected to know how to pray through the inspiration of the Holy Spirit (Romans 8:26-27). In the CAC mission premises, there are specfic hours of worship. The prayer hours are 6.00a.m., 9.00a.m., 12.00 noon, 3.00p.m., 6.00p.m.,9.00p.m., 12.00 midnight and 3.00a.m.

3.4.2 Prayers and Fasting

The church members believe in the efficacy of prayers, which form the focal point of all their doctrines and practices. To appreciate the place of prayers, we may refer to a comparison made by the former church General Evangelist, D. O. Babajide, that:

> Prayer to CAC members is like a power-house built by
> God and the saints in heaven, like a source of water for
> all to be refreshed, an everlasting fire to give light and
> heat to all who need it (Babajide, 1959)[192]

In Christ Apostolic Church, Prayers, when accompanied with fasting are believed to be able to accomplish the impossible and produce untold spiritual results. Praying or prayers represent the distinctive features of the Aladura Pentecostals.[193] Babajide also refers to prayers as the main way to defeat Satan (Babajide, 1959:19). Also, Oshun remarks on the praying life in the Church as follows:

> As prayer is regarded as multi-dimensional so it is
> multi-functional....Prayer in the Pentecostal tradition,
> is a conversation with God fired by inspiration,
> sharpened by fasting and embellished/reinforced by
> songs. It also forms the citadel as well as the
> ammunition of Pentecostals especially among the

---

[192] D. O. Babajide,Ibere Ise Woli Joseph Babalola ati ti Woli Daniel Orekoya ni 1930 (Ilesha: Olalere Press 1959), p.18

[193] An Interview conducted with Dorcas Ajayi at Ile-Ife on 04-04-2011. Aged, 61 years.

Aladura adherents in Nigeria (Oshun, 1983)[194]

Furthermore, there are daily, weekly and quarterly prayer meetings in every local assembly throughout the year except Saturdays when church members are expected to have time for domestic work and prepare for Sunday worship (Oshun, 1981).[195] Daily prayers in the Church usually take place between 6.00am and 6.30am for about an hour or half an hour, and again in the evening between 5.00pm and 6.00p.m for another hour or two. Special weekly meetings are held during the week outside these normal hours for those who need spiritual help and comfort. In our interview with Oluwamakin, he remarked:

> Prayer is essential for all CAC members. There are special prayers for pregnant women, nursing mothers and barren women. The results are marvelous.[196]

In CAC, prayers go along with fasting. In some assemblies, congregational prayers are observed in the last three days of each month. Such meetings may carry the same obligation to fast. In general, the CAC observes the period of Lent as a time of prayer and fasting; and during this period, all other meetings might be suspended during the Lenten period to enable church members to participate in the exercise.

3.4.3 Church Meetings

One of the most practical aspects of the CAC's Pentecostalism is the revival service. The service (which sometimes includes gospel outings (ode-iwasu) either as a separate

---

[194] C. O. Oshun, "Nigeria's Pentecostalism: Dynamics and Adaptability," Journal of the Nigerian Associated for the Study of Religions, Vol.8, (1983), p. 48

[195] See C. O. Oshun, (unpublished Doctoral Thesis,..., 1981), p. 380

[196] An interview conducted with D. O. Oluwamakin on 20/7/2008, at CAC, Pisgah, Akure. Aged, 68 years

or subsidiary programme) forms a recurrent theme and becomes the main preoccupation of the Church since 1940.[197] The CAC revival service is mostly deliberately organized by some assemblies to serve certain purposes. Most importantly is to increase the numerical strength of the Church and also to create a forum for healing and receiving Holy Spirit Pentecostal baptism. The CAC makes it mandatory for church members to aspire for the spirit baptism particularly during tarry meetings. The process of spirit baptism always starts with spiritual songs and repeated clappings of hand. This may result to speaking in tongues and prophesying.

Other revivals include open-air revival and church revivals. One feature of the revivals in the Church is the echoes of hallelujah. The Hebrew word *hallelujah* designates praises and all that is connected with praising God (Oshun, 1981:386). The word *hallelujah* has become an acceptable mode of salutation, identification mark or pass-word among Aladura Pentecostals. As the people shout *hallelujah* and *ogo* (glory), they wave hands and fists in the air. This is prolonged until the bell is rung. The corporate shouting of both hallelujahs and '*ogo*' is a special characteristic of the Aladura Pentecostals and constitutes standard practice in worship. Hence, both terms have become concomitants of each other in the sense that the one usually presupposes the other and both together form a single act. [198]

In addition, most active unit for the sustenance of the revivals in the Church is the praying-band. The unit comprises of believers especially among the youth in the Church. Their aim is to

[197] An interview conducted with Pastor Joel Akintunde at CAC Ilare on 20-2-2011. Age-61 years

[198].An interview conducted with C. O. Oshun at Ikeji Arakeji on 17-11-2011. Aged, 62.

meet for prayers (Matt.17:21). Historically, the first praying-band in the Church was the *"Egbe Afadurajagun"* (The Praying Battalion). This unit emerged in the early 1950s under the leadership of Prophet Babajide, who was then an assistant to Joseph Ayo Babalola and later the second General Evangelist of the Church. In 1965, the name was changed to *"Egbe Imole-Aye"* (the Light of the World) and later to *"Egbe Odo"* (Youth Fellowship)- (Oshun, 1981:388).

The Youth Fellowship, which now is recognized as the only unit to function as praying band for the youth is well organized and composed by the Church authority. It now constitutes the largest unit in the Church. The Fellowship holds its annual meeting between June and August according to the CAC zonal arrangements. Based on this development, the Fellowship contributes immensely to the building and growth of the Church. From the foregoing, it is clear that the contemporary situation in the CAC tallies with the dream of Max Weber when he postulates that society has meaning with its development. The CAC grows into maturity with the dictate of its youths.

3.5 General Remarks

At this juncture, it is essential to examine the importance of various practices in the growth and expansion of the Church (CAC). As earlier mentioned in this book, church members are groomed to develop spiritually. Members, therefore, are to undergo baptism by immersion and also aspire to receive the Holy Ghost baptism.More often, emphasis is on spiritual baptism. The idea is that believers can only experience power encounter after receiving Holy Ghost baptism.

From the above discusssion, it is convincing that the spiritual baptism is an evidence of possession and demonstration of spiritual gifts related to dreams, visions, trance, healing and prophecy. However, the manifestations of these gifts among the

Aladura churches may differ from one another. In the CAC for example, the spiritual manifestation must comform with the teachings in the Bible. The Bible therefore forms the plumb line for visionary experiences and prophetic utterances in the Church.

Finally, on this note, it is important to relate the role of music in the spirituality of the Church. From all indications, music has become a great tool in the spirituality, evangelization and proselytisation processes of the Church. The CAC mission through this practice has not only influenced Nigerian music greatly but has also dominated the gospel music circle. The CAC music is now one of the most popular music genres in Nigeria.[199] In addition, the Church carries its music beyond the nation's frontiers as it expands to foreign countries through migration with modifications. Its music has been instrumental to the diverse operations which is acceptable in the global world.

---

199. For detail, see Femi Adedeji "The Theology, Practice and Evolution of Indigenous Music of Christ Apostolic Church in Nigeria and the Diasporas: Issues in Christian Transformative Musical," a paper presentation at the 1st International Conference on the Origin of Christ Apostolic Church, the First Pentecostal Churches in Nigeria and Ghana, held on 6th-8th August, 2012 at Joseph Ayo Babalola University, Ikeji Arakeji, Osun State, Nigeria

CHAPTER FOUR

THE PLACE OF REVELATIONS AND HEALINGS IN THE GROWTH OF CHRIST APOSTOLIC CHURCH

4.1 The Place of Revelations in the Growth of the Christ Apostolic Church

In the course of this study, we shall discuss the role of revelation in the growth of the CAC from the following contexts:

➢ Revelations Prior to the Inception of the CAC (Prelude to CAC)

➢ Revelations at the Inception of the CAC

➢ Revelations from 1960 – 1994

4.1.1. Revelations Prior to the Inception of CAC (Prelude to CAC)

The CAC, right from its inception, is popularly called *Ijo Aladura*, meaning Prayer Church. The reason is that the Church is prophetically founded on the word 'thou says thy Lord' (*bayi L'oluwa wi*) in the early twentieth century. Tracing the history of spirituality in the Church right from the 20th century, the Prayer Group carried weight in people's mind because of their teachings and spiritual practices. They believed in divine healing and

126

reliance divine instruction (Oshun, 1981).[200]

Furthermore, history confirms further that the Prayer Group shared visions with the American Faith Tabernacle Congregation when it arrived in Nigeria in 1922 after thorough conviction. Take for instance; the teachings of the Faith Tabernacle became fascinating to the Nigerians because they were more akin to African thought patterns concerning the basic issues of life. These beliefs and issues pertaining to life were later built upon by the founding fathers of the CAC.

The Prayer Group and Faith Tabernacle worked under the directives of the Holy Spirit and also screened themselves spiritually in matters relating to dreams, visions and prophecies. Also, healing by faith contributed to the tremendous increase in membership of the Faith Tabernacle between 1918 and 1929. The membership started with about twelve (12), rose to thousands with the Babalola's revivals (Adegboyega, 1978). [201]

Also, the arrival of the British Apostolic strengthened the spirituality of the Nigerians. It is noteworthy that both The British Apostolic leaders and the Faith Tabernacle in Nigeria were Pentecostal and they believed in divine healing, vision, dreams, baptism by immersion, and the baptism of the Holy Spirit and attendant signs.

All these developments culminated in years later to the formulation of practices related to revelations and healings in the CAC. Indeed, the Nigerian Faith Tabernacle did not express any reservations like the British Apostolic leaders did on spiritual matters. They (Nigerian Faith Tabernacle) outrightly rejected the

---

[200]. See C. O. Oshun (unpublished Doctoral Thesis), p.26

[201] S. G. Adegboyega, *A Short History of the Apostolic Church in Nigeria...*, p.7

use of any kind of medicine based on the divine instructions and revelations from God. They had total reliance on God for healing and other personal needs. This belief they claimed rested on both scriptural and experiential foundations.[202] However, the British Apostolic missionaries had different opinions about faith healing. The different beliefs on healing led to controversy and division.

4.1.2   Revelations at the Inception of the CAC

The phenomena of revelations and healings as religious practices in the CAC became prominent with the revivals of Joseph Ayo Babalola between 1928 and 1930. His prophetic ministry, the most accomplished and famous in the "Aladura" communion, was not only epochal in ushering in a period of effectual prayer and divine healing; it was also held to have confirmed both the claim of the Faith Tabernacle to divine healing and their long expectation of a mighty revival.

David Babajide, one of the patriarchs in the CAC, testified to the events of 1930 revival which shook the entire nation of Nigeria.[203] He confirmed that many of the prophetic revelations were unique and real with series of healings and deliverance. According to Babajide, the 1930 revival was a turning point in the history of the Church because since then the emphasis on spiritual matters became so strong and prominent among its leaders and adherents.[204]

202. An interview conducted with C. O. Oshun at Joseph Ayo Babalola University on 17-02-2011. Age- 62 years

203 An interview conducted with David Babajide at CAC Theological Seminary Ilesha on 19-06-2008. Age-101 year

204 This view was also shared by Pastor T. Aromibose, the Chairman, CAC Oke'sa, Ilesha on 2-3-2011. Aged 77 years

Oluwamakin, in his write-up, stated that Babalola made some prophetic revelations during his revival at Ilesa in 1930 and which have come to fulfillment in recent years. Some of these revelations are translated thus:

> *Ijo ti Emi Oluwa ti owo iranse mi Apostle J.A. Babalola da sile yii, yoo lo aadorin odun laye (70 years), lehin aadorin odun..., a o gbe omi ijo na ka ori ina.Itumo eyi ni wipe, opolopo ayipada ni yoo de ba ijo naa.* (Oluwamakin, 2007:13).[205]

Meaning:

The Church that I, the Lord, founded through My servant, Apostle J.A. Babalola, will be in existence for seventy years: after seventy years… Its water shall be put on the fire. The meaning is that many changes will happen in the Church.

Also, the writer (Oluwamakin) cited another revelation thus:

> *Ni ojo kefa, osu kini ni odun 1945,ni Oluwa fihan mi (Babalola) ni gbangba pe gbogbo ojo Jimoh (Friday) je ojo atunse aye yii; ojo yii gan ni Olorun tun aye yii da. Ojo yii gan-an ni Noah so kale ninu oko si ori ile aye; ojo yii ni Olorun sure fun eniyan nigba aye Noah. Ojo ti o dara fun adura gbigba ni ojo Jimoh* (Oluwamakin, 2007:17).[206]

Meaning:

The Lord revealed to me (Babalola) clearly in 1945 that the day Friday is the day of redemption of the world in its history; the Lord on this particular day (Friday) re-made the earth. On this particular day, Noah disembarked

---

[205]. D. Oluwamakin, *Olododo yoo wa ni Iranti Titi Aye* (Ilorin: Amazing Grace, 2017), p.13

[206] Ibid, p.17

from the ship on to the earth. God on this day blessed man during the time of Noah. Friday is a very good day to pray.

Another prominent figure who promoted revelations as practices at the inception of the Church was Daniel Orekoya. His activities became very outstanding in Ibadan, Abeokuta, Lagos, Warri and Sapele. Orekoya laid down the prophetic validation of revelations and other spiritual gifts as part of the requirements for church growth and development in the CAC, particularly in Lagos and Ibadan,[207]

Surprisingly, Orekoya, who was a cripple, managed the faith home in the surburbs of Lagos for over four years before his calling. His revelation in 1931 was basically on Church transformation. In addition, Orekoya claimed to have had divine encounter with angels who informed him about the restoration of spiritual gifts and faith healings among ministers and members of the Christian fold if they could abstain fromwordly things. Such things include idolatory, adultery, fornication, the use of ornament, earrings and other bodily adornments like strong perfume and bleaching creams. All these revelations formed the bedrock of the practices in the CAC in later years after its incorporation in 1943.

The revivals of these two great personalities drew people from all walks of life and also promoted evangelism as many joined the Christian fold. Ajisafe, a church planter in the CAC confirmed that Babalola and Orekoya laid legacies in the spiritual

207.Orekoya also had other divine encounter with angels about the restoration of spiritual gifts and healing ministry if the people could shun idolatory, abstain from adultery and fornication; and abstain from the use of gold ornaments, earrings and other bodily adornments in obedience to biblical injunctions. All these revelations formed the bedrock of practices in the CAC in later years. For further detail, see E.H.L. Olusheye, *Unity of Christ Apostolic Church*: A Must (Ibadan: Gideon Global Press, 2011), pp. 39-40

practices of the Church. Other practices put on ground by these two persons include: praying seven times daily – 6:00am, 9:00am, 12:00 noon, 3:00pm, 6:00pm, 9:00pm and 12:00 midnight. Also, they introduced that ministers and members in the Church must jingle bell before and during prayers to acknowledge the presence of the angels of God and thereby send off strange spirits. The lives of the two patriarchs have been very impressing. They showed love to members and other leaders in the Church. Their preachings on faith healing and trust in God definitely formed the background to the spiritual practices in the Church up till this moment. J.A.Alokan has a strong conviction that the CAC derives its practices and teachings from many sources, namely the Holy Scriptures, the touching and soul-inspiring sermons, lectures of its founding fathers and the spiritual guidance of the Holy Spirit. [208]

4.1.3   Revelations from 1960 – 1980

The place of charisma in the demonstration of spiritual gifts became more prominent in the Church between 1960 and 1980. The period marked the appearance of different gifted ministers as church planters and administrators. Also, the period saw the emergence of ministries within the church setting. These gifted ministers claimed the ownership of the assemblies and ministries they established. The operations during this period were completely different from the time of Joseph Ayo Babalola, Daniel Orekoya and Isaac Akinyele, when the focus was only on church planting and expansion.

The position of CAC, according to its motto, is "One fold, one shepherd." The laid down rules in the CAC are that gifted

---

[208] .The information was divurged io an interview conducted with J.A. Alokan, a reknowed author in the Church

ministers should use their gifts to draw people into the Church and that they should operate under the directives of the Church authority. The situation became otherwise when these gifted ministers invested heavily on their ministries and planted churches without any financial support from the CAC authority. It became virtually difficult for the CAC leaders to have full control of the independent ministries because they did not have any financial commitment with their leaders.

Due to the lapses on the part of church leaders, many of the gifted ministers who hold independent ministries do not follow the laid down rules of the Church. For instance, it has been discovered that some pastors and their wives are in control of church finances and the administration of their assemblies. Some couples engaged in sitting at the chancel/altar. This practice is unallowed in the Church. Only ordained ministers are allowed to sit in the chancel.[209]

However, it must be stated here that the charismatic leaders who formed independent ministries in the Church have really contributed to the spread of the gospel and promoting the name 'CAC' in Africa and overseas. They invest heavily on evangelism through the use of media such as the television, radio and the internet. The prophetic gift of revelations became more prominent as people trooped out for revivals to receive breakthroughs, healings and deliverance.

One of such recognised ministry in the CAC is the World Soul-Winning Evangelistic Ministry. It was established by Timothy Obadare in May 1974.[210] The Ministry of course took off

209 An interview with Samson Obaseki on 14-11-2010 at CAC Camp, Ikeji Arakeji. Obaseki is 83 years old while Odutuga is 75 years old.

210 See *CAC Year Book* (Lagos: CAC Printing Press, 1985), p. 285.

under the name World Soul Evangelistic Group (WOSEGRO) and later World Soul Evangelistic Ministry (WOSEM). One of the prominent leaders is Oluranti Akinola. He assisted Obadare to organize youths for revivals and prayers. He also assisted Obadare to set up revival grounds in Ado Ekiti, Efon Alaaye, Akure and Ilesa. The youths of the Church on the other hand contributed substantially to support the ministry of Obadare.[211] In due time, the World Soul-Winning Evangelistic Ministry expanded tremendously with over one hundred branches at home and abroad (CAC Year Book, 1985, 286)

In addition, the emergence of Christ International Evangelical Ministry (CIEM) under S.K. Abiara in 1977 is a living testimony to the CAC and other indigenous Pentecostal churches in Nigeria. The membership of the ministry cuts across denomination and racial differences. The prophetic ministrations of Abiara spurred the CIEM to greater heights. The record of attendance showed that for the first three years of its establishment, the ministry recorded regularly an attendance of 200 people. (CAC Year Book, 1985, 306). But after its 5th year, the attendance became astronomical. Take for instance, a total number of fifty-one thousand, one hundred and twenty (51,120), were recorded between 6th and 27th January, 1985 (4 Sundays)- (CAC Year Book, 1985, 306)

Similarly, the Christ Message Ministry – (CAC Kii Baati) was established in March 13, 1982, under the leadership of Lt. Col. L.J. Odeleke (President of the Ministry) and Mrs. Bola Odeleke as the Vice President. Through divine inspiration, the ministry took off with about 303 members in 1982 and increased to a number of 2,500 in 1984 (CAC Year Book, 1985, 302).

---

211 An interview with Oluranti Akinola, a former Secretary to WOSEGRO, on 5-11-2011 at CAC Holy Spirit, Akure. Aged 73 years.

The 1985 CAC Year Book confirms thus: "The Year 1984 marked a remarkable improvement in this Ministry. We started the year with two Radio Stations in Lagos and Ogun States. God in His infinite mercy added two Television Stations to our area of propagating the word of God. Today, people in Lagos, Ogun, Oyo, part of Kwara, Bendel and Ondo can now see us preach the word of God to them in their homes at their most convenience. Praise God" (CAC Year Book, 1985, 303).[212]

4. 2. The Place of Healings in the Growth of the CAC

At the inception of the Church, the patriarchs really did significant work in the healing of lands designated for idol worship and in the deliverance of evil powers that controlled the cosmos. Elder Ademakinwa in an interview said that Pastor Latunde and his prayer group in 1936/37 annulled all the evil powers attached to *Igbo* Olose, a very terrible forest not up till that time utilized for hundred of years. He also conducted healing on land which later became revival grounds. The land is now the site of the present CAC Headquarters at Ile –Ife.[213]

In a similar way, at Efon Alaaye in the present Ekiti-State, it was Joseph Ayo Babalola that conducted deliverance on the land called *igbo* airo (uncultivated land). This was a sacred forest reserved for rituals and burial ground of people killed by sanponna (chicken pox), ara (thunder) etc. The *igbo airo* was at the backyard of the king's palace.

---

[212] See CAC Year Book...1985, p.303

[213] Information collected from Timade Ademakinwa, a CAC Elder at CAC Moore District Headquarters, Ile-Ife on 9-3-2012. Interview conducted at CAC Moore Headquarters. Age-58.

Plate 14: CAC Ile Ife Moore Assembly Erected on the Annulled Land

Source: Chairman's Office, CAC Moore District Coordinating Council 14/5/2011

Interestingly, the forest was a forbidden place for the king even though it was directly at the back of his palace. However, after deliverance had been conducted on the ground by Joseph Ayo Babalola, the reigning king (Aladejare Agunsoye). [214] was led into the bush and no mysterious thing happened to him. The *igbo airo* since then has become an attractive place where modern structures are erected.[215]

---

[214]. Information divulged through an interview with Elder Taiwo Olagunju of the CAC Oke Ayo Efon Alaaye, 17-2- 2012, Aged 64.

[215] See J. A. Ademakinwa, *Iwe Itan Ijo Aposteli ti Kristi*, pp.64-65.

Plate 15: The Front View of the Palace of Efon- Alaaye Leading to *Igbo-Airo*

Source: Oba's Library, Efon-Alaaye, 17-2-2012

4. 3. Instances of Healings through CAC Prophets and Healers

The CAC is known as a prayer and revivalist church. Those that named it as a prayer and revivalist church have reasons to support their arguments. Perhaps, one of the reasons is the revivals and miracles that came up in the Church between 1930 and 1980\. These revivals convinced eye witnesses that the CAC is a spiritual Church. [216]

Adedej is of the opinion that the power of God resides in certain humans called prophets who demonstrate the power of God through healings. At this juncture, it is important to discuss these prophets and prophetesses that possess the gift of healing in the Church from the context of the following: healings at the inception

---

[216].In an interview with Dr. Femi Adedeji on 25-10-2010. He stated that the phenomena of revelations and healings have been majorly responsible for the proliferation of the CAC. He also remarked that the duo phenomena have contributed to the tremendous expansion of the Church in the contemporary times.. Dr. Femi Adedeji was interviewed in his office. Age–54 years.

of CAC 1930-1960, healings from 1960-1980 and healings from 1980-1994.

4. 3.1 Healings at the Inception of the Church (1930-1960)

Records in the CAC archives indicate that there are cases of documented miracles and healings from 1930 till present times. [217] However, in the course of this discussion, attempt shall be made to examine among others, the healing ministries of three important personalities who featured as healers and prophets between 1930 and 1960. They are, Joseph Ayo Babalola, Daniel Orekoya and Josiah Aderibigbe Adelaja.

Joseph Ayo Babalola

Joseph Ayo Babalola's revivals, which began in 1928 and ended in 1959, brought about series of testimonies and deliverances. He conducted deliverance and healings in many towns and villages in Yoruba land and adjoining areas. Joseph Ayo Babalola was born in Odo-Owa, Nigeria, to the family of David and Martha Rotimi on April 25, 1904.

He grew up as a farm boy until January18, 1918 when his uncle, Moses Oni Rotimi, registered him at an elementary school at Oto-Awori along Badagry Road in Lagos State. However, he completed Standard Two at Oto-Awori before his uncle transferred him to Ebute Meta. He started Standard Three at Methodist School, Ago-Ijaye, Ebute-Metta in 1921 and completed it at the age of 17. Unfortunately, he had to drop out of school in 1922 when his uncle was transferred to Iwoye, near Ilesa. He had to find an alternative

---

[217] See *Official Organ of Christ Apostolic Church* ...1978, pp. 11-19. Also see, *Official Organ of Christ Apostolic Church...*, Vol. 21, No.1, 1988, pp. 9-10. And see *Official Organ of Christ Apostolic Church*, Vol. 33, No.2, 2000, pp. 11-19.

to his livelihood by opting for apprenticeship as a drug dispenser.

In June 1927, Babalola started another apprenticeship. This time he joined the Public Works Department (popularly called PWD) at Osogbo to learn steamroller, driving and operating. He was still working with the Ministry of Works when God called him in October 28th, 1928. Since then, he had series of encounters with the Holy Spirit. These encounters produced spiritual encounters of healing and deliverance in his ministry.

Babalola started evangelizing at Ipetu-Ijesa and its environs, teaching and praying for people. Because his area of call was distinct (divine healing), his ministry attracted a lot of people. At Erin-Ijesa, he prophesied the immediate return of a prince that ran away for 15 years and it was so. At Omu, a town near Ikeji-Arakeji, he prayed for a woman who had been pregnant for four years and was delivered after drinking water that was sanctified by the prophet. [218]

In June 1930, Babalola came to Ibadan and wrote to the Faith Tabernacle leaders about his intention to join the Group. Odubanjo replied him to join in the deliberation at Ilesha which was scheduled for July 10, 1930 after the General Council meeting. However, the meeting ended abruptly with a revival as he (Babalola) raised a 10 year old boy from death.

---

[218] An interview conducted with Pastor J.A. Alokan, a re-knowed writer in the Church on 20-6-2010 at Oke Ijebu Akure.

Plate 16: Joseph Ayo Babalola.

Source: CAC 1986 Almanac

Undoubtedly, the 1930 Revival serves as a turning-point in the history of indigenous Pentecostalism and in fact, Christianity in Nigeria. Moreover, the Revival introduced Babalola to many places which he had never imagined he could reach. The Revival took him to many villages and towns. Available records in the CAC Sunday School Library show that as Babalola preached the gospel, many people surrendered their idols and charms for burning.

Plate 17: Charms and Amulets at Ilesha Revival in 1930

Source: CAC Sunday School Library, Akure.

Plate 18: Surrendered Charms and Amulets at Efon Alaaye Revival in 1930

Source: J. A. Medaiyese, *Itan Igbedide Woli Joseph Ayo Babalola*, p. 34

Evangelist George Oripeloye was of the opinion that through the revivals of Joseph Ayo Babalola, many prayer grounds, camps and mountains were established. According to him, he felt that the purpose for the establishment of these mountains and prayer grounds was to give chance to people to wait upon the Lord. Babalola, through the help of the Holy Spirit, established popular prayer mountains in many towns such as Erio, Ido Ajinare now Ido-Ile, and Efon-Alaaye in Ekiti State.

Also, with the assistance of David Babajide, the popular mountain at Ikoyi near Ikire in Osun State was established. This mountain (CAC Oke Ikoyi) provides a veritable avenue for Church ministers of all religious denominations to seek God's face, for spiritual and physical blessings, deliverance of all sorts, family problems and breakthroughs. In the same way, the venue where Joseph Ayo Babalola received God's call, Ikeji Arakeji, has been turned to a New Jerusalem in Nigeria.

This prayer ground, which was established by Joseph Ayo Babalola for people to receive healing and breakthroughs, has become a resort for the generality of people. The ground is today used as a prayer ground for solutions to people's diverse problems. Also, the flowing river (Ariran) at Ikeji is useful for faith healing for all callers. Babalola, according to writers, had the divine instruction to bless the water for healing and deliverance of people. In this regard, many people have been coming to bath and drink the water with faith for healing and deliverance. The water has two compartments, one for drinking and the other for bathing (See pictures below)

Plate 19: The Divine River Ariran

Source- Photograph Taken By the Author at CAC Camp, Ikeji Arakeji on 14-10-2010

Plate 20: The Divine River Ariran

Source- Photograph Taken By the Author at CAC Camp, Ikeji Arakeji on 14-10-2010

It must be noted that the Ariran water has been a source of blessings for many people after Joseph Ayo Babalola had passed to the great beyond. This divine spot has become more pronounced since 1990 as many eminent people (including kings and prelates) have been coming from all over Nigeria and the rest of the world to receive healing at the Miracle Center. According to Olowe:

> Specifically, 1992 was a vibrant year at the Miracle Center. People of different religious denominations are usually seen at the Center for bathing sessions. There are rules for bathing at the stream; People with physical wounds, leprosy, issue of blood, and other infirmities are not allowed to bathe directly at the stream. They would fetch water from the stream and bathe in designated bathrooms (Olowe, 2007:60).

Plate 21: The Divine River Ariran

Source- Photograph Taken By the Author at CAC Camp Ikeji Arakeji on 14-10-2010

Also, it is necessary to mention here that all the healing miracles that occurred at the Center were without the assistance of a minister; that is, there were no specific prayer sessions with the assistance of any Pastor. The following few examples of miracles, are worth mentioning:

1. Eunice Morolayo Igbalajobi, a woman who was lunatic and roamed the streets for 33 years was healed, and delivered from insanity after taking the Ariran water that was blessed by Joseph Ayo Babalola.

Plate 22: Healing From Insanity

Source- Abi Olowe, *Joseph Ayo Babalola Miracle Centre* ..., p. 63

2. In January 1990, while work on the construction of the stream was in progress, two men from Osogbo brought one lunatic Alhaji for healing at the stream. Their intention was to dip him into the stream but he managed to escape from them and ran to the bush. Olowe confirmed in his writing that as the lunatic took off, one of the men managed to sprinkle the water from the stream on him. Surprisingly, the lunatic according to the writer received his healing through the water sprinkled on his body. He appeared to the two brothers in Osogbo and narrated how two angels appeared to him and poured water on him and led him home (Olowe, 2007: 60-61)[219].

3. A woman who was suffering from a bloated stomach was

---

[219] See A. Olowe, *Joseph Ayo Babalola Miracle Centre...*, pp. 60-61

delivered after drinking and bathing with the Ariran water. The woman was said to be a daughter of a prominent traditional herbalist in Ikeji-Arakeji. [220]

4. Kehinde Fakoya, who was deaf and dumb, received healing, having suffered for several years at the Lagos University Teaching Hospital (LUTH) and other failed attempts from various traditional healers. She received healing in March 1992 after having her bath and drinking from the Ariran stream.

Plate 23: Healing from deaf and dumb

Kehinde drinking another cup of water from the Ariran Stream

unde responding to calls after her healing

Source: Abi Olowe, *Joseph Ayo Babalola Miracle Centre...*, p. 65

---

[220] An interview conducted with Pastor D.O. Alabi - a lecturer at Joseph Ayo Babalola University Ikeji-Arakeji on 17-11-2011. Aged 48

Apart from the use of the water for healing, part of the spot where Babalola received his call has been converted to a Mission University named Joseph Ayo Babalola University, Ikeji-Arakeji, located in Osun-State, Nigeria. The Ikeji Arakeji prayer ground gave birth to other praying mountains established by Joseph Ayo Babalola. These mountains have become grounds for healings, deliverances and places of safety for people who encounter spiritual problems. A few of the mountains founded by Babalola were as follows; CAC *Ori Oke Ikoyi* (*Ikoyi* Mountain) in Osun State, Nigeria, CAC *Ido Ajinnare* (now Ido-Ile) Mountain and CAC *Oke Anu* Erio in Ekiti State.

In addition, we also learnt in the course of this research that Joseph Ayo Babalola, through his healing ministrations, founded many assemblies in CAC. For example, Babatope of Ilesa (now retired from service) confirmed that Babalola planted the Christ Apostolic Church, Okesha, Ilesa in 1931; Christ Apostolic Church, Oke-Igbala, Efon Alaaye in 1942; Christ Apostolic Church, Ebute Metta, Lagos in 1944; Christ Apostolic Church, Irefin, Ibadan in 1949 and others. Surprisingly, all these assemblies have produced many other big assemblies after them.

Apart from the afore-mentioned, the Christ Apostolic Church, by its doctrine, forbids its members and workers from going to the hospital for medical treatment. The core of its doctrine is the entire belief in divine healing and complete reliance on God for all needs. Joseph Ayo Babalola, in his days, according to history, taught members of the Church about cleanliness and the principles of hygiene. His teachings about conception and care of a new born baby can be equated to ante-natal and post-natal care in modern medicine. According to Alabi, the late Apostle gave out the order of prayers for pregnant women, and also the regular psalms to read for safe delivery. This teaching became known in the maternity center at Ede and other maternity centers in CAC

146

assemblies.

Pregnant women, from all walks of life and from near and far, willingly went to the maternity for safe delivery. The maternity home equally developed as a centre of revival and evangelism. Many women who had been barren went there and had children; some others who had complications in their pregnancies were safely delivered of their babies; many children were born without surgical operation; and women with protracted pregnancies also delivered their babies. Also, a woman with seven years' pregnancy delivered a normal, living male child. Likewise, the water from the prayer meeting at the Ede centre was sent to a woman who was barren at Gusau and she became pregnant. [221]

Many indigenous Pentecostal churches have adopted the use of maternity centres. Take for instance; Pastor Sadela of the Gospel Apostolic Church, Lagos has established Ile-*Agbebi* (Maternity Home) for expectant women and a clinic for those waiting for the fruit of the womb. Also, the Church of the Lord, Aladura has established faith homes for pregnant women.

Following this pattern, the Christ Like Assembly Akure, Ondo-State under the leadership of Ketiku, organizes prayers for pregnant women and also looks after women's delivery. The Church of God Mission, founded by late Benson Idahosa, does not only take care of pregnant women, but also has a standard hospital where pregnant women and the sick are given medical attention.

In précis, Joseph Ayo Babalola has contributed greatly in the building of healing ministries in the CAC. He conducted healing deliverances in many towns and villages in Yoruba land and beyond. At Efon Alaaye, a land at the back of kings' palace which was

---

[221].The detail of this event is found in the *Official Organ of Christ Apostolic Church*, Vol. 23, No. 1 (1990), p. 21

forbidden for the king was consecrated through prayers. At Usi Ekiti now Ekiti State, he singled handedly cut down the forbidden tree which was regarded as sacred tree (Ojo, 1988). [222]

Daniel Orekoya (February, 1930 – August, 1930)

We are yet to ascertain the exact date when Daniel O. Orekoya was born. But records indicate that he was born and bred in Ijebu-Ife and that he was a professional tailor. Originally, he was an Anglican Church member before joining the Faith Tabernacle in Lagos (Babajide, 1975).[223]

Here, his sterling spiritual qualities became manifest and for over four years, he was engaged as a sexton of the Idi-Oro Faith Tabernacle centre; and later appointed as the care-taker of the maternity centre at Idi-Oro in 1926. A hired house was then used as the maternity for the group. Adegboyega confirms that Orekoya was a man of faith and was mightily used of the Lord to perform signs and wonders to mankind through his prophetic healing (Adegboyega, 1978).[224]

On 28th August, 1930, Daniel Orekoya attended the revival of Babalola at Oke-Ooye, Ilesha with the view to discussing his calling with him (Babalola). He (Orekoya) was there for one week. However, from the time the revival began, Joseph Babalola made it a practice to pray to God to raise other prophets who could assist him in the ministerial work. The arrival of Orekoya at Ilesa was a blessing in disguise for Babalola .He warmly received and prepared him for ministerial work.

---

[222] John Odunayo Ojo, *The Life and Ministry of Apostle Joseph Ayodele Babalola (from 1904-1959)*, (Lagos: Prayer Band Publications, 1988), pp.78-79

[223] D. O. Babajide, *Ibere Ise Woli Joseph Babalola ati Woli Daniel Orekoya*, p.22

[224] S. G. Adegboyega, *Short History of the Apostolic Church in Nigeria*, p.16

On 4th September, Orekoya left Ilesha for Lagos via Ede and Ibadan. But when he got to Ibadan, he called to give a report of his divine experiences to Akinyele. Surprisingly, his encounter with Akinyele led to the Oke Bola Revival.[225] There are series of records of healings and the resuscitation of dead people in the revival. The case of a dead pregnant woman Alice Abeo (later Alice Adisa) was a wonderful miracle of the Ibadan revival. Abeo was from the village of Kute near Ibadan. Her husband brought her to the revival to be abandoned there after the third day of her death (Adegboyega, 1978).[226]

Plate 24: Evangelist D.O. Orekoya

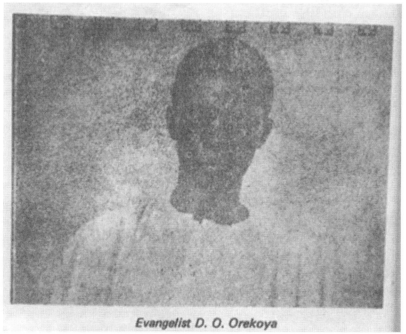

Evangelist D. O. Orekoya

Source: S. G. Adegboyega, *Short History of the Apostolic Church in Nigeria...*, p. 16.

---

[225] An interview with T. Omjuwa-the CAC Zonal Chairman for Oke Alafia District Headquarters on 17-4-2010. Age-55 years.

[226] See S. G. Adegboyega, *Short History of The Apostolic Church in Nigeria,* p.19

The dead body was brought to the revival ground because Abeo's husband had no money to propitiate the gods against a recurrence of that bad fate. All he wanted was to invoke God to stop such a bad incident among the remaining members of his household. But ringing his hand-bell, Daniel Orekoya prayed on her corpse for about half an-hour and she, thereafter, came back to life (Adegboyega, 1978).[227] Ehindero confirms that: "from every part of Ibadan and surrounding towns, people came carrying bottles filled with water…" Also, people began to surrender their charms, charm belts, rings, armlets, potions and idols for destruction and burning.[228]

As the revival progressed, more people came to surrender their charms and lives to Jesus Christ. One of such people was a middle-aged woman called Ajike.[229] During the revival programme, Ajike loosened her wrapper as if she was under a powerful spell, removed a charm-amulet (Yor. *Onde)* from her waist and dropped it near the spot where the prophet was standing. As she turned back to go, the charm cried out in clear voice, pleading that Ajike should not leave her. However, Ajike got her deliverance on that day.

Records show further that 341 known people were cured during the first two weeks at the Oke-Bola revival. The number increased between September 14 and October 4, 1930. The number of the sick people who were cured had jumped to 2,538. The breakdown is as follows: Miscarriage: 49, pregnancy without giving birth: 202, hunchbacked: 15, gonorrhea:19, bellyache: 87,

---

[227] *Ibid*, p. 18

[228] An interview conducted with D. O. Ehindero at Ikare-Akoko on 16-12-2009. Age-78 years

[229] Information divulged from W. Aladejare, a retired Chairman in CAC D.C.C. Oke Ijebu, Akure on 7-6-2010 in Akure.Age-74 years.

witchcraft: 41, backache: 161, blindness: 24, coughing: 22, infertility: 11, dead bodies raised: 22, women's sickness: 24, rashes and blemishes: 11, leprosy: 58 and the like (Babajide, 1959)[230]

Apart from the regular revival sessions at Oke-Bola, public processions were held within the municipality as well as open air services at Agodi, Sabo, Ita Bale, Agbeni, Oje, Ayeye and Dugbe (Oshun,1981).[231] It was common for Orekoya during prayers to request his audience to recite a scriptural passage thus:

Oluwa womi san, emi o san,
Oluwa gbami la, emi yoo la.(Babajide, 1959)[232]

Meaning:

Heal me o Lord, I will be healed. Save me, I shall be saved

After the recitation of this passage, Orekoya prayed with faith for his audience and those who received healing would inform the recorders accordingly.

From October 1930 to March 1931, Orekoya began a revival in Abeokuta. The revival brought closeness with Ifakoya Dawodu Oshitelu, of the Church of the Lord Aladura. Oshitelu had been on an evangelistic mission in Abeokuta and its suburbs before the arrival of Orekoya. However, the relationship was short lived.

At the end of January 1931, it was decided that Orekoya and Oshitelu should part ways because of differences in their spiritual approaches and methods. Nevertheless, Orekoya pulled

---

[230] D. O. Babajide, *Ibere Ise Woli Joseph Ayo Babalola ati ti Woli Daniel Orekoya ni 1930* (Ilesha: Olalere Press, 1959), p. 22

[231] C. O. Oshun, (unpublished Doctoral Thesis…,1981), p.122

[232] See D. O. Babajide, *Ibere Ise Woli Joseph Ayo Babalola…*, p. 13

crowds in thousands at the revival. An estimated number of over 2,000 persons testified to God's work.[233]

Orekoya, in March 1931, returned to Idi Oro where he continued his revivalistic activities until his departure to the Delta areas of Warri and Sapele in the present Delta State. Orekoya was invited for revival in Warri and Sapele by a certain lady who witnessed the miracles at Oke Bola, Ibadan. Unfortunately, Orekoya had an accident in the course of the revival. The prophet was involved in a gas-lamp explosion which inevitably brought the revival to an abrupt end and later caused his death at Ijebu-lfe, his own town (Oshun, 1981)[234]

To round off this piece, it is necessary to mention that Orekoya did not live long to enjoy the fruits of his labour. However, the little time he spent for God's work indicate clear evidence that he was anointed for ministerial assignment.

Josiah Aderibigbe Adelaja

Another great personality in the history of the CAC between 1930 and 1960 was Adelaja. The actual date of Adelaja's birth is unknown but records show that his birth could be between 1910 and 1916. His activities in the spread of the gospel shared this. Adelaja worked as a pastor in one of the congregations of the Faith Tabernacle in Kano after the fall of Pastor Clark in 1926.

It must be noted that prior to the advent of the 1930 revival movement, the Faith Tabernacle group of Nigeria had made incursions into some big towns of Northern Nigeria. But at the advent of the new revival movement in 1930, Faith Tabernacle had

---

[233] J. A. Ademakinwa, *Iwe Itan Ijo Aposteli ti Kristi* (Lagos: Agege CAC Press Ltd, 1971), p. 63

[234] C. O. Oshun, (unpublished Doctoral Thesis…, 1981), p. 12

gradually lost its popularity among people. The disintegration of its leadership with the fall of A. Clark had badly affected its members not only in the South but also in the North of Nigeria (Ademakin, 1971).[235]

Providentially, the revival movement provided solutions to that religious impasse, more so that Adelaja as pastor in charge of that area readily identified himself with the revival movement. In response to the need of the area, the revival leaders led by Joseph Babalola and Joshua Medaiyese, in cooperation with other revival leaders in the South, launched revival crusades at different principal towns of the Northern Region.[236] They preached the gospel to the people and made many converts. Soon, Kano became the District Headquarters and the seat of Adelaja, who was then acting as the Superintendent of that area.

Adelaja started the ministry in Kano as a part-time minister. He was a businessman. He engaged in selling name-tags and labels for identifying luggages at major railway towns of Kano, Nguru, Kafanchan and Gashua. He was known for his high standard of integrity, honesty, righteousness and holy living. He worked relentlessly in that area to establish and consolidate the new Faith.

He successfully performed the church duties of baptizing converts, conducting harvest services, preaching the gospel and winning souls, organizing prayer meetings and fasting sessions as well as performing wonders and miracles. Through his untiring zeal and with the cooperation of his ministers and the church members, the new Faith quickly spread to the nooks and crannies of Northern Nigeria.

---

[235] J. A. Ademakinwa, *Iwe Itan Ijo Aposteli ti Kristi*..., pp. 50-51.

[236] An interview conducted with Pastor J. R. Mangai, the Zonal Chairman CAC Makurdi at Ikeji Arakeji on 13-11-2009, Age-56 years.

Plate 25- J. A. Adelaja.[237]

Source- CAC Secretariat, Bashorun, Ibadan

Furthermore, the pioneer missionary gave prominence to the training of his workers. To that end, Adelaja established in the North a Religious Training Institute, similar to the C.A.C. Bible College in the South, in order to teach English and Hausa languages to the Northern youths. The Institute has now become one of the thirteen satellite campuses of the church main seminary at Ile–Ife. The seminary was first established in Kano before it was permanently established at Bokkos in Plateau State.[238]

Not only that, Adelaja pioneered many assemblies in the

---

[237] *Ibid*

[238] An interview conducted with Pastor G.Ehindero, Coordintor, CAC Kaaba campus on 17-2- 2009. Aged 49 years.

Northern parts of Nigeria. In an interview with Waleola, a prophetess who had lived in Kano before she re-deployed to Erio Ekiti remarked that Adelaja laid a very solid foundation for the Christ Apostolic Church in Northern Nigeria. During his lifetime, virtually all C.A.C. assemblies in Kano and suburbs remained united. However, after his death on 31st October 1969, the large district was split into four districts of Kano, Kaduna, Zaria and Jos. The area was designated "Section C", consisting of some fourteen autonomous districts. Seven of them were supervised by senior pastors in the rank of Assistant General Superintendent (now chairman), and the others coordinated by pastors not below the rank of a District Superintendent.[239]

To sum up this section, Adelaja steadily identified with the 1930 Revival. Through him, Joseph Ayo Babalola visited Kano to conduct revivals. There were series of miracles wrought through the revivals of Adelaja in the Northern part of Nigeria. He was able to introduce the practice of faith healing among the CAC members in the North particularly in some areas like Kano, Jos, Kaduna and Sokoto. Apart from his spiritual contributions, he also laid a solid administrative structure for church leaders in the North to emulate.

4. 3. 2 Healings in the CAC from 1960-1980

This section will also discuss the activities of three personalities who have contributed to spirituality in the CAC. The names are as follows; David Olulana Babajide, Samson Oladeji Akande, Godwin Nwoye and Patrick Abu Ayewo Egabor.

---

[239] An interview conducted with prophetess M. A. Waleola at Erio Ekiti on 26-06-2011.Aged 66 years.

David Olulana Babajide

Babajide was the second General Evangelist in the CAC between 1951 and 1991. He was born at Oke Mesi in the present Ekiti State in 1907. He was a school teacher before his call to divine service. Babajide claimed that the Lord spoke to him to leave the teaching profession for full gospel ministry. He said that he first resisted the directive for sometime, until 1937 when he resigned his work in obedience to that divine call.[240]

Having received the call of God, David Babajide received training as a church worker under the leadership of Jacob Odusona (the second President of CAC) in Ibadan. In 1941, he graduated from his training and was ordained as an Evangelist. In the same year (1941), he was married to Dorcas Adebanbe and the marriage was blessed with six children.

Furthermore, due to the involvement of Babajide in evangelical work, he was recommended for ordination as a pastor in 1949. In 1959, after the death of Joseph Babalola, he was appointed as the second General Evangelist of the Church. David Babajide has a unique style of evangelism. He was a good singer and also an accomplished composer of Pentecostal choruses.

H. O. Oladejo likened him to the biblical David because of his keen interest in songs.[241] He used to burst into spiritual songs during revivals. These songs often led to healings, deliverance and testimonies of all sorts.[242] He launched evangelistic campaigns in

---

[240] An interview conducted with Pastor David Babajide on 19-06-2008 at CAC Theological Seminary, Ilesha. Aged 101

[241] H. O. Oladejo, "A Vision Turns to Reality," in *Christ Apostolic Church School of Prophets and Magazine*, vol. 1, (2003), p. 1

[242] S.A. Fadola (80 years) and S. Daramola (60 years) confirmed during my interviews with them that Babajide was a singer and during his ministrations,

Ilesha, Ibadan, Oyan, Lagos, Ilorin, Kano and Enugu. He was popularly called the 'Singing bird' (Aoko) of Jesus. One of the popular songs of Babajide is:

> Lojo Ologo gbogbo wa, yo duro, niwaju oba ogo
> Gbogbo ise wa la o duro so, pelu orin lawa yo dahun;
> A o korin, a o korin a o korin

> On that glorious day, we shall stand before the king of glory, we shall testify to our work, through song we shall answer all questions through song. We shall sing, sing, and sing.

David Babajide contributed substantially to the growth of the CAC through effective evangelism. He was a lover of the Bible. This is much reflected in his works. He is a renowned author of many booklets containing the tenets and practices of the Church, with emphasis on Love, Prayer, Holy Spirit and Righteousness. He was also author of biographies of Church Leaders, namely Joseph Babalola and Daniel Orekoya. Many of these books are still in circulation.[243]

---

there were records healings. Fadola was interviewed on 07/03/2008 at CAC Olugbode Ibadan, while Daramola was interviewed on 2-6-2012 at CAC DCC Owo, Ondo State.

[243] An interview conducted with T. O. Bolatioto at CAC Mukuro, Ile-Ife on 17-6-2008.Age-60 years.

Plate 26- David Babajide

Source: CAC Library, Sunday School Akure, Ondo State

David Babajide planted many CAC assemblies all over the country. But unlike some other planters, he did not lay claim to them as his own. The 'Light of the World Society' (*Egbe Imole Aye*) that has played prominent roles in promoting evangelism in the Church, was his brain-child. Babajide carried out the vision, which God revealed to him about the establishment of a school of prophets and evangelism at Ilesha in 1931.[244]

Surprisingly, without soliciting for funds from anywhere, Babajide rallied round the Prophets and Evangelists in the Church to support his vision, by sending ministers who had God's calling to attend the institution. The response was very encouraging with the following figures below: 1959 (19), 1963 (15), 1970 (18) 1971 (39), 1975 (50) and 1978 (24).[245] (Medaiyese, 1956: 46). The

---

[244] An interview conducted with B. Folaju, a CAC Pastor at Oka-Akoko, Ondo State on 12-7-2010 at CAC D.C.C Headquarter Oka Akoko. Age-63 years

[245] See J. A. Medayese, *Itan Igebedide Woli Joseph Ayo Babalola* (Ibadan: Oluseyi Press, 1956), p. 46

school has produced crops of great ministers who occupy prominent positions in the Church. The school has moved to its permanent site with the view to running a degree programme as soon as possible. The school is named 'Babajide School of Prophets and Evangelists'.

Samson Oladeji Akande

Another great personality for discussion as a prophet and healer in the CAC between 1960 and 1980 was Samson Oladeji Akande popularly known as Baba Abiye. He was born and bred by poor parents between 1896 and 1902 at Kusi compound in Ede, now Osun State of Nigeria. The actual date of his birth is not known because some writers claimed sometime around 1896 while some claimed 1902. However, most writers agreed on 1902. His father's name was Joseph Moronkola Akande while his mother was Mariam Oyemoni Akande.

In 1929, Oladeji Salami Akande, who was a devoted Muslim, met a woman named Ayisatu Mojirade. She was a daughter to a popular man in Ede town known as Lawani, from Ojisun Compound in the same town. The courtship was for about three and a half years when a calamity befell Oladeji Akande, who was otherwise called Salami after conversion. The unfortunate incident happened when suddenly he became blind. His condition became critical as he consulted the herbalists and native doctors for solutions. But all efforts to regain his sight proved abortive. At last, he was referred to Ilorin for the attention of medical doctors. Many herbalists in Ede tried to get the problem solved but all proved abortive.[246]

However, Oladeji Akande had an encounter with Jesus

---

[246] This information was divulged from the following people, Kunle Oluwatukasi, a CAC pastor at CAC Kosohuntoluwakoleese Akure. Aged 31

Christ in 1936 through one Mrs. Mary Oni , a lady evangelist, who brought the gospel of Christ to Ede after the revival activity of Babalola in 1935. Oni's evangelical outreach started gradually. It was initially a house-to-house evangelism. Later, the lady evangelist moved about the town, ringing her hand bell and proclaiming Jesus as saviour. It was during this campaign that Oladeji Akande met Oni, who later convinced him of attending church programs at Ede. Oladeji Salami Akande followed the woman to the revival organized by her. That was the beginning of his encounter with Christ.

In 1938, Oladeji Akande underwent baptism by immersion through a Senior Pastor, J. B. Odusona. The rest of the families, including his wife, were also baptized during this period. That same year, Odusona visited the CAC assembly, Ede, and baptized other members of the Church who had given their lives to Christ. The conversion of Oladeji Akande to Christianity precipitated serious threats and persecution from the Muslim society in the town. Oladeji Akande was initially a strong Muslim in Ede. Members of his entire family were Muslims as well.

However, with his conversion, all his family members became Christians. Other Muslims who looked at Akande as mentors also got converted and became Christians. This development, therefore, created fear among the Muslims, particularly as Akande embarked on evangelistic missions in Ede and environs.[247] Ololade confirmed that many Muslims were converted to Christianity during the revivals of Akande.

---

[247] This information came from Evangelist M. A. Ololade at CAC Oke Igan Akure on 16-`10-2011. Age-85 years

Plate 27: Oladeji Akande

Source- CAC 1980 Almanac

This led the Muslim leaders to oppose the revival movements. They incited the king of Ede and the Police District Officers (D.O.) of the town against Akande. Like the allegations against Babalola during his revivals, Akande was also accused of bringing lepers into the revival for healing and for disturbing the peace of the town.[248]

The history to the revival of Akande began in January, 1943, when Akande claimed that God commanded him to go to Osogbo to observe a Marathon prayer with fasting to last sixteen months (Akande, 2006).[249] He was to observe the Marathon prayer under Prophet Komolafe of Osogbo. At the end of praying and fasting,

[248] Information from Prophetess Maria Olabintan at CAC D.C.C. Headquarter, Ile Ife on 5-11-2011. Age 71 years

[249] Funso Akande, Itan Igbesi Aye Woli ati Ajihinrere Samson Oladeji Akande (Baba Abiye), 1896-1992 (Ibadan: Olalere Press, 2006), p. 28

Akande discovered that he had been endowed with the prophetic gifts of vision and healing. Here are the records of some miracles God performed through Prophet Oladeji Akande:

1. Many sick and infirmed people were brought to him and they all received their healings.

2. After returning to Ede from Agberi's evangelistic crusade, the corpse of a man who had died for four days was brought to him. God restored the man to life. The man and his entire family became members of the C.A.C.

3. Many barren women became mothers of children through the prayers and prophetic gift of Prophet S.O. Akande.

4. A woman from a town known as Edunabon, called Maria, had been carrying a pregnancy for over fifteen years. The woman went to collect bath water flowing from where Prophet S.O. Akande was bathing. She drank the water, believing that the Lord would heal her. In the evening of the same day, she got rid of the still born baby. After her deliverance, the woman was blessed with male and female children later.[250]

5. At Masifa, a man's penis was shrunk. His name was Joseph. The penis was hardly visible. Only the head of the penis was visible. After many days of persistent prayer of faith, Joseph's organ became normal. He later married and had many children.

7. A hunchback attended the Ode-Omu crusade in 1964. After incessant prayers, the hunch disappeared. The man later became a

---

[250] Information revealed through M. O. Adeosun a lady evangelist who worked under Akande for about eight years before planting a church at Ilesha. Interview conducted on 26-6-2011 at CAC Miracle Ground, Ilesha. Age-68 years

minister of God (Ojo, 2008)[251]

From the foregoing, it is discovered that Akande was able to excel in the ministry because he was a man of prayers. He subjected himself to hard discipline by fasting and praying. He used to pray a lot before attending any programme. This habit enabled him to hear God's voice and directives before the commencement of the programmes. He developed a prayer ministry by establishing Ori Oke Ede (Ede Mountain top). Here, people from various places came to seek God's face for deliverances and all sorts of breakthroughs. Benjamin Adeniyi of the African Church remarked: "Prophet Oladeji Akande was a great man of prayers. He prayed many hours continuously and tirelessly. His prayer life had no equal. He, on several occasions, would withdraw himself to the hills or mountains to fast and pray. Those who have witnessed him testified to his prayer life that he could pray for three hours non-stop."[252]

Not only that, Akande lived an exemplary life of holiness. He did not only preach the life of holiness, he also practised it. Close associates of the prophet confirmed that he lived a life of sanctification and purity. He believed that the only obstacle for prayers to be answered is sin. So, Akande spent so much time with people by praying on forgiveness. [253]He had an insight to this prayer because of the past experience he had with his step mother. It was confirmed through an interview that his step mother

---

[251] J. O. Ojo, *The History and Ministries of Some Past Leaders in Christ Apostolic Church* (Ile-Ife: Timade Ventures, 2008), pp. 56-57

[252] An interview conducted with Benjamin Adeniyi, a priest at the Holy Trinity African Church, Ogba Parish, Agege, Lagos State. Age-38 years. Date of interview-15-4-2010

[253] An interview conducted with Pastor G. A. Adio, a family friend to Akande during his life time and now a retired Pastor at Ile –Ife (Interviewed on 15/5/2010).Age-78 years.

confessed that she was responsible for Akande's blindness through diabolic means. (Ojo, 2008: 57). She regretted this action

Another factor that helped Akande to excel in his ministerial assignment was obedience and humility. He gave respect and honour to the leaders of the Church (CAC).[254] He was found kneeling down before the church leaders (those in higher post) when speaking to them. He spoke gently and reverently to his superior, colleagues and subordinates.[255] This habit, however, formed the basis of the practice of humility and respect to superiority in the Church.[256] Also, his relationship with friends and those who came for healings served as pacesetters for prophets and prophetesses particularly in the areas of handling of revelations and human relations.

Godwin Nwoye

Godwin Nwoye, a native of Isigbo Nara in the old Nkanu was a traditionalist before his conversion to Christianity in 1934. Nwoye was said to be one of the opponents of the gospel before conversion (Okoronkwo, 2003).[257] He believed so much in his culture and tradition; and would never permit other new religion to infiltrate. This generally has been the habit of the Igbo indigenes. They Igbo cherished their culture and tradition. This perhabs accounted for the reason why Christianity was very difficult to penetrate to Igbo kingdom in the nineteenth and twentieth centuries (Kalu, 1978: 305).

The book, "Christianity in West Africa" by Ogbu Kalu, has

[254] An interview with Pastor G. A. Adio on 15-5-2010

[255] *See above, n. 97*

[256] Ibid

[257] S. N. Okoronkwo, Christ Apostolic Church (Enugu: El-Demak Publishers,2003), p. 17

the following to say about the unholy zeal of the people, and how it was quenched:

> It was after the destruction of the Arochukwu Oracle by the British expedition … from December 1901 until March 1902, the whole of Igboland was opened up to British rule, that both the Roman Catholic and the Protestant denominations vied with each other for prior occupation of Arochukwu and the surrounding district (in Igboland). In this interdenominational scramble, all tactics were used. Schools and hospitals were freely opened in order to attract the Igboland (Kalu, 1978)[258]

The above quotation summarizes the severe opposition faced by the early Christian missionaries, and how they finally triumphed and had the Church planted in Igbo land.

This was the exact situation before the advent of the Christ Apostolic Church in Igbo land in 1950. Nwoye got converted through one Miss Violet Lazarus. She came all the way from Port Harcourt in order to open the CAC branches in Enugu that year. The Lady Evangelist succeeded in opening a branch at No 40, Carter Street, Ogui, Enugu.

In 1960, Godwin Nwoye started evangelical outreaches as he moved to Agbani from Nara. Here, there were lots of miracles wrought through Nwoye and his assistant, Job Ani. Here, an assembly was planted within few months. In regard to the Lord's works at Agbani, Godwin has the following to say;

> Miracles, healing, signs and wonders were the result of our crusade in halls and car parks at Agbani. Many testified of God's healing touch, God's grace in special ways, forgiveness, love from above and real joy of salvation in their hearts. As the lame walked,

---

[258] *Ibid*, p. 305

the dumb spoke; there arose as always has been, great opposition, oppression and suppression. As great were the battles, so great were the victories (Okoronkwo, 2003).[259]

The miracles helped to spread the Church to other places such as Amuri, Akpugo, and Ugbawka.

Furthermore, through the revival of Godwin Nwoye, the CAC assemblies were planted in Ndiagu in 1961. The person who monitored the progress of these assemblies was Kingsley Ogbodo, a native of that village. Similarly, CAC reached Obinagu Akpugo (Nkanu Zonal Head-quarters) the same year (1961) through Godwin, Anthony Ifedigbo, Paul Onwuakagba and others. The Ogbozine and Umuzzi villages caught the fire of the revivals and ended with the emergence of five assemblies; some later became District Coordinating Councils in 1987.[260]

It must be noted that apart from the gift of ministration, Godwin demonstrated the spirit of humility and endurance which many people emulated. Both young and old admired him when addressing them. Ugoagha remarked: "Godwin Nwoye knelt down when greeting and discussing with his superiors, a tradition strange to pastors in Igbo land."[261] It was also stated that Nwoye adopted the style of singing and dancing during his revivals before any ministrations; and in most cases took about twenty to thirty mi[263]nutes. This process was to make people happy and prepare their hearts for the interference of the Holy Spirit.

[259] *Ibid*, p. 25

[260] Interview with P. C. Ugoagha at Ikeji Arakeji on 17-8-2009. Age-56 years

[261] *Ibid*

[263] *Ibid*

Also in 1962, the revival of Nwoye resulted in the establishment of the CAC in Ugbawka town. This event led to the establishment of the CAC, Ugbawka II in 1964, while Ugbawka III and IV started in October 4, 1980 and September 7[th,] 1981.[264] The Assemblies mentioned have recorded huge successes in Ugbawka, in such a way that the number of her assemblies have now tremendously increased to twelve or more.

In addition, Nneogbu Nwaonyiba also founded CAC assembly at Nkerefi I in 1960. Two years after, she invited Godwin Nwoye for a three-week revival. The outcome of the revival was the establishment of an assembly named Nkerefi II in 1967; followed by Nkerefi III in 1972 and Nkerefi IV in 1984. Also, The Ogui brethren organized a crusade at No. 1 Awkuzu Street, Uwani Enugu in 1965. Subsequently, the Christ Apostolic Church, Uwani was established. Godwin Nwoye dedicated the Church.

Furthermore, the gospel also got to Abakpa through Nwoye. Here, he was able to pioneer an assembly. Thereafter other CAC assemblies were opened through the financial support of the church leaders in October, 1971. Recently, there are CAC assemblies at Enime, nine miles away from Enugu. There are also established churches in Ugwuogo, Ugboezejio, Awka, Okposi, Uburu and Ishiagu, including that of Nkalagu, which was opened in 1961, but was taken over by the dissident group in 1979.

[264] *Ibid*

Plate 28: Godwin Nwoye

Source: Okoronkwo, S. N. *Christ Apostolic Church, Igbo land*, p. 24

Patrick Abu Ayewo Egabor

Patrick Egabor was born at Agenebode (now in Edo-State) in the early 1900's. The actual date of birth is unknown. He was from a polygamous family. Egabor grew up in a very tense environment where only his mother catered for his education and upbringing from the primary to secondary school. He had his education between 1936 and 1941. He was on government scholarship between 1942 and 1945 to study Book-keeping and Accounting in a higher institution of learning. Thereafter, he taught in a secondary school for one year (1945-1946).

In 1941, Egabor was baptized and later became a strong member of the Christ Apostolic Church, Warri. Today, the Church has now become the District Coordinating Council of Christ Apostolic Church headquarters in Warri. In April 1944, it was confirmed that Egabor had a dream which prompted him to ministerial work.

Also, after two years precisely, (1946) he had another revelation that he should contact Joseph Ayo Babalola who was then conducting revivals in Warri. In his interactions with Joesph Ayo Babalola, it was confirmed that God wanted to use him. Babalola prayed for him and thereafter directed him to meet David Babajide, the then Assistant General Evangelist of CAC for counseling and ministerial tutelage before starting his theological training at CAC Bible Training Institute, Ibadan.

It was at the Bible Training College that he was endowed with the power of healing and prophecies. In 1956, he prayed for his mother who was sick for a long time (for she had constant chronic stomach pain) and she was cured. The prophetic gift of healing on Egabor drew many people particularly from his family, especially from his mother's side, to accept Christ as their Lord and Saviour.

In 1957, he graduated from the CAC Bible Training Institute, Ibadan and got ordained as a pastor in 1958, a year before the death of Joseph Ayo Babalola. He got married in 1967. The marriage was attended by late Bishop Benson Idahosa, Elijah Olusheye (CAC former president), Joseph Olu Alokan (retired CAC General Evangelist), Pastor Anthony Imevbore (retired University Professor) e.t.c. Egabor was happily blessed with three children; Solomon, Gloria and Blessing

In September 1958, Egabor was posted out as a full time minister by the CAC Authority to work in the defunct Mid-Western State of Nigeria, before he became an itinerant evangelist all over Nigeria. Between 1979 and 1981, Egabor was recognized in the CAC circle as a gifted minister noted for healing and deliverance. The reason for this recognition was that his ministry was followed by signs and wonders. The Lord endowed him with the gift of laying of hands for healing of diverse diseases like headache, fever and epilepsy.[265]

In addition, Egabor was always noted for his activeness during revivals. Records showed that in Ekpoma, there were miracle-working and healing deliverances through the revivals of Egabor. Also diverse ailments that defiled orthodox medicine were healed during the revivals. Diseases so dreadful as stroke, cancer, migraine, diabetes, bronchitis etc, were healed.[266] Again, it was also noted that people who were under firm grips of demon spirits were dispossessed of their malignant spirits. Not only that, other malevolent spirits of sins like melancholia, sex-mania and nymphomania were said to have been exorcised

Also, at the Ekpoma revival, many witches and sorcerers surrendered their lives to Christ and embraces the Christian faith. It was also claimed that during the Ekpoma revival, some witches vomited their birds of divination at the revival ground.[267] Also, in Auchi, Egabor stormed the town with his evangelical campaigns.

---

[265] An interview conducted with Pastor S. F. Babalola, one of the converts of Egabor but now a lecturer at Joseph Ayo Babalola University, Ikeji Arakeji. Date of interview- 17-11-2011. Age-47 years.

[266] An interview conducted with Jacob Alokan, one of the disciples of Egabor and also ex- General Evangelist of the Christ Apostolic Church now based at Efon- Alaaye, Ekiti State. Interview conducted on 14-01-2010. Age-77 years

[267] *Ibid*

Here, he prayed for a pregnant woman who had not delivered for a period of two years and the woman gave birth to the child safely.

Egabor had different methods through which he healed ailments. First, he used to conduct prayers and fasting for his patients in secluded places. He believed so much in isolating people for prayers and fasting. Also, most times he stayed in secluded places according to divine instructions for prayers. The word 'secluded' is interpreted scientifically by Olayiwola as 'incubation', meaning '*Abe-Abo*'. It means a solitary place where the sick or those in spiritual bondages seek God in prayers and fasting (Olayiwola, 1991).[268]

He also used hydrotherapeutic method. The practice involves praying over water for members to drink for healing. Also, such water can be used for bathing. He also made use of psalms for deliverance and healing. At times, Egabor would anoint his patients with oil. This is generally known as anointing oil. This idea is in accordance with the stipulation of the Epistle of James in the scriptures.

Before concluding this section which deals with healings in the Church between 1960 and 1980, it is pertinent to know that apart from the three afore-mentioned prophets who had contributed in one way or the other to the building of healing ministries in CAC, the year 1975 in particular was noted for series of miracles, healings and deliverance in different CAC assemblies both in Nigeria and abroad. The records of such healings are as follows:

1. At CAC District Headquarters, Okitipupa in Ondo State, under Pastor Z. A. Ajayi, many who were insane were healed. Also, a

---

[268] D. O. Olayiwola, "Hermeneutical- Phenomenological Study of the Aladura Spirituality in Ijesa Social History, '' Asia Journal of Theology, Vol. 6, No2, (1991), p. 260

man who was deaf received his healing. Also, in the same town, an herbalist surrendered all his charms and armlets for burning.

2. At CAC Headquarters, Abeokuta, Ogun State, under Pastor S. O. Siwoku, there was a young man who was poisoned and had spent so much time and money at the hospital and who was miraculously healed received healing during one of the revivals. Also, a pregnant woman who was to undergo surgical operation gave birth to twins at the CAC maternity home.

3. J. Olu Young, the District Superintendent for Oshogbo gave reports of how revival services had brought about divine healings, and series of miracles. Consequently, the number of the congregation increased from 2,200 to 4,356. Also, the number of assemblies in the District increased from 37 to 55.[269]

In addition, the 1978 was also noted for outstanding miracles of signs and wonders in the Church (CAC). At CAC Oke-Igan, Akure in Ondo State, a woman who was pregnant for six years forcefully delivered a monster child. The monster baby had the body of a human being with abnormal structures all over him without a distinct neck. The arms were without fingers. The monster child had very large eye balls. (See picture overleaf)

Apart from this, there were series of recorded miracles in CAC Kaduna District Headquarters in 1978. The Official Organ (1978) of the CAC mentioned some of these miracles and testimonies as follows: (Also, see pictures overleaf)

[269] *CAC 1975 Year Book*, pp. 4748

Plate 29: Monster Child Born

Source: *Official Organ of the Christ Apostolic Church*, 1978, p. 19

Plate 30- A barren woman giving testimony for delivering a baby boy

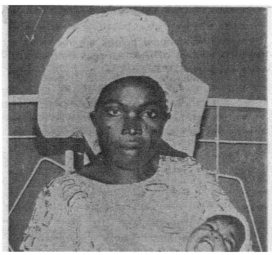

Source- *Official Organ of the CAC*, 1978, p. 12

Plate 31: Testimonies from once barren women

Source: *Official Organ CAC*, 1978, p. 12

4.3.3   Healings in the CAC from 1980-1994_

The second half of the twentieth century witnessed the emergence of prophets and prophetesses like Timothy Obadare, Samuel Abiara and Bola Odeleke. In the course of this discussion, attempts shall be made to discuss the relevance of these prophets and prophetesses in the development of healing ministries in Nigeria and abroad.

Timothy Obadare

The World Soul Winning Evangelistic Ministry (WOSEM) pioneered by Obadare in the late 1970s spread into many places of the world in 1980. One of the notable CAC assemblies established by the World Soul Winning Evangelistic Ministry led by T. O. Obadare in 1981 is the present CAC Odubanjo Memorial Church, Ketu. It accommodates thousands of people during Sunday service.[270]

In an interview with Obadare, he confirmed that series of

---

[270] Information received from Pastor Adeware Alokan during an interview with him at No 125, Oke Ijebu on 20-5-2010. Age- 87 years

CAC assemblies had emerged in 1982 through WOSEM in America and Europe, as a result of the healing ministry endowed him through the Holy Spirit.[271] The confirmation of this tremendous expansion was published in the 1986 CAC Year Book in the column of the report from Obadare. He (Obadare) remarked thus: "Many CAC assemblies have now been established in the Unites States.... In New York, many people including black Americans had been converted to the Church, Wonders of healing, Salvation and infilling of the Holy Spirit took place among the people during the revival crusade organized by T.O Obadare."[272]

Most services at the WOSEM always start with thanksgiving choruses to God. Prayer and congregational hymn follow this. The message of God follows simultaneously. The message is mostly reserved for Prophet T.O. Obadare. The man of God usually starts his message with '*Ogo ni fun Olorun loke Orun*' (Glory be to God in the heaven). He systematically repeats this in another style – 'mo tun wi lekan si pe ogo ni fun Eledumare' (I say once again Glory be to the Almighty God).

During his messages, Obadare prophesies directly into the lives of the people. His messages are always direct without any reservation for church leaders, top government officials and other dignitaries in different offices. The healing and prophetic power endowed on Obadare has made his followers proud of him. They, therefore, refer to themselves as WOSEM members. These followers are proud to be called this name because people from all walks of life have been thronging the prophet's revival center at Akure and Ilesha, for God who never fails (Koseunti) would meet their needs.

---

[271] An interview conducted with Prophet T. O. Obadare at CAC Koseunti Akure on 17-5-2011. Aged 82

[272] See *CAC Year Book*, 1986, p. 303

Many prominent personalities had been healed through his crusade. Usually after sermon, Obadare prophesied into the lives of people, and there were reports of healing here and there. Oba Akinla of Erin-Ijesa (a traditional ruler) was healed through Obadare's ministry. Also, Obadare's programme on the television and radio also presented series of healings and testimonies during this period.

Not only that, Obadare performed healing during his peripatetic preaching and open air crusade. This informed the reason why Olayiwola reported that: ".....Miracles were reportedly performed by Prophet Obadare during the 1978-81 revival meetings. Also,it was recorded by Olayiwola that many cripples walked, deaf and dumb were healed" (Olayiwola, 1993).[273] The case of a woman who was healed of a long breast was a living testimony in WOSEM and CAC at large (See picture below)

Plate 32: Healing from Swollen breast Disease at Obadare's crusade

Source: WOSEM Library, on 15-11-2011

---

[273] D. O. Olayiwola, "Ilesha as and Obadare movement compared," *Journal of Ecumenicalns,* (1993), p. 88.

Plate 33: The conversion of a wizard-Solomon Olujide Ajayi

Source: *Official Organ of Christ Apostolic Church*, p. 11

Apart from this, there are records of healing in the CAC Year Book and other related documents in the archive. (See appendix III for details). Based on the foregoing, it is necessary to outline a few out of the numerous wonderful works of God through Obadare at the Osogbo revivals of 12th May, 1984 as follows:

1. Jide Ogunmodede, of Latona Street, Osogbo renounced his membership from eight different cults.[274]

2. Nike Oladimeji of No.7, Kolawole Street Osogbo who was deaf and dumb got healed.[275]

3. Michael Oladele of No.20 Ayetoro Street, Osogbo was delivered

---

[274] See *Official Organ of the CAC*, Volume 15, No.3, p. 33

[275] *Ibid*, p. 33

from the torment of evil spirit.[276]

4. Comfort Oluwakemi of Ayetoro Street, Oshogbo was delivered of her 7 years delayed pregnancy.[277]

5. Julianah Makanjuola from Iwo regained her senses after many years of insanity.[278]

6. Comfort Alao from Benue State who met her problem in 1973 after she was fought by a horse in her dream and was taken to many specialist hospitals in Nigeria and later to a London famous specialist but was not healed, received instant healing during the Oshogbo revival.[279]

Samuel Abiara

The ministry of Abiara became known in the CAC in the early 1980s. Records in the CAC Year Books and CAC Organ have shown that Abiara was indeed a prophet endowed with the healing power. Samuel Abiara founded the Christ International Evangelical Ministry (CIEM) in 1977.[280]

The membership of the ministry cuts across denominational and racial differences. Its objectives include preaching the Gospel to the whole creation; strengthening brotherhood among all Christians; cooperating with Africans and International Religious Organizations designed to promote the Gospel; and publishing religious literatures that would lead to a sound understanding of the

[276]*Ibid*, p. 33

[277] *Ibid*, p. 33

[278] Ibid, p. 33

[279] *Ibid*, p. 33

[280] *Official Organ of the CAC*, 1985, p.16.

word of God.

Samuel Abiara, the founder of the Christ International Evangelical Ministry was born into a humble family of Abiara at Erin-Ijesa in present Osun State of Nigeria in 1942. He lost his father at a very tender age, so he did not have the privilege to study beyond primary school because of financial situation. Hence, after primary education, he engaged in farming and later in minor commercial engagements. However, after his divine call in 1963, he had contact with David Babajide (the second General Evangelist in Christ Apostolic Church) for counseling.

David Babajide later became his (Abiara) mentor. Here, Babajide instructed him to attend the School of Prophets and Evangelists at Ilesha for proper training. Following his training there, he was ordained as a prophet in 1982. In the process of evangelical work, God used him to perform works of healings and miracles both in and outside Nigeria through the Christ International Evangelical Ministry (C.I.E.M.). The CAC bulletin of April 1985 states that:

> For the first two years of its establishment, the ministry recorded regularly an attendance over 200. But after its 5th year, the attendance became astronomical (Alokan, 1991)[281]

Thus, the record of attendance from the inception of the Ministry in the last Sundays of January of each year between 1977 and 1985 were as follows: 1977 (48), 1978 (108), 1979 (218), 1980 (472), 1981 (3, 164), 1982 (7, 857), 1983 (9, 395), 1984 (9, 409) and 1985 (19, 062). 51, 120 worshippers were recorded between 6th

---

[281] See Adeware Alokan, CAC, 1928-1988, p. 240

and 27th January 1985 (4 Sundays). Record of converts for 1984 was 3, 070.[282]

The CIEM has spread the gospel to many towns and cities in Nigeria. Like WOSEM, CIEM propagates the Gospel through the use of Radio and Television broadcasts in States such as Ekiti, Oyo, Ogun, Ondo, Lagos and Osun. The ministry also enjoyed the grace of God through its founder (S.K. Abiara) as the blind see; the lame walk; the barren blessed with children; the sick healed of their various diseases. The detail of the report was as follow:

> A woman at Bere Street, Ibadan was cured of 17 years' ailment of sleeplessness whilst another woman was delivered of a crocodile after 8 Years of abnormal pregnancy (Alokan, 1991)[283]

The C.I.E.M. has a standardized worship and administration. The overall Director, which is usually referred to as General Overseer, is S.K. Abiara, followed by the Deputy Director and other Directors. The C.I.E.M. does not have a stereotyped style of worship. At times, the General overseers and other Directors may officiate in mufti and at times in clerical suits.

The style of prayer follows the new Pentecostal churches; and programmes such as Jesus festival; one hour with Jesus; washing of feet etc are well packaged for people. These programmes are claimed to come up through divine revelations and are sponsored by wealthy people in the society. Records in the CAC Year Books and CAC Organs have shown that Abiara was indeed a prophet endowed with the healing power. Find below some of the pictures of Abiara during his revivals and ministrations of healing and deliverance in Nigeria. They are as follows:

---

[282] See *Official Organ of CAC* (April, 1985), p. 17.

[283] See CAC, 1928-1988, pp. 240-241

Plate 34: A Woman Giving Testimony

Source: *CAC 1984 Year Book*, p.17

Plate 35: A Man Giving Testimony on Breakthrough

Source: *CAC 1984 Year Book*, p. 18

Plate 36: A Woman Giving Testimony of Healing

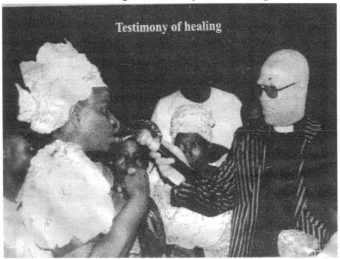

Source: *CAC 1985 Year Book*, p. 18

Plate 37: Testimony of Deliverance from Insanity

Source: *Nigerian Tribune*, April 17, 1993, p. 31

Bola Odeleke

Christ Message Ministry popularly known as *Kii-baa-ti* was established on 13th March, 1982 through the activities of Lady Evangelist Bola Odeleke. The Ministry was strictly managed by the family. Lt. Col. L.J. Odeleke (Pastor) now late, was the President of the Ministry and Lady Evangelist Bola Odeleke was the Vice President. They were assisted by a number of evangelists.

The seat of the Ministry is at Okota Layout, Isolo, Lagos where within seven days of its existence, it had acquired an acre of land at a cost of ₦24, 000.00. Revival on the ground began under a canopy with 303 people in attendance in February 1983. Soon, a Church building measuring 210 feet by 60 feet was completed for worship. By February, 1983, the revivals of Odeleke had covered many areas in Lagos State. The Ministry enjoyed many miracles, healings and moving power of the Holy Spirit. Find below some of the miracles as recorded in the CAC *Official Organ* and *Year Book*:

1. On Saturday, March 7, 1987, Isiaka Aladokun was delivered from the power of darkness at the Kii-baa-ti Crusade in Ibadan.

2. In Lagos, a woman who had been lame for six years dropped her crutches; her ankles received strength and she walked as the prayers were being said. She testified to the power of God after the prayers and people sang and glorified the Lord.[284]

3. Another notable miracle was the confession and repentance of three young girls, namely Bosede, Adekunbi and Alatise. They surrendered their weapons as seen in the picture below. The first weapon surrendered (as seen in the left picture) is the bag (red with blood) which they used in collecting blood from people until they

---

[284] See *Official Organ of the Christ Apostolic Church*, Volume 15. No.6, (1985), p. 22,

become pale and die. When the Ox-tail is pointed to any house, the house will be set ablaze and burnt down. The ring in the calabash was used, they claimed, in spoiling pregnancies. Also, many charmed rings and belts were left behind on the revival ground.

Plate 38: Weapons Surrendered By Bosede, Adekunbi and Alatise.

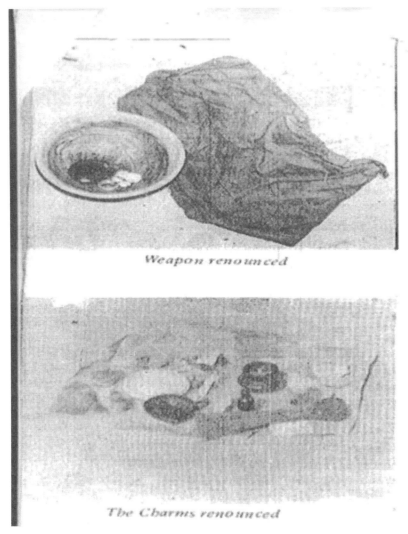

Weapon renounced

The Charms renounced

Source: Official Organ of the CAC, p. 23

Plate 39: Mukaila Adedeji Renounces his Charms and Surrenders them

Mukaila Adedeji renounced his Charms & brought them

Mukaila Adedeji rejected the Charms

Source: *Official Organ of the CAC*, 1985, p. 23

4. Moses Olawale Fapohunda, an herbalist and a member of secret society renounced his secret society membership of Roscrucian since 1985 and surrendered his life to Christ. He also surrendered his charms and other instruments used to harm other fellows who had offended them. (See pictures below)

Plate 40: Moses Fapohunda Praising God for his Deliverance

Source: *Official Organ of the CAC*, p. 23

4.4 Summary

The CAC emerged in the twentieth century in an environment where the spiritual exposures of the people were limited to the traditionalists and the foreign missionaries from mainstream churches of the Anglican, Catholic, Methodist and Baptist. However, before the arrival of the missionaries, the indigenous people especially the Yoruba believed in consulting *Ifa* oracle and the *Ifa* priest to discover some mysteries concerning marital, jobs and other vital issues of lives. The *Ifa* priest popularly known as *babalawo* also derived their own word of knowledge and wisdom from the manipulation and interpretation of the *Ifa* corpus.

According to Max Weber, the structure of every society at every given time has its meaning. The period under discussion had its meaning. The *babalawo* virtually solved all problems affecting the people in the society. In the Yoruba setting, the *babalawo* or *baba awo* at times perceived the problems of their client even before they opened their mouths to say them. They also prescribe solutions to these problems through their divine means. This is the indigenous people's version of revelatory manifestations and it had aided them in solving many problems of life.

However, the spiritual operations of the foreign missionaries prior to the emergence of the *Aladura* were quite different from the traditional healers who attended to the spiritual needs of the people through consulting higher powers or media. Most solutions offered by the traditional priests were in the form of sacrifices to God through appeals to ancestors or malevolent and benevolent spirits who controlled the cosmos.

Definitely, there were gaps to be filled as the Christ Apostolic Church emerged in Yoruba land early in the twentieth century. Accidentally, the stages of growth in the CAC have its meanings as Max Weber has rightly stated in his theory about the society. His theory perfectly fits the situation of the CAC which developed and grew in a society where the need for spiritual search-lamp was needed to find lasting solutions to unprecedented existential problems. The first set of prophets and leaders in the Church laid a solid foundation as they prepared the ground for subsequent leaders to work upon. The founding patriarchs of CAC to some extent have provided the spiritual lamp needed for its generation in the early and mid-twentieth century as they expanded their ministries, severally and jointlys in Nigeria as well as foreign countries like South Africa, Europe and America.

Joseph Babalola and Daniel Orekoya were excellent in accuracy in the use of prophetic ministrations. However, it is glaring from the available record that Daniel Orekoya would have been very outstanding in the healing and prophetic ministry even more than Joseph Babalola if he had lived longer than the time he had spent. For example, 22 dead bodies were raised in a revival

187

meeting of Daniel Orekoya; and 240 dead bodies were raised within one year in his ministry.

Apart from the duo, there were other prophets whose emergence was within the CAC or during Babalola's revivals. Two prominent ones among them will include: Peter Olatunji and Emmanuel Omotunde. Similarly in the 1960s, there were notable CAC prophets in Ibadan, e.g., Pastors Durojaiye and Olowere.

As Max Weber has rightly proposed about the theory of society and its meaning, the 1960 through 1980 experienced another dynamic set of prophets and leaders in the CAC. These gifted leaders were noted for great expansion of the Church to many places in Nigeria. David Babajide who was a teacher before taking up the ministerial assignment spread the Church to non Yoruba areas particularly in Bendel, Warrri and Anambra. His prophetic ministry opened up CAC in all these areas. Also the CAC for the first time enjoyed the presence of a physically challenged person through his gifts. Samson Akande had deficiency because he was blind but he was noted for accuracy in his prophetic ministrations. The CAC acknowledged his (Akande) worth by appointing him as one of the executives of the Church. He was given the position as the prophet for the CAC Executive. This office was not in the constitution but it was created just to recognize his (Akande) worth in the Church.

The periods late 1970s and 1980 upwards definitely were very significant in the history of Nigeria. First, in the area of agriculture, development was very spectacular. Nigeria's production of palm oil and kernel, cotton, cocoa, ginger and groundnut was enormous. It was a period of Operation Feed the Nation. Also the discovery of crude oil made the economy so buoyant. Nigeria became the leader producer of Columbite and Tin in the world. Lead, Zinc, Coal and of course, the black gold were amongst the many minerals that were prospected, processed for local use and exported to boost our foreign exchange earnings.

In addition, technology became advanced. The transport sector was also dynamic. It was adequately developed to meet national needs. In the field of medicine, there were series of awareness about health care. Scholarships were offered to students to read medicine, law and pharmacy in reputable universities in the western world. All these developments have changed the reasoning of the people in the society. The level of exposure was very high. The situation tallies with the reasoning of Max Weber when he examines the structure of the society through meanings.

Thus the CAC operations during the era of the founding fathers may not fit in into the milieu of the development in the late 70s and early 80s in Nigeria. There was another vacuum to be filled by the CAC. This perhaps accounted for the emergence of charisma from different quarters of the Church and with independent ministries. Timothy Obadare established *The World Soul Winning Evangelistic Ministry* (WOSEM) in August 1974 and it spread into many areas of the world in the 1980s. Also, Samuel Abiara established *Christ International Evangelical Ministry* in 1977.

This ministry became international as from the 80s. The *Christ Message Ministry* (CMM)/ *Power of God Never Fails Ministry (Agbara Olorun Kii Baati)* was established on March 13, 1982 by Lady Evangelist (Mrs) Bola Odeleke. Even though these ministries operated independently, they have filled the vacuum of the yearnings of the laity in the Church for expansion and modernizations. Take for instance, record showed that the WOSEM as at 1985 had over one hundred branches at home and abroad.[285] In the same way, Abiara has many branches of his ministry in Nigeria and abroad.[286]

---

[285] *CAC Year Book* (Lagos: CAC Printing Press, 1985), p. 285

[286] See http://www.pctii.org/cyberj18/adewale.html

It will be right to say here that the emergence of different ministries in Nigeria had its effects in the development of the Church. First, it lifted the name of CAC from local to international countries in Europe, United Kingdom, United State of America and Asia. It became a trans-national and global church. Second, it marked the beginning of crises and divisions in the Church. Many of the independent ministries operated individually and this affected the administrative control the practices in the Church. The CAC practices were undermined as foreign practices from other denominations particularly from the Pentecostal churches in America were brought into the Church. An attempt to checkmate the operations of these independent ministries resulted into crises.

Another area which the Christ Apostolic Church has contributed meaningfully to the lives of the people by promoting the gospel is in music. The Church at its inception came with its peculiar Christian music to replace the accustomed music of the indigenous. Most songs were composed in the local tunes and fine tuned to meet the needs of the people. In contemporary time, not only has Christ Apostolic Church influenced Nigerian music greatly, but has also dominated the gospel music circle, and offered one of the most popular music genres in Nigeria.

The Christ Apostolic Church music, therefore, is highly functional and possesses deep metaphysical connotations. From indigenous native airs, anthems, hymnody, art music and lyric-airs to gospel music. Its style forms one of the manifestations of indigenous Pentecostalism; as it has been instrumental to the diverse operations in its spread and its acceptability throughout the world. As Max Weber has rightly proposed that there is a correlation between religious beliefs and practical ethics of the society; the totality of the Yoruba people is based on the expression of joy through songs. The society has its meaning as people express joy and unhappiness through music. Take for instance, during war, wedding ceremony, burial, festival, crises etc, songs are rendered to express sympathy, joy, passion, comfort and boldness.

The Christ Apostolic Church gospel singers at its inception were able to separate the sacred from secular music. However, there were some local songs that were injected into the sacred space and music. Such music has been fine tuned to meet the demands of the sacred music. The Church from this standard possesses its uniqueness and identity in liturgy which are again hinged on praying and singing of hymns, anthems and choruses

(www.cacworldwide.net/history.asp. Accessed on 12/01/2012).

Thus, the evolution of music in CAC followed the metamorphoses of the Church. The music consisted of prayer songs and hymns from the CMS. Later, Rev Ola Olude composed songs in native airs. The arrival of gifted ministers and revivalists under Apostle Joseph Ayo Babalola and Daniel Orekoya transformed the gospel music to inspire and admonish; and thereby resulting to healing and deliverance. Ayo Ogunranti (1980:8) revealed that Apostle Ayo Babalola always sang a lot of hymns and lyric airs including one that no one had heard before.' He also listed about 80 songs used in the early period of the Church (18-21). All these have contributed to the growth and development of the spirituality of the Church in the contemporary time

CHAPTER FIVE

THE PLACE OF REVELATIONS AND HEALINGS IN THE CHANGES/CRISES OF THE CHRIST APOSTOLIC CHURCH

5.1 Background to Changes and Crises in the Church

The Christ Apostolic Church has a very humble beginning. It was administered by the founding fathers that manifested exemplary lives of integrity, love, industry, loyalty and tenacity of purpose. However, the issue of crises has been long in the Church; it first began to surface gradually in the 1960's until it reached its climax in 1991 (Olusheye, 2010).[287] There are many factors responsible for the CAC crises which have very strong link with the religious practices of revelations and healings.

The second quarter of the 19th century after the demise of Joseph Babalola and Daniel Orekoya marked the mass arrival of ministers of God from other denominations in the CAC. The reasons for the sudden increase in the number of these ministers was as a result of the sudden growth in the numerical strength of the Church. The Church became popular and therefore drew the attention of gifted men, youths and the like.

However, this development had negative implication on the Church. Many people with different doctrinal backgrounds had to find their ways into the Church because of its wide popularity. At that time, CAC had emerged as one of the giant indigenous churches in Nigeria. The revivals of 1930 and afterwards spurred

---

[287] E. H. L. Olusheye, *The Legacies of our Church Patriacrhs* (Ibadan: Gideon Global Press 2010), p. 66

the name of CAC to greater heights, both in and outside the country.

The expansion of the Church, which was engendered by the influx of converts, therefore, later gave rise to administrative complexities and strange religious practices. Different kinds of people came to join both the clergy and the laity. Soon, there were series of conflicting ideas and teachings as a result of different theological backgrounds of ministers in the Church. Some of the laid down rules pertaining to the practices of revelations and healings were altered. The practices of the CAC that ensure that sick people should be handled with care and should not be involved in long fasting were altered.[288] Instead, the prophets and prophetess used to gather the insane patients, chain them, put them under torture, fasting, enchantment etc..[289] Hence, through this process, the power of the Holy Spirit was undermined.

Unlike the time of Joseph Ayo Babalola where the sick, oppressed and the like received instant healings through prayers and divine revelations during revivals; the 1960-1980 witnessed prophets and prophetesses turning assemblies to hospitals where people with diverse problems were pilled up.[290] The implication of the change in the religious practices of healing through divine instruction could be seen in two forms. First, the originality in the practices of revelations and healings became diminished. Many who had absolute trust in the healing faith now doubt the power of God as their sick ones were chained, molested, and abused in the course of healing.

Thus, the families of the sick who failed to receive healing

---

[288] See *Iwe Eto Ilana ti Ijo Aposteli Kristi Nibi Gbogbo* (Ilesa: Ilesanmi Press, 1968), pp. 27-54

[289] An interview conducted with Akinola Oluranti in his assembly CAC Holy Spirit, 5-11-2011. Age-73 years

[290] *Ibid*

were taken to hospital and native doctors for healing as their last hope. This was a challenge to the teaching on faith healing, accuracy in prophetic diagnosis of visions, dreams and discerning spirits for the edification of the church. Two, some ministers decided to set up independent ministries within the Church bringing in their own foreign method of healing. In 1970, T.O Obadare established the World Soul Evangelistic Ministry (WOSEM) and the ideas were copied by several other ministers like S.K. Abiara, Bola Odeleke and Bola Are. Also, there were other ministers who planted separate assemblies in the name of CAC but operated different doctrines, teachings and practices not constituted by the founding fathers.[291] All these discrepancies in the religious practices within the church brought internal conflicts, divisions, and indiscipline to pollute the revered doctrinal practices of the CAC (Olusheye, 2011).[292]

Thus, many vocal members of the leadership of the Church viewed the activites of these gifted ministers who operated within the Church and also those that planted assemblies as inimical to its progress.[293] Prophecies warning against the continued errant tendencies of these separate ministries, particularly of WOSEM's independent operations in the CAC, were repeatedly given, and both the ministers and members of the Church were becoming restive (Olusheye, 2011:47).

Towards the end of 1989, a set of pastors of the Church

---

[291] An interview conducted with Pastor Joel Akintunde of the CAC Glory of God Assembly, Ile-Ife on 20-2-2011 Age 61 years. Also Pastor Fesojaye Adedeji confirmed that the CAC Guiding Rules and Regulations contradicts the operations of the pastors, prophets and prophetesses in the Church particularly from 1980 to 1994. Adedeji is 76 years. Age-76 years

[292] See E. H. L. Olusheye "Unity of Christ Apostolic Church: A must (Ibadan: Gideon Global Press 2011), p. 47

[293] An interview with Fesojaye Adedeji

formed a group called "Christ's Initiative Forum for the CAC". The Forum under the leadership of late Pastor E.O. Makinde, presented some suggestions to the Church during the CAC Pastor's Conference of September, 1990 which generated some controversies.[294] In their paper, the group drew the Church's attention to the obvious lapses in the Church's administration, most especially, the foreign and strange practices and doctrines of "Churches within Church" introduced by some gifted and influencial evangelists. These practices have negative impact on the laid down policies and practices of Joseph Ayo Babalola and the other founding fathers of Christ Apostolic Church. The end result of this move by the Forum were rifts and divisions.

Apart from this, the rejection of revelations by leaders in the Church as a result of power tussle also contributed to the crises in the CAC. At the inception of CAC, emphasis had been laid on 'thus says thy Lord' (prophecy in particular) and no leader dares kick against the visions or voice of God when it had been proved as real. Take for instance, the final split between Joseph Shadare (Esinsinade), the Nigerian faith Tabernacle leader and the General Executive Council of the CAC in 1935 (when the name was adopted) was as a result of revelation.

Joseph Shadare was initially offered the post of President of CAC before its take off, but he rejected it on account of divine revelation he had before contact with the Faith Tabernacle. According to the revelation, he said that God gave him the instruction to head the Faith Tabernacle in Nigeria and not any other group. This was the true nature of the founding fathers, believing strongly in visions, prophecies, dreams and discerning spirit as the ultimate in piloting their ministerial assignment.[295]

---

294 See C.O. Oshun, "Rediscovering and Fostering in the Body of Christ: The Experiences of Christ Apostolic Church...," p. 159

[295] See above reference no-.127

However, in the course of time, this practice of relying on revelation gradually became a thing of the past. As it has been mentioned earlier, church leadership was based on seniority and divine revelation. However, priority is placed on divine revelation rather than appointment based on seniority. This is similar to the installation of kings in Yoruba land. The divine must be consulted through Ifa oracle to discover the best person for the kingship. Thus, in CAC setting, the church leaders and gifted ministers consult God through prayers and fasting to discover the right persons for the posts.

In one of the comments made by C. O. Oshun during his valedictory service in Joseph Ayo Babalola University, he was of the opinion that David Odubanjo ought to have been the first President of Christ Apostolic Church; because of seniority, commitment and services rendered to humanity and the Church before incorporation.[296] But due to divine consultation and revelations, Oba Akinyele was chosen when Joseph Shadare rejected the offer on the ground of revelation received through God.

Similarly, the issue of succession to the post of the president after the demise of Jacob Odusona in 1966 became controversial among the church executives. The leaders of the Church were divided on whether he should be succeeded by either Elijah Titus Latunde or Joshua Medaiyese because they were both ordained the same day. This was, however, later amicably resolved through prayers and divine instruction. Elijah Titus Latunde was however appointed as the president based on the leadings of the Holy Spirit in 1966 while Joshua Medaiyese became the General Superintendents between 1966 and 1975.

The peaceful era in the Church continued till the early 80s when J. B. Orogun took the mantle of leadership as the President

296 A speech by C.O. Oshun (Vice-Chancellor, Joseph Ayo Babalola University, Ikeji) at the send-off valedictory Service organized by the College of Humanities, JABU on 16-2-2011, Time 11.30am.

196

of the Christ Apostolic Church in 1983. It happened that there was a controversy that raged after the demise of Elijah Titus Latunde in 1983. The question was whether he should be succeeded by Joseph Orogun or Abraham Ade Olutimehin. Orogun was ordained before Olutimehin. So, by CAC regulations, he had an edge over Olutimehin but on the other hand, divine revelation was in favour of Olutimehin.

However, the Church later became politicized. But the question of whether CAC regulation or divine instruction should be given priority arose. There was overwhelming spiritual support for Abraham Olutimehin; nonetheless, 'the Lord says' consideration should be given to the erstwhile practice in favour of Joseph Orogun, the then General Superintendent in 1983.

Not too long after the induction of Orogun as the President of CAC in 1983 that crises began in the Church. It began in 1988 with the ordination of wealthy and influential people in the Church. However, these categories of people claimed to have been inspired to seek for positive change particularly, in the practices of the Church. The crisis was gradually reaching a climax in the following pastoral conference at Ilesha in 1989.

Thus many observers within the Church regarded the erstwhile precedent as a major contributor to the crisis plaguing the Church. It may be a coincidence, but really, the situation of things in the Church became worsened since the time of Orogun. However, in my interview with Pastor Oluranti, he was of the opinon that Orogun refused to hearken to the revelation that he should not take the mantle of power for two main reasons. First, that the revelation was politicized. He (Orogun) sensed that the revelation came mainly from the supporters of A. Olutimehin. Second, Orogun believed that based on the tradition of seniority in the Church, he was next to assuming power. [297]

---

297 An interview with Akinola Oluranti at CAC Holy Spirit Assembly on 5-11-2011

Another factor that contributed to the crises based on religious practices in the Church was faith healing itself. It was the belief of the founding fathers that healing should be via the power of God, and not through medication. The seriousness in faith healing could be seen in the metamorphorical stages of the Church right from 1939 to 1943.[298]

One of the fundamental reasons for the separation between the Nigerian and European members of the Apostolic Church in about 1939 was the issue of healing.[299] The African brothers and sisters parted in less than ten years with the British Apostolic Church on the grounds that the white missionaries were using medicine (quinine) and not relying on faith for protection against malaria.[300]

Thus, there are records in which the leaders of the Christ Apostolic Church agreed with the submissions of Ayegboyin and Ishola. Take for instance; Ogunranti confirmed in his paper that C.B. Sercombe, a one time Secretary to the Apostolic Movement in the Gold coast (later Ghana) and Nigeria, stated that the break up was on the account of the use of medicine and the interpretation of the doctrine of divine healing and revelations.[301] Similarly, in the Golden Jubilee celebration of The Apostolic Church in 1981, S.S. Jemigbon, the then Vice Chairman of the Church stated in part:

298 The CAC regulations says that no CAC member or leader should make use of orthodox or native medicines to cure any ailment as stated in II Chronicle 16:12 and II Kings 1:1-4 but should rely on faith healing as promised by Jesus Christ in Mark 16:18 or call on the elders of the church for prayer and anointing as stated in James 5:15.

299 Oral interview conducted with Mrs. D.O. Adebule, the leader of CAC Good Women Association, Nigeria on 17-9-2010. Age-68 years.

300 For more detail, see Deji Ayegboyin & S. Ademola Ishola, *African Indigenous Churches...*, p. 76

301 Ayo Ogunranti, A paper presented to the Young Men League at CAC Ebute-Metta in October, 1980.

"Between 1938 and 1939, there was misunderstanding, over divine healing and certain aspects of church administration." [302]

However, this practice of faith healing gradually became a thing of the past particularly as from 1990. Unlike the time of Joseph Ayo Babalola and others (1930-1970) when members held firmly to divine healing,[303] the attitudes of leaders in the Church towards faith healing as from 1990 upwards were lookwarm. Many of them (Church leaders) visit hospitals and some have personal doctors in Nigeria and abroad.[304]

In addition, there were series of problems even among the few prophets and prophetesses who still practiced faith healing in the 1990s. However, within that circle, there were cases wherein healings were not forthcoming. Many people who came for healings died unnecessarily. Taye Akintoye narrated how his mother died during birth delivery in 1991 due to loss of blood at the Mission house in CAC Oke Alaafia, Akure.[305] Apostle Gama also narrated how his

---

302 The Apostolic Church Golden Jubilee Message, October 1981, published by *Nigerian Tribune.*,on November 18,1981, p.18

303 See C.O. Oshun "The Pentecostal Perspectives of the CAC ...," p. 109. See also S.G. Adegboyega, *Short History of the Apostolic Church in Nigeria...*, p. 26

304 The following personalities testified to the trend of development in the CAC, particularly as from 1990 upwards, i.e. Prophet Sunday Aderanti (52 years) from CAC Power Chapel, Ile-Ife on 20-02-2010. Age-52 years. Also, T. Adeniyi, a CAC Elder at CAC Oke-Alaafia, Akure confirmed that CAC leaders as from 1990 (when the youths and wealthy ministers took over the affairs of the church) were noted to change the practices of faith healing and some even clamoured for orthodox medicine. T Adeniyi is 48 years. Interview conducted at Joseph Ayo Babalola University Ikeji on 20-05-2011. Other ministers who opted out from CAC but who confirmed this fact included Rev. S. Abodunrin (44 years) now the founder of Christ Bible Evangelistic Ministry, Ilesha; and Rev. Benjamin Adeniyi (54 years), a priest at the African Cathedral, Lagos. Interview was conducted with Abodunrin on 10-2-2011 at Ilesha while interactions with Adeniyi took place in Lagos on 15-04-2010.

305 Taye Akintoye is an elder in CAC Pisgah, Akure. Age: 37. Interview conducted on 14-11-2011.

parents, because of faith healing, lost three children within two months in Ghana because of chicken pox, a deadly disease which could be cured by medicine within some couple of days.[306]

Also, there were instances of false revelations or mis-interpretations of revelations which have negative influence on the practices of revelation in the Church. Prior to the registration of CAC in 1943, it was confirmed that Sakpo's prophecy led to the splitting of the church coffers, which were jointly held by Lagos and Ebutemeta. Thus, it also precipitated the final break between the Ebutemeta and Lagos Assemblies.

Oshun believed strongly that the prophecy was fake because, prior to Sakpo's prophecy at Ebutemeta, two independent prophecies at the Ipaja Assembly confirmed that a false prophecy was imminent and that S.G. Adegboyega (the leader of Ipaja Assembly) should take action and handle the prophecy appropriately to avoid confusion and chaos. However, Adegboyega took no action when Sakpo's prophecy came out.[307] This oversight was to further complicate an already complex situation.

Similarly, in 1989, a group of people who claimed to be divinely inspired to reorganize the Church finally ended in splitting the Church into three using the same name "Christ Apostolic Church". At least all the sides are expressing their legitimacy and the justness of their causes to the outside world. The mainstream is known to the public as the CAC led by the General Executive Council under the leadership of E.H.L Olusheye. The second group is referred to as

---

306 An interview conducted with Gama, I. during his visit to Nigeria on 10-1-2012 at Joseph Ayo Babalola University, Ikeji Arakeji.

307 An interview conducted with Christopher Oshun the former vice chancellor of Joseph Ayo Babalola University, Ikeji Aarakeji on 17-11-2011.Age -62 years.Also,G. Okegwemen, the CAC General Secretary supported this view in an interview conducted at CAC Camp Ikeji Arakeji on 17-02-2011. Age: 68 years. This view was also narrated by Joe Jacobs the CAC Youth Officer on 6-3-2011 at Ikeji Arakeji on 17-2-2011. Age – 53 years.

CAC Supreme Council led by J.O. Adegoroye and later by Ayo Ogunlade, while the third group was under the leadership of Odunaiya and O. Ige.[308]

However, M. Ogunniyi was of the opinion that there was a misplaced priority in the visions of the Forum group who claimed to embark on church reforms.[309] In the first place, the CAC regulation does not allow young pastors who were ordained within a year to be in charge of church affairs.[310] Also, that the decisions of the reformers did not augur well with the scriptural principles of peace resolution. Take for instance, Pastors N.E. Udofia (General Secretary), J.O. Adegoroye (Akure Chairman) and T. Obadare were suspended from the Church.[311] Also, the three aged Principal Officers of the Church, Pastors J.B. Orogun (President), A.O. Olutimehin (General Superintendent), and D.O. Babajide (General Evangelist) were compulsorily retired.[312]

However, the church members and leaders could not react against these moves of the group of reformers because they claimed to be divinely led by the Spirit of God. In CAC, the tradition is that ministers and members hold firmly to divine instruction- 'Thus says the Lord'. However, the actions of the so called reformers called for suspicions.[313] Thus, various challenges came up as a result of

308 Information collected from the secretary of WOSEM, Pastor Oluranti Akinola who happens to fall under the Supreme Council. This view was confirmed by T. Folarin (62 years) at Obafemi Awolowo University, Ile Ife on 20-10-2011. Also, S. A. Fadola (80 years) and Elder E. O. Egunlae (72 years) testified to this fact through interviews on 2-7-2010 at Ado Ekiti.

309 Interview conducted with M. O. Ogunniyi at CACTS, Ile-Ife, on 3-5-2011. Aged–49 years.

310 See *Iwe Ilana ati Eko ...*, pp. 19, 20, and 58.

311 Interview conducted with M.O. Ogunniyi

312 *Ibid.*

313 *Ibid.*

reforming the Church. Take for instance; there were court cases over the ownership of the Church. The General Supreme Council under the secretarialship of Udofia was claimed to have the incorporated church certificate issued in 1947. There were also disputes over the assets of the Church particularly the Babalola International Miracle Camp, Ikeji-Arakeji.[314]

The uncontrolled proliferation due to the increase in numbers of members and ministers contributed to the crises which affected the religious practices of revelations and practices in the Church. Statistically, in 1931, two persons (A.O. Omotosho and J.A. Medaiyese) were presented by Joseph Ayo Babalola through divine instruction for ordination. J.B. Orogun and other five persons were ordained in 1937. Also, six persons were chosen in 1938 as evangelists with the view to promoting evangelism in the Yoruba region of Nigeria. They were Benjamin Adefabijo, Joshua Apata, David Adio, John Oye, Titus Alade and Simeon Babatunde.[315]

In 1946, the number of church workers increased tremendously over the records between 1931 and 1938. For instance, at Efon-Alaaye (now in Ekiti State), the ministers were about eighteen.[316] Between 1955 and 1960, many people who now serve as leaders in the contemporary CAC arrived for one reason or the other in the Church. Take for instance, Obadare came to CAC as a result of the divine revelation he had when he was at The Apostolic Church Ilesha to meet Joseph Ayo Babalola for spiritual counseling. It was here Joseph Babalola revealed to him about his divine assignment in

---

314 Interview conducted with Pastor M.A. Ololade from WOSEM 16-10-2011. Age – 85 years. Also, Prophetess M. O. Igbalajobi made a confirmation of this fact in an interview conducted on 10-04-2011. Age-78years.

315 See J. A. Medaiyese, *Itan Igbedide Woli Joseph Ayo Babalola* (Ibadan: Oluseyi Press, 1956), p. 58.

316 *Ibid*, p. 58

the Christ Apostolic Church.[317]

Also, Olusheye arrived in the Christ Apostolic Church for spiritual consultation with Joseph Ayo Babalola in 1955. It was here that God revealed to him about the assignment he had in the Church.[318] Other reknowed Pastors that arrived in the Church from 1960 included; T. Babatope, G. Aguda and Akintola who was the former principal of CAC Theological Seminary before decamping to the General Supreme Council side, a faction of the Christ Apostolic Church.[319]

The number of ordained pastors in the Church in 1960 was thirty two. It increased to forty in 1962. The number jumped to 65 in 1975 when the would be pastors received pastoral training at the CAC Theological Seminary, Ile- Ife for a period of two years. In the same way, in 1982, ordained pastors were 102. However, as from 1993 upwards, the General Executive Council ordained 400 people (both full time ministers on the field and part time ministers) were considered for ordination. Between 1994 and 1995, more than one thousand were ordained. In 1997, 60 were ordained. In 1999, 2000 were ordained. Also, between 2001 and 2010, 5100 were ordained.[320]

Consequently, the uncontrolled ordained ministers embarked on proliferation of assemblies without control from the central ruling

---

317 Interview conducted with Pastor Oluranti Akinola at CAC Holy Spirit Church, Akure, on 17-9-2011. Age-71 years. Others that were interview in connection with this discussions were: Evangelist Ohon (63 years) on 17-11-2009, Ruth Peter (61 years) at Ikere Ekiti on 17-3-2011 , Evangelist Olubode Hezekiah (54 years) at Ikeji Arakeji on 17-11-2011 and J. Miller (53 years) at Ikeji Arakeji on 17-11-2011

318 *Ibid*

319 *Ibid*

320 Information got from Pastor Isaac Olutimehin, the personal assistance to Pastor Abraham Olutimehin, the ex General Superintendent CAC world-wide. Age-48 years.Date of interview-17-5-2011.

body. In addition, the Church could not come up with a definite position of how exactly the business of church planting should be carried out; hence there were ideas and factions. Thus, due to inadequate training of ministers particularly those that came from other Christian faiths, the operations in the Church were contrary to the founding fathers of the Church. It consequently affected faith healing as many of these leaders (unlike the founding fathers) visit hospitals while some lay little emphasis on revelations of dreams, visions etc.

Lastly, the Church's constitution which was set aside (not used) also contributed to the crises. As earlier mentioned, the focus of the CAC is on spiritual matters and not on the constitution. The constitution was not reviewed nor referred to when the situation called for it. The church's only constitution has been the Article of Incorporation of 1946. From 1966 onwards, successive administrations have embarked on making administrative changes. In the 1980s, several regional and national meetings were held. Unfortunately, the exercise was aborted before its full usefulness became un-known. Hence, matters relating to abuse of prophetic gifts, such as, fake healing, unfulfilled and inaccurate prophecy and interpretation of dreams could not be addressed since the constitution has not been upgraded. Oshun remarks:

> The Church had not endorsed a new constitution that could make necessary changes possible when, in May 1989, at a national ordination service, the first signal of trouble emerged.[321]

With the administrative defects in the Church, many ministers operate individually. There are many assemblies with the logo and name of CAC without having any attachment or link with the central administration in Ibadan, CAC Headquarters. However, as earlier discussed, the situation in the Church prompted some young pastors

321 *Ibid,* p. 160

to actions by constituting themselves into a reformist group for the Church with promises to raise money and restructure the administration. Somehow, the leading figure in the group, Pastor (former Elder) Tewogbade hijacked the reformation programme and soon became the lone voice; soon, also he hijacked the leadership of the Church by wielding enormous financial influence over the members of the Supreme Council which later became the General Executive Council.

5. 2 Negative Effects of the Crises

5.2.1 Schism and Secession

The intervening years between 1930 and 1988 marked a period of relative peace and stability for the Christ Apostolic Church. It was a period of consolidating its gains from the revival years and commuting its losses from the struggle. The Christ Apostolic Church, Nigeria, also maintains a link with the Christ Apostolic Church, Gold Coast now Ghana, until 1960.[322] After the incorporation (CAC), the first set of principal officers (1943-1964) were- Isaac Babalola Akinyele (President), David Osmond Odubanjo (General Superintendent), Jacob Odusona (Vice-President), Joseph Ayo Babalola (General Evangelist) and David Olulana Babajide (Assistant General Evangelist).

Also, the second set began (1964-1966) with Jacob Odusona (President), Elijah Latunde as Vice-President, Joshua Medayese as General Superintendent and David Olulana Babajide as General Evangelist. The third set (1966-1983) consisted of Elijah Latunde as President, Joshua Adeniran Medayese and Joseph Bolade as General

322 C. O. Oshun, "The Experience of Christ Apostolic Church," in Ademola Ishola and Deji Ayegboyin (eds.), *Rediscovering and Fostering Unity in the Body of Christ: The Nigerian Experience,* (Lagos: ATF Publications 2000), p. 158

Supretentent and David Olulana Babajide as General Evangelist

With the death of Babalola and Odubanjo in 1959 and Akinyele in 1964, CAC was set to have a new leadership. For a short time, Pastor Odusona led the church in succession. Pastor E.T Latunde, whose long tenure ushered in a period of organizational restructuring for the Church, soon succeeded both.[323]

However, the scenario for the final breakup, as earlier discussed, occurred in May 1989, at the national ordination service of new ministers in the Church. Consequently, a group known as 'Forum' emerged. Their actions led to schism in the Church. However, Oluranti was of the opinion that the Church was at the verge of collapsing before 1989. According to him, two personalities (Olusheye and Obadare) were directly involved in the crises.

The root of misunderstanding according to Akinola started between them (Olusheye and Obadare, both residing in Akure, section B) as a result of Sunday school pamplets which was under Olusheye. He was accused of mis-appropriation of Sunday school funds and Obadare attempted to use the opportunity to checkmate the power of Olusheye as he became the leader of the panel to investigate the accusations alleged against Olusheye. However, the panel did not come up with any concrete result pertaining to the allegation. It was only discovered that Olusheye bought some equipment for the Sunday school without proper permission from the Supreme Council.

Thus, Olusheye was reprimanded for his action. Olusheye, on the other hand, hit back at Obadare some couples of months after this incident by exposing the secret operations within his (Obadare) ministry particularly in the areas of establishing seminary for the training of ministers, the running of a big printing press, the gathering

323 Information from Pastor Oluranti Akinola on 5-11-2011 at the CAC Holy Spirit Church, Akure.Age-71 years.

together of influential and wealthy people in the CAC for sponsoring his ministry.[324] The end result was schism.

5.2.2 Waste of Resources

The court cases which started about twenty six years ago have gulped a lot of money. Huge sums of money had to be spent by leaders of both groups on securing bails, payment of lawyers' fees and transportation. Money also had to change hands on many occasions between the church leaders and law-enforcement agents. This action runs counter to the provisions of the scripture.[325] In 2006, J.O.Alayo, Chairman, Peace Committee of Supreme Executive Council made a report at the CAC conference held at Oniyanrin, Ibadan that the CAC had lost billions of Naira on court cases. His report stated thus:

> Millions of naira had been spent on prosecuting court cases and engaging the services of legal practitioners. Also, millions of naira had been spent on travelling and obtaining documents. In all, the church has lost a lot of fortunes running into billions.[326]

Also, properties were destroyed. At the CAC Secretariat at Oniyanrin in 1992, a group of people suspected to be thugs came to the premises, drove away people residing in the premises. Window louvers were broken and iron gates were forced open, but no records of casualty or death were discovered. In Abeokuta, doors to the church were broken at broad-day light and some pastors were driven away from the premises. Some of these victims as Akobere explained were physically assaulted. Many were admitted in the hospitals.[327]

---

324 *Ibid*

325 Holy Bible, I Cor.6:5-7. Also see Matthew 18:15-17

326 J. A. Alayo, "CAC Cases," in *Nigeria Tribune,*Wednesday,27 September, 2006, p. 40

327 Information about this incidence was received from Pastor Akobere Kehinde from CAC Headquarters, Ibadan on 17-9-2011.Age-45 years.

The implication of this is that the CAC has wasted resources, time, knowledge and money that could have been devoted to the expansion of the Church through effective evangelism and crusade on irrelevant matters. The concentration on court cases and avoidable disputes on CAC landed property adversely affected the time for preaching the Word and saving of souls.[328] The purpose of the Church has been defeated because it has deviated in promoting the instruction of Jesus Christ on the Great Commission of bringing people into the Kingdom of God.

5.2.3 Decrease in Membership and High Death Rate of Church Leaders

One of the negative effects of the crises in the CAC was the reduction in membership. Though, it was a gradual process, many youths in the Church had to shift base to younger but more settled and peaceful Churches. Many of the youths of the church became members of the new generation churches such as Mountain of Fire and Miracles, Redeemed Christian Church of God, Faith Mission Church, and Deeper Christian Life Ministry, etc

Another negative effect of the crises was that a large number of CAC valuable ministers moved away to the older and new generation churches. Since a huge sum had been diverted into court cases, it was difficult for the Church to sustain the ministers and give them good welfare like it happened in other churches. Most gifted ministers were attracted with fat salaries to churches like Anglican and Redeemed churches.[329]

In CAC, a pastor who was ordained within a period of ten years

328 *Ibid*

329 The information was received from an Anglican priest Ven. (Dr) Paul Ojo, a lecturer at Uyo University, 2-5-2012. Also, S. Borokinni, the Provost of the Anglican Church Cathedral, Akure confirmed this information. Interview conducted at Akure on 17-6-2008. Age-62 years.

from the time of the incident (1984-1994) received between 7000 naira and 10000 naira per month. In the recent time (2012), an average salary of a pastor is between 18,000 naira and 20,000 naira. On the other hand, in the Angilcan Church, an average minister received between 20,000 naira and 25,000 (1984-1994) and about 60,000 naira to 70,000 naira in the recent times.[330]

In addition, the interview conducted in the course of this work points to the conclusion that during the last two decades, many pastors in the church seem to have either fallen by the wayside or suffered avoidable death as a result of the long crises in the Church. From 1990-1994, information received showed that many church leaders died of stress, hypertension and sicknesses as a result of the calamity that erupted in the Church. The details of records of the deceased in the Church between 1990 and 1994 are as follows: In 1990, (87), 1991 (104), 1992 (120), 1993 (75) and 1994 (81).[331] Also between the years 1995-2009, record revealed that the death rate of ministers was still very high, even though it was not as higher as that of 1990 to 1994. (See Appendix IV for detail)

Apart from high death rate, the number of prophets and propheteses posted to CAC assemblies reduced considerably. Many left CAC because of the ugly situations to stand on their own by planting churches. Thus, Bola Odeleke, who was one of the gifted lady evangelists, opted out of the Church in the '90s and established her ministry. Dorcas Siyanbola of CAC Agbala Daniel also pulled out of the Church and founded a ministry. Joshua Ketiku of the present Christ Like Assembly opted out of the Christ Apostolic Church, Kosehunti and established his ministry.[332] Many also run independent

---

330 Information received from Ven. (Dr.) Paul Ojo, Dept. of Religious Studies, University of Uyo. Age-44 years. Interview conducted on 2-5-2012.

331 Information collected from CAC Library, Bashorun, Ibaban, on 17-5-2010

332 Oral interview conducted with Mrs D. O. Adebule, the leader of Good Women Association, Nigeria on 17-9-2010.Age-68 years.

ministries with the name of CAC. Such people do not attend the district monthly meeting and they refuse to send their monetary due to the central authority.

In the course of this research, attempt was made to do a survey of prophets and prophetesses by examining their numerical strength in their various assemblies between 1989 (before crises) and 1990-1991 (the climax of crises) in the Church. About four towns in three states of the country (Nigeria) have been considered for survey, namely: Akure in Ondo State, Omuo and Ado Ekiti in Ekiti State, Warri in Delta State.

Let us consider the following analysis:

Table 1- Number of Prophets and Prophetesses in CAC Assemblies, Akure Ondo State

S/N	CAC Assemblies	Total No. of Prophets in 1989	No. of Prophets In 1990	No. of Prophets in 1991	% of Proph In 1989	% of Proph. In 1990	% of Proph. In 1991
1.	Cathedral, Warri	16	5	11	100.0	68.7	31.3
2.	Mount Bethel	22	8	14	100.0	63.6	36.4
3.	Shalom District	5	2	3	100.0	60.0	40.0
4.	Oke Ibukun	15	6	9	100.0	60.0	40.0
5.	CAC Refinary Road	13	6	7	100.0	54.0	46.0
6.	Oke Iyanu	2	2	1	100.0	100.0	100.0
7.	Oke Ayo	9	2	7	100.0	77.8	22.2
8.	Ekpan District	8	2	6	100.0	75.0	25.0
9.	Power Chapel	13	2	11	100.0	84.6	15.4
10.	Oke Igbala No. 1	5	2	3	100.0	60.0	40.0
11.	Oke Igbala No. 2	15	3	12	100.0	80.0	20.0
12.	Miracle Centre	5	1	4	100.0	80.0	20.0

Source- Data collected from CAC Assemblies, Akure

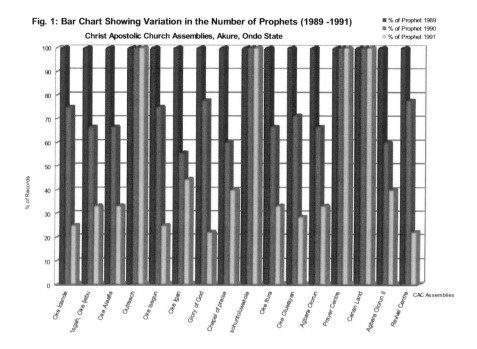

Fig. 1: Bar Chart Showing Variation in the Number of Prophets (1989 -1991)

Christ Apostolic Church Assemblies, Akure, Ondo State

Table 2- Number of Prophets and Prophetesses at CAC Asemblies, Omuo Ekiti

S/N	CAC Assemblies	Total No. of Prophets 1989	No. of Prophets 1990	No. of Prophets 1991	% of Proph In 1989	% Of proph 1990	% of proph 1991
1	Oke Igbala	8	6	2	100.0	75.0	25.0
2	Oke Igbala (2)	15	8	7	100.0	53.3	46.7
3	Oke Ayo	2	2	1	100.0	100.0	50.0
4	Mount. Bethel	6	5	1	100.0	83.3	16.7
5	Mountain of Peace	4	3	1	100.0	75.0	25.0
6	Oke Ilaata	2	1	1	100.0	50.0	50.0
7	Omuo DCC	4	3	1	100.0	75.0	25.0
8	Oke Idande	5	1	4	100.0	20.0	80.0

Source- Data collected from CAC Assemblies, Omuo Ekiti

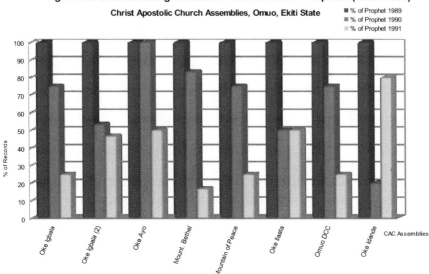

Fig. 2: Bar Chart Showing Variation in the Number of Prophets (1989 -1991)

Christ Apostolic Church Assemblies, Omuo, Ekiti State

■ % of Prophet 1989
▓ % of Prophet 1990
▒ % of Prophet 1991

Table 3- Number of Prophets and Prophetesses at CAC Assemblies, Ado Ekiti

,S/N	CAC Assemblies	Total No. of Prophs. in 1989	No. of Prophets in 1990	No. of Prophets In 1991	% of Proph In 1989	% of proph In 1990	% Of Proph In 1991
1.	Ogba Alaafia (DCC)	15	2	13	100.0	86.7	13.3
2.	Oke Itunle	7	4	3	100.0	57.1	42.9
3.	Mountain of Power	3	3	0	100.0	100.0	0.0
4.	Power Chapel	4	3	1	100.0	100.0	0.0
5.	Housing Estate	8	6	2	100.0	75.0	25.0
6.	Oke Igbala	4	3	1	100.0	75.0	25.0
7.	Oke Enphoh	5	2	3	100.0	60.0	40.0
8.	Oke Iye	7	3	4	100.0	42.9	57.1

Source- Data collected from CAC Assemblies, Ado Ekiti

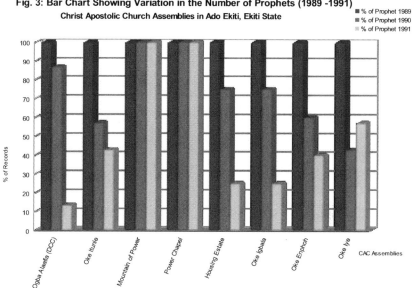

Fig. 3: Bar Chart Showing Variation in the Number of Prophets (1989 -1991)
Christ Apostolic Church Assemblies in Ado Ekiti, Ekiti State

■ % of Prophet 1989
▨ % of Prophet 1990
▧ % of Prophet 1991

Table 4- Number of Prophets and Prophetesses in CAC Assemblies, Warri, Delta State

S/N	CAC Assemblies	Total No. of Prophets in 1989	No. of Prophets In 1990	No. of Prophets In 1991	% of Proph. In 1989	% of Proph. In 1990	% of Proph. In 1991
1.	Cathedral, Warri	16	5	11	100.0	68.7	31.3
2.	Mount Bethel	22	8	14	100.0	63.6	36.4
3.	Shalom District	5	2	3	100.0	60.0	40.0
4.	Oke Ibukun	15	6	9	100.0	60.0	40.0
5.	CAC Refinary Road	13	6	7	100.0	54.0	46.0
6.	Oke Iyanu	2	2	1	100.0	100.0	100.0
7.	Oke Ayo	9	2	7	100.0	77.8	22.2
8.	Ekpan District	8	2	6	100.0	75.0	25.0
9.	Power Chapel	13	2	11	100.0	84.6	15.4
10.	Oke Igbala No. 1	5	2	3	100.0	60.0	40.0
11.	Oke Igbala No. 2	15	3	12	100.0	80.0	20.0
12.	Miracle Centre	5	1	4	100.0	80.0	20.0

Source- Data collected from CAC Assemblies, Warri, Delta State

213

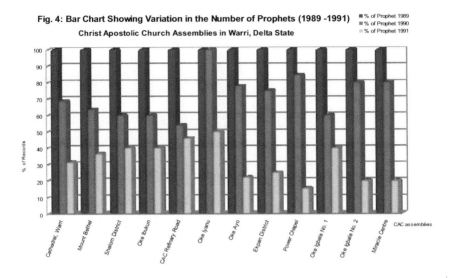

Fig. 4: Bar Chart Showing Variation in the Number of Prophets (1989 -1991)
Christ Apostolic Church Assemblies in Warri, Delta State

Thus, from the analyses above, one could see that even though the CAC has a number of gifted ministers to serve as gospel bearer to out-stations or other distant places, yet records show that some have left their primary assignment for greener pastures or to pioneer churches to operate individual ministries within the Church.

5.2.4   The Beginning of Church Politics

One of the effects of the crises on Christ Apostolic Church was the organizational restructuring of the Church. As earlier stated, the activities of the Forum Group brought a lot of changes and development into the administrative structure of the Church. It led to the creation of more districts or coordinating councils and thereby gave the Church a new face-lift since many offices were created in the Church. On the other hand, it marked the beginning of struggle for power within the Church. Positions and promotions were not placed according to the traditions and constitutions of the church. Medaiyese submits: "The promotions of staff after the death of President Latunde in the 80s was based on who you

214

know".[333] Oshun remarks: "The Orogun-led Forum Administration was incapable of total control, and therefore most of its policies were ineffective, or inconclusive, or perhaps biased".[334]

First in the history of the Church, after the death of Latunde, the Church leaders jettisoned the prophecy that Orogun should not hold the mantle of power because of the calamity foreseen to befall the church during his tenure. There were several prophecies on the appointment of a President to succeed the late Pastor Latunde in 1982. The Good Women Society played a prominent role and for the first time the CAC witnessed a situation in which women almost lorded it over the majority, including the authority of the Church, even if it means using unprophetic legitimations whichever way this tended towards. However, the resultant appointment was, therefore, viewed with suspicion.[335]

Thus, in 1992, Orogun was retired by the Forum Group and Faniyan was appointed as Acting Chairman of the General Executive Council.[336] However, there were other senior officers such as I. Ajuwon and O. Babafemi who could stand in that direction. But, the Forum Group dictated the affairs of the Church and their favourites were considered for Church appointment. [337] This was the position of things up till 1995 when the General Executive Council and Supreme Council appointed their officers

---

333 An interview with E. O. Medaiyese, the chairman CAC Southern D.CC.London, on 4-6-2010 in London. Age-65

334 Christopher Oshun, "The Experience of Christ Apostolic Church,"..., pp. 161-162

335 *Ibid*, p. 171

336 See C.O. Oshun "CAC of Nigeria," in Oshun (ed.), *The Spiritual Standard of the Nigerian Faith Tabernacle Fathers,1918-1930*, (Lagos: ATF Publications, 1997), p. 7

337 G. Omitinde, is a Pastor and a worker at Joseph Ayo Babalola University, Ikeji Arakeji. Interview conducted on 20-5-2011. Age-48 years.

respectively. However, between 1992 and 1995, there were series of court cases to settle the rifts but all efforts proved abortive. The detail of the court cases is discussed in the footnote.[338]

5.3 Positive Effects of the Crises

5.3.1 Church Organizational Restructuring

As earlier mentioned, one of the positive effects of the crises on the practices of the Church is the restructuring of the organization of the church setting. One, through the influence of the Forum Group, there was the adoption of the use of the General Executive Council to replace the Supreme Council. The General Executive was used at the point of registration of the Church (CAC) in 1943. So, this move was a reversion to tradition.

This development necessitated the creation of more Districts and Zonal Coordinating Councils within the church setting. The implication is that promotion became rapid in the Church, as ministers in the lower cadres were raised to higher posts. Thus, the situation automatically opened doors for the non-ordained ministers to be ordained en-masse.

The development in the Church with the creations of Districts from different levels and the mass- ordination brought a partial and peaceful reconciliation of some groups in the divided Church. On October 23, 2001, E. O. Adelekan, the General Superintendent of the Supreme Council Group decamped to the General Executive Group. He was warmly received by the General Executive Group and reinstated to his appropriate rank in

338 The court summons further included: (i) Suit No. 1/15/93 of 6th July 1993 at the Ibadan High Court, No5. (ii) Suit No. AK/42/92 of 16th September, 1993 at the Akure High Court (iii) Suit No. AK/42/92 of 22nd September 1993 at the Akure High Court. (iii)Suit No. AK/42/92 of 28th September at the Akure High Court. (iv) Suit No. AK/42/92 of 41th November, 1993 at the Akure High Court

the Church. Following this pattern, Adio, a reknowned prophet from Ilorin through divine instruction decamped from the Supreme Executive Group to the General Executive Council Group. And being a church founder, his assembly was upgraded to a special district.

Other developments that took place between 1990 till present time in the Christ Apostolic Church are seen in the establishment of infrastructure and also the deep interest of leaders in education. The donation of 3 million in 1992 by the reformers for the development of the Church and its administration widened the practice of embarking on costly developmental projects in the Church. In the imitation of the reformers, some other financiers within the Church emerged to work for the Church. Examples of such projects are the International Revival Camp at Ikeji-Arakeji promoted by I.O.Ogunbomehin and his Church; and the establisnment of satellite campuses of the CAC Theological Seminary, Ile Ife in Ilesha, Lagos, Ibadan, Bokkos, Kano, Kabba, Warri, Enugu and London.

The Christ Apostolic Church has a seminary with twelve viable satellite campuses in Nigeria and one in London with Pastor Rufus Thomas as the coordinator. The Chairman for the Board of Council of the seminary in Europe is Pastor A. O. Fashina. Not only that, the Church has established a University at Ikeji Arakeji, Osun-State. Billions of Naira has been expended on these projects particularly in the building of roads and the erection of gigantic buildings. This is the part of the church that has been passing through some turbulent times in the last eighteen years. Many gigantic auditoria and chalets for ministers have been constructed while buildings were erected for conferences, prayer meetings and revivals.

5.4. The Implications of Changes/Crises on Christian Groups of Missions and New Pentecostal Churches

5.4.1 Cordial Relationship

One of the effects of schism occasioned by the practices of revelations and healings in CAC is the bridging of gaps between the different sides in the Church (CAC) and other Churches. When the crises erupted in the first quarter of the twentieth century, it was a shock to the Christian communities in Nigeria and Diaspora. To return peace to the Church was no ast easy, it has to be a gradual process.

Some of these Christian communities namely, Oyo State Branch of Christian Association of Nigeria (CAN) and Nigerian Association of *Aladura* Churches (NAAC) sent delegates to contact the church leaders from all sides of the factions and appealed to them to settle their scores and withdraw cases that were already in court. The steps to put an end to conflicts by these Christian bodies have brought a sort of mutual understanding and closeness within the leaders of the Church

In addition, several appeals were made by these Christian communities to leaders of the Church to accept peaceful resolution and resolve their differences based on these considerations. First, that the church founding fathers, namely David Odubanjo, Isaac Akinyele and others had suffered and laboured greatly for the establishment of the Church. Second, that, these leaders have demonstrated to the Christian world a level of spirituality which enhanced the fame of the Church and had succeeded in handing over the Church to their succeeding officers as a united, God-fearing and soul-winning Church; that a departure from the original practice would project the Church bad image.

All these appeals have gone a long way in bringing a sort of love, understanding and respect between the peace settlers and the two parties involved in the long crises. It has also served as an eye opener to promote peace and discourage disunity in their various churches. Now, in the contemporary CAC, the issue of crises is becoming a forgotten issue.

5.4.2 Outburst of Revivals in the Church

In our earlier discussion, we discovered that one side effect of the schisms arising from practices in the CAC was the mass movement of members to older churches and new Pentecostal churches. However, the restructuring in the Church has also brought a new wave of revival which attracted thousands of people. In the year 2000, the General Executive Council organized a millienium revival at Ikeji Arakeji with the view to promote evangelism in the Church.

All CAC members and ministers both in Nigeria and abroad, were invited to attend the programme.In adition; other dignitaries from CAC were invited to attend the programme. The revival lasted for three days. There were series of testimonies and miracles during the revival. Also, many youths who had left the Church began to find their ways back to the Church.

Similar revivals took place in several locations in Nigeria such as Lagos, Port Harcourt, Ibadan and Odo Owa in Kwara State. Prominent members of the Church who returned to CAC were: Elder Isaac Durodola who left the Redeemed Christian Church back to CAC. Also, Raphel Oguntimehin left Gospel Faith Mission to join CAC and Taye Akintola left Christ Embassy to CAC.[339] It is also on record that many people came back to CAC from churches like Redeemed Christian Church of God, Deeper Christian Life Ministry, Faith Mission Church and Mountain of Fire and Miracles.[340] All these developments led to an outburst of Holy Ghost revivals in many assemblies in the CAC.

---

339 Information got from Mrs Toyin Fadola from CAC Pisgah Akure on 10-03-2011. Age-43 years

340 Joshua Adeware Alokan, *CAC at 90* (Ile Ife: Timade Ventures 2010), p. 422

5.5 Findings

From the research, it was discovered that the Christ Apostolic Church patriarchs were major contributors to the growth of indigenous Pentecostalism in Nigeria. Their activities also contributed to the birth of Christ Apostolic Church in Nigeria and abroad up to 1980. The uniqueness of the works and activities of those great heroes sustained the practices of revelations and healings in the Christ Apostolic Church to the 21st century.

From the foregoing, it is obvious that the CAC patriarchs, no doubt, contributed greatly to the building of the Church through its practices and thereby place it as one of the leading indigenous Pentecostal Churches in Nigeria. Thus, the CAC has continued to be relevant among other indigenous Pentecostal churches as it continue to meet the needs of the people for healing, deliverance and prophetic revelations in a dislocated society searching for meaning.

In addition, the study discovered that the CAC has a long record of multifarious encounters with the Holy Spirit in power and in might. This spirit encounter has played significant roles in establishing members in the Christian faith. This is because these encounters have met the spiritual needs of the Africans particularly in terms of guidance and explanation to every problem of life. It is clear to a large extent that African indigenous way of life during the advent of western missionaries was underrated, blacklisted and disrupted. All these gaps were filled with the initiative of some founding fathers of CAC. Through their efforts, indigenous Christianity came to incorporate these values to their faith to give it relevance and meanings before Africans.

Not only that, the study discovered that the CAC crisis which started in 1988/89 and has persisted till date had its root in the practices of revelations and healings. The expansion of the

Church, which was created by the influence of converts, therefore, gave rise to administrative complexities and strange religious practices. Different kinds of people joined the clergy and the laity; and their conflicting ideas affected the standard of the Church on the practices of revelations and healings.

Furthermore, the study revealed that the CAC, in spite of the on going crises and schisms, has continued to expand because of its emphasis on prophecies, visions, dreams, speaking in tongue, prayers and faith healings, which have provided solutions to the peoples' prevailing problems. The statistics as at 1980 shows that the Christ Apostolic Church has expanded tremendously to Europe, America and other places in the world.

In London for example, there are fifteen Assemblies. The large congregations among them are CAC Outreach under Pastor A.O. Fashina with 620 members, the CAC Stockwell under Pastor Thomas with 418 members, the CAC under Pastor S. A. Okunola with 206 members and the CAC under the chairmanship of Pastor J. T. Bandele with 56 members. From these analyses, it is obvious that the prophetic gifts of healing, spirit of discernment, dreaming and prophecy have been blessings to individuals, churches, society, nations and humanity at large.

The findings showed further that the irregularities in the CAC constitution after its incorporation in 1943 was a major factor responsible for poor administrative structure and policy of the Church particularly in the areas of Church organization and centralization, promotion pattern, discipline, training of ministers and funding.

In addition, the study revealed that music plays vital role in the practices of revelation and healing in the Church. It also helps in establishing many people in the faith. It has become a great tool in the spirituality, evangelization and proselytisation processes in the Church. CAC through this practice has not only influenced Nigerian music greatly but has also dominated the gospel music circle, which has now become the most popular music genres in Nigeria.

Finally, the study discovered that Christ Apostolic Church operated a brand of Christianity that is deeply rooted in the African culture. The world-view of the CAC just like other Aladura adherents is taken into consideration, particularly in their beliefs towards the operation of the malevolent spirits, forces of evil, witches and wizards. This perhaps accounts for the reasons why the Christ Apostolic Church places much emphasis on revelations and other forms of spiritualities to help in identifying spiritual problems, fears of life as well as providing lasting solutions to them.

5.6. Summary

From the foregoing, it is essential to examine the role of revelations and divine healings as instruments of promoting unity and growth in indigenous Pentecostalism, particularly in the Christ Apostolic Church. The term "unity" stands for stability, love, commitment and cooperation that exist among a group of people living in a community or society.

Based on this, the practices of revelations and healings will be relevant to keep the standard and unity of the Church intact. Christ Apostolic Church was initially administered by the founding fathers that manifested exemplary lives of probity, love, industry, loyalty and tenacity of purpose. These qualities show that the practices have a place in bringing solidarity and integrity among church leaders in the Christian communities.

In view of this, the Church in the new millennium needs to prepare ministers who are capable of meeting the challenges in the contemporary society and who will also be relevant, responsive, sensitive, creative, imaginative, dogged, determined, aggressive, bold, courageous, knowledgeable, resourceful, vibrant, dynamic, undaunting, selfless, spirit-filled and spirit-directed to meet up the daily spiritual needs of people in the society. On this, Oshun remarked:

> Definitely, there will be no room for mediocrity, pretension, self-centeredness, pious-frauds or priest crafts, indiscipline (moral, spiritual and administrative) especially among the ministerial class, young and old, men and women, ordained and un-ordained, stipendiary and non-stipendiary.[341]

From this background, unity in the CAC is bound to occur if the leaders from the various divided camps could let go the weaknesses of the past borne out of a reckless lowering of standards, undue compromise, flagrant indiscipline and nonchalance for serious learning in both secular and spiritual matters. The Christ Apostolic Church must put more efforts in its recent peace moves to bring some of the scattered assemblies together, particularly with the establishment of a citadel of higher school of learning Joseph Ayo Babalola University. The University has given employment to both Christians and Muslims; and also admits students from different denominations and sects.

---

341 See C.O. Oshun, "The Experience of Christ Apostolic Church,"…, p. 166

CHAPTER SIX

CONCLUSION

6.1 Introduction

It is note-worthy that the Christ Apostolic Church since its inception contributes positively to the growth of indigenous Pentecostalism in Nigeria Olusumbola reveals in his book that the growth of the Christ Apostolic Church stems from the works of the pioneering fathers, particularly Joseph Ayo Babalola, who worked relentlessly to lay a solid foundation for the Church. According to the writer:

> The pioneering work of Apostle Ayo Babalola, seventy two years after Christianity had been introduced to Nigeria, could be likened to the European missionaries who were said to have been part of the opening up of the so called Dark Continent.[342]

For the first thirty years of the advent of CAC, the older churches, particularly the Anglican Church, looked down on the religious institution. Why? First, the colonial power did not accord recognition to the Church. In addition, the pioneering members of the Church were assumed mostly to be uneducated. Third, the prophetic gifts of healing and breakthrough through persistent prayers were strange to the Protestant churches.

However, by the early 1950s, the CAC had demonstrated to the Protestant churches that it had a valuable message for the

---

342 O. Olusumbola, *The Growth of Christ Apostolic Church in Erin-Ijesa* (Ibadan: Ayo Press Publishing Company, 2001), p. 35

community. The practices in the CAC, which were attributed to faith healings and prophetic gifts, have prompted G. A. Oshitelu to summarize in his writings that:

> The Christ Apostolic Church, to a large extent practices faith healing alone. Hence, the CAC forbids the use of the medicine in any form. For the CAC in particular, sickness is recognized as the result of sin or satanic attack. Thus, they maintain that medicine is a human means which is against the ways of God..[343]

This development could be seen as people trooped to the Church. Based on this, it is evident that CAC plays a significant role in the development of Pentecostalism in Nigeria. In the history of African Pentecostalism, CAC, according to some writers, almost took the leading role in terms of the number of local assemblies and worshippers. The confirmation of this is seen in the submission of Olusheye in the Christ Apostolic Church Year Book of 1980 that:

> We of the Christ Apostolic Church have to thank God immensely for the establishment of this great organization which is one of the largest African indigenous missionary establishments in the world and it has been the most rapid growth in the history of African Pentecostalism.[344]

Moreover, the religious revolution of CAC revivalists at the inception of the Church contributed immensely to the tremendous growth of the new Pentecostal Churches in Nigeria. It is observed that many of these new Pentecostal churches are the offshoots of the CAC. J. Falope, Bishop of the Anglican Diocese of Ilesha had

---

343 G. A. Oshitelu, *History of the Aladura (independent) Churches,1918-1940: An Interpretation* (Ibadan: Hope Publications, 2007), p. 102

344 See *Christ Apostolic Year Book* (Lagos CAC Printing Press 1980), p. 52

this to say to complement the above:

> ...there are pockets of virile evangelization here and there all over the country. These pockets of evangelization have their roots mostly outside 'older' denominations. Such evangelization has its roots principally in the 'Apostolic' bodies (churches) which sprang up in the last fifty years and have spread phenomenally throughout the country. In pursuit of their programs of virile evangelization, they see to it that, as far as possible, places of worship are sited.[345]

In addition, there is no doubt that the works of the pioneering fathers of the Church have indeed contributed tremendously to the rapid growth of the charismatic- Pentecostal revival of the twenty-first century in Nigeria. The history could be traced to the happenings in the 1970s, with the activities of some CAC students who studied abroad. They laid much emphasis on the baptism of the Holy Spirit. These students after completing their studies came to spread the ideas of Pentecostal revivals in Nigerian universities

From 1970, the Pentecostal revival group at University of Ibadan made advancement to hold evangelistic retreats in some towns in mid-western and Eastern Nigeria. The first evangelical activity, which was later called 'Congress' was held at the University of Ibadan in May 1970. By the middle of 1970, the leaders of the congress formed an independent and permanent organization tagged 'World Action Team for Christ'. Other universities followed the example. All these developments were as a result of the influence of CAC and other indigenous leaders in the early twentieth century.

345 See *The Growth of Christ Apostolic Church in Erin-Ijesa,* p. 35

The emphasis of the CAC patriarchs and other subsequent gifted leaders on the practices of revelations and healings has gone a long way in replacing the tradition of people from consulting the diviners for one reason or the other. The Yoruba tradition in particular encourages the indigenous practices of conjuration, sorcery and enquiry from diviners. However, the CAC patriarchs and gifted ministers to some degree of confidence have effectively substituted the indigenous practice of consulting diviners, witches and sorcerers by unraveling secrets and mysteries through revelations and divine healings from Christian faith perspective.

6.2. Conclusion

From the findings, it has been discovered that CAC has got a long record of multifarious encounters with the Holy Spirit in power and might. These Holy Spirit encounters have established many people in Christian faith. These encounters have also met the worldview of Africans particularly in the areas of spiritual consultations and interpretations, explanations and guidance to every problem of life. The Holy Spirit encounters have therefore gone a long way to bridge the gap that existed between African indigenous religious consciousness and the type of Christianity introduced by the early missionaries into Nigeria before the colonial period. Through the Holy Spirit encounters, CAC has been able to incorporate indigenous African taste in interpreting the spiritual gifts of revelations through dreams, discerning spirit, prophecy and the healing power.

To this end, it is evident that from the works of the CAC pioneering leaders, divine healings and revelations are real. The stability and growth that the Church incurred in the past was as a result of the untiring efforts of the pioneering fathers of the Church (CAC). They had diligently sought the scripture to discover the gifts that could profit the Church for spiritual and numerical growth; and they had also explained how these gifts could be delivered without distortion or abuse to the entire populace. These attitudes have really promoted peace and harmony within the society and Christian communities

Finally, this study has made contribution to knowledge as it provides more information on the relevance of revelations and healings to the growth and development of the Christ Apostolic Church in Nigeria. It also broadens our understanding about the implications of revelations and healings in the CAC and on other Christian faiths in Nigeria. The study is, therefore, significant as it gives full details of beliefs and practices in the Church, the contributions and the legacies of patriarchs in the Christ Apostolic Church and their connections to the development of the Church through practices attributed to revelations and healings.

BIBLIOGRAPHY

Books

Abioye, N. O., *Uses of Psalms and the Words of God Inspired from Apostle J.A. Babalola* (1904-1959), Ilesha: Hope Publications, 2000.

Adegboyega, S. G., *Short History of the Apostolic Church in Nigeria,* Ibadan: Rosprint Industrial Press Ltd, 1978.

Ademakinwa, J. A., *Iwe Itan Ijo Aposteli Ti Kristi,* Lagos: Agege CAC Press Ltd, 1971.

Adeniyi, M. O. and Babalola E. O., *Yoruba Muslim-Christian Understanding in Nigeria,* Lagos: Eternal Communications Ltd, 2001.

Ajayi, J. F. A., *Christian Missions in Nigeria, 1841-1891,* London: Longman Press, 1965.

Akande, F., *Itan Igbesi Aye Woli ati Ajihinrere Samson Oladeji Akande (Baba Abiye) 1896-1992,* Ede: Gospel Promotion Outreach, 1989.

Alokan, A., *The Christ Apostolic Church (1928-1988),* Lagos: Ibukunola Printing   Press, 1991.

_____, *Cradle and Beyond,* Ile-Ife: Timade Ventures, 2005.

_____, *Christ Apostolic Church at 90,* Ile-Ife: Timade Ventures, 2010.

Anderson, A., *Zion and Pentecost*, Pretoria: University of South Africa Press, 2008.

Anim, P. N., *The History of How Full Gospel Church was Founded in Ghana (Then Gold Coasts Colony),* Accra: Graphic Press

_____, *An Introduction to Pentecostalism,* Cambridge: Cambridge University Press, 2004.

Ayandele, E. A., *The Missionary Impact on Modern Nigeria, 1842-1914: A Political Analysis,* London: Longman, 1966.

Ayegboyin, Deji and Ishola, Ademola S. A., *African Indigenous Churches, an Historical Perspective,* Lagos: Greater Heights Publications, 1997.

Babajide, D. O., *Ibere Ise Woli Joseph Babalola ati ti Woli Daniel Orekoya ni 1930*, Ilesha: Olalere Press, 1959.

Babalola, E. O., *Current Research Studies in Religious Institution,* Ile-Ife: 2001

Babalola, J. A., *Eto Iranti Ajodun ti a o maa se ni Odoodun Nipa Ibere ati Isoji Nla Christ Apostolic Church,* Lagos: Ibukunola Printers Nig Ltd, 1954.

Babatope, J. A., *The Hero of Faith: The Apostolic Church,* Ilesha: Haastrup Press, 1993.

Baille, J., *The Idea of Revelation in Recent Thought,* New York: Columbia UP, 1956.

Barr, J., *Fundamentalist,* London: Macmillan, 1977.

Beetham, T. A., *Christianity and the New Africa,* London: O.U.P.1967.

Best, T. and Dagmar, H., (eds.), *Worship Today: Understanding, Practice, Ecumenical Implications*, Geneva: WCC Publications, 2004.

_____, *So We Believe, So We Pray*, Geneva: WCC Publications, 1995.

Boer, H., *Pentecost and Missions*, London: Lutterworth Press, 1961.

_____, *A Short History of the Church*, Ibadan: Daystar, 1976.

Brunner, F. D., *A Theology of the Holy Spirit; The Pentecostal Experience and the New Testament Witness,* New York: Paulist Press, 1991.

Chamber, M., *Jesus of Oyingbo*, London: New Society Publications, 1964.

Dulles, A., *Models of Revelation*, New York: Image Press, 1985.

Dzurgba, Akpenpuun, *The Sociology of Religion*, Ibadan: Wemilore Press, Nig. Ltd, 1991.

Edwards, D., *Christianity, the First Two Thousand Years*, London: Redwood Publishing Book, 1998.

Ekundayo, C., *History and Ministerial Life of Joseph Ayo Babalola (1904-1959),* Ibadan: United Christian Publications, 2004.

Engelbert, B., *New Christian Movements in West Africa,* Ibadan: Oluseyi Press, 1997.

Erivwo, S. W., *A History of Christianity in Nigeria: The Urhobo, the Isoko and the Itsekiri,* Ibadan: Daystar Press, 1979.

Evelyn, F., *Christian Healing: A Consideration of the Place of Spiritual Healing in the Church of Today in the Light of Doctrine and Practice of the Ante-Nicene Church:* London: Mobray and Co, Ltd,

1940.

Fashola-Luke, E. et al. (eds.), *Christianity in Independent Africa*, London: Rex, Collings, 1978.

Geerhardus Vos, *Biblical Theology, Old and New Testaments*, Michigan: Eerdmans, Publishing Company, 1991.

Grimley, J. B. and Robinson, G. E., *Church Growth in Central and Southern Nigerian,* London: Grand Rapids, 1966.

Harvey, C., *Fire from Heaven: The Rise of Pentecostal Spirituality and the Reshaping of Religion in the Twenty-First Century,* London: Oxford University Press 2008.

Hastings, A., *African Christianity,* London: O. U. P., 1967.

Heschel, A. J., *God in Search of Man: A Philosophy of Judaism,* New York: Noonday Publications, 1955.

Hexham, I., *Christianity Today,* London: Eerdmans Publishing Company, 1977.

Hodges, M. A., *A Guide to Church Planting and Development,* Chicago: Moody Bible Institute. 1973.

Hollenweger, W. J., *The Pentecostals,* London: SCM Press, 1972.

Idowu, E. B., *Olodumare: God in Yoruba Belief,* Ikeja: Longman Publications, 1962.

_____, *Towards an Indigenous Church*, London: Edwards Arnold Press, 1968.

Idowu, M. O., *Joseph Babalola, Thoughts of an Apostle,* Lagos: Artillery Christian

Publications, 2000.

_____, *Joseph Ayo Babalola, the Mantle of an Apostle,* Lagos: Artillery Christian Publications, 2009.

Ishola, Ademola and Ayegboyin, Deji (eds.), *Rediscovering and Fostering Unity in the Body of Christ: The Nigerian Experience,* Lagos: ATF Publications, 2000

Isiramen, C. O., (ed.), *Religion and the Nigerian Nation: Some Topical Issues,* Ibadan: En-Joy Press and Books, 2010.

Iwe Ilana ati Eko Ti Ijo Aposteli Kristi Nibi Gbogbo, Ilesha: Ilesanmi Press, 1968.

Kalu, O., *African Pentecostalism: An Introduction*, New York: Oxford University Press, 2008.

_____, *The History of Christianity in West Africa,* London: Longman, 1980.

Lucas, P., *New Religious Movements in the 21st Century*, New York: Routledge Publications, 2004.

Marshall, R., *Political Spiritualities: The Pentecostal Revolution in Nigeria,* Chicago: University of Chicago Press, 2009.

Mbiti, J. S., *African Religions and Philosophy*, London: Heinemann Press, 1969.

Medaiyese, J. A., *Itan Igbedide Woli Joseph Ayo Babalola fun Ise Ihinrere*, Ibadan: Oluseyi Press, 1956.

Mcgrath, A., *Heresy, a History of Defending* the *Truth*, London: Ashford Colour Press, 2009.

Ndiokwere, N., *The African Church Today and Tomorrow: Prospects and Challenges*, Onitsha: Effective Key Publishers, 1994.

_____, *Prophecy and Revolution: The Role of Prophets in the Independent African Churches and in Biblical Traditions,* London: Camelot Press Ltd, 1981.

Nyamiti, C., *Studies in African Theology: Some Contemporary Models of African Ecclesiology: A Critical Assessment in the Light of Biblical and Church Teaching*, Nairobi: CUEA Publications, 2007.

Ogungbile, D. O. and Akinade, A. (eds.), *Creativity and Change in Nigerian Christianity,* Lagos: Malthouse Press Limited, 2010.

Ojo, J. Odunayo, *The Life and Ministry of Apostle Joseph Ayo Babalola,* (From 1904-1959) Lagos: Prayer Band Publications, 1988.

Ojo, J. O., *The History and Ministries of Some Past Leaders of Christ Apostolic Church,* Ile-Ife: Timade Ventures, 2008.

Okoronkwo, S. N., *Christ Apostolic Church, Igbo land, 1952-2002*, Enugu: El-Demak Publishers, 2003.

Olayiwola, D. O., *The Anglican Church in Egbaland, History of its Genesis, Development and Impact,* Abeokuta: Gbemi Sodipo Press Ltd, 2009.

Olowe, A., *A Great Revival, Great Revivalist: Joseph Ayo Babalola,* Texas: Omega Publishers, 2007.

Oloye, D. O., *Itan Ibere Isin Igbagbo Ni Ijo Aposteli Ti Kristi ni Ilu Owo,* Lagos: Kemington Onabanjo Enterprise, 1974.

Oluwamakin, D., *Olododo Yoo wa ni Iranti Titi Aye,* Ilorin: Amazin Grace, 2007.

Olusheye, E.H.L., *A Short History of the Christ Apostolic Church,* Lagos: Artillery Christian Ministry Publications, 1993.

_____, *The Legacies of Our Church Patriarchs,* Ibadan: Gideon Global Press, 2010.

Olusumbola, O., *The Growth of Christ Apostolic Church in Erin-Ijesa,* Ibadan: Ayo Press Publishing Company, 2001.

Olupona, Jacob and Toyin Falola (eds.), *Religion and Society in Nigeria: Historical and Sociological Perspectives,* Ijebu Ife: Adeyemi Press Ltd., 1991.

Olujobi, D. O., *Awon Isotele Woli Giga Josefu Ayodele Babalola, 1928 – 1958,* Abeokuta: CAC Owode-Egbado Press, 1992.

Oluyoung, J. O., *Awon Oro Isotele lati Enu Woli Josefu Ayo Babalola: Bere lati 1930-1959,* Oshogbo: Owonifari Printing Works, 1965.

Omoyajowo, J. A., *Cherubim and Seraphim: The History of an African Independent Church,* Lagos: NOK Publications, 1982.

_____, *Church and Society,* Ibadan: Baptist Press, 2002.

_____, *Diversity in Unity: The Development and Expansion of the C&S Church in Nigeria,* Lanhan: UP of America Press, 1982.

_____, *Religion, Society and the Home,* Ijebu Ode: Vicoo International Press, 2001.

Onovughakpo, S., *History and Doctrine of the C &S (Nigeria),* Warri: Midland Press, 1971.

Oshitelu, G. A., *History of the Aladura (Independent) Churches, 1918-1940, an Interpretation,* Ibadan: Hope Publications Ltd, 2007.

Oshitelu, R., *African Instituted Churches: Diversities, Growth, Gifts, Spirituality and Ecumenical Understanding,* London: Hamburg, 2002.

Osiegbu, John, *Prophet Obadare-a Brief Profile,* Akure: Wosem Press, 1985.

Peel, J. D. Y., *Aladura: A Religious Movement among the Yoruba,* London: Oxford Press, 1968.

Pollock, J., *Billy Graham: Evangelist to the World,* New York: Harper and Row, 1979.

Porterfield, A., *Healing in the History of Christianity*, New York: Oxford University Press, 2005.

Rouse, R. and Neill, C. (eds.), *A History of the Ecumenical Movement 1517-1948,* Volume 1, Geneva: WCC Publications, 2004.

Simpson, G. E., *Yoruba Religion and Medicine in Ibadan,* Ibadan: University Press, 1999

Starkey, L. M. (Jr.), *The Holy Spirit at Work in the Church*, London: Macmillan, 1980.

Steward, B., *Historical Background of Churches in Nigeria,* Lagos: Interwale Press Limited, 1980.

Sundkler, B., *Zulu Zion and some Swazi Zionists,* London: O.U.P., 1976.

Tasie, G. O. M., *Christian Missionary Enterprise in the Nigeria Delta,* 1864 – 1918, London: Brill, 1978.

Thorogood, B., *Gales of Changes; Responding to a Shifting Missionary Context,* Geneva: WCC Publications, 2010.

Tillich, Paul, *Systematic Theology I*, Chicago: University of Chicago Press, 2005.

Turner, H. W., *History of an African Independent Church, The Church of the Lord Aladura*, London: O.U.P., 1967.

Turner, H. W., *Religious Innovations in Africa: Collected Essays on New Religious Movements*, London: G. K. Hall and Company, 1979.

Vaughan, I. J., *The Origins of Apostolic Church Pentecostalism in Nigeria*, London: IPSWICH Book Company, 1991.

Webster, J. B., *The African Churches among the Yoruba*, Oxford: Clarendon Press, 1964.

Westberg, G. E. *Theological Roots of Wholistic Health Care,* Hinsdale Illinois: Wholistic Centre Inc., 1979.

Wilson, Bryan and Jamie Cresswell (eds.), *New Religious Movements: Challenge and Response,* London and New York: Routledge, 1999.

Articles in Books and Journals

Abney, L. L., "Demons in the First Century," Ogbomosho *Journal of*

Theology, No 2, 1987, pp. 27-42.

Adedeji, S. O., "The Theology and Practice of Music Therapy in Nigerian Indigenous Churches: Christ Apostolic Church as a Case Study," in *Asia Journal of Theology*, India 22 (1), 2008, pp.142-154.

Adelowo, E. Dada, "A Comparative Study of the Phenomenon of Prophecy in the Bible and the Qur'an," *Ife Journal of Religions*, Vol. 11, 1982, pp. 38-55

Adewale, S. A. "African Church Movement and Impact on Socio-Religious Life in Nigeria," in Emefie Ikenga Metuh (ed.), *The Gods in Retreat: Continuous and Change in African Religion*, Ibadan: Claverianum Press, 1985, pp. 174-183

Asaju, D. F., "Noise, Fire and Flame Anointing and Breakthrough Phenomena among the Evangelicals," in Ogungbile, David O. and Akintunde Akinade (eds.), *Creativity and Change in Nigerian Christianity*, Lagos: Malthouse Press Limited, 2010, pp. 95-108.

Ayandele, E. A., "The Aladura among the Yoruba: A Challenge to the 'Orthodox' Churches," in Kalu, O. (ed.), *Christianity in West Africa: The Nigerian Story*, Ibadan: Daystar Press, 1978, pp. 20-25.

Babalola E.O. "The Phenomenon of Medicine and Healing," in M. O.Adeniyi and E. O. Babalola (eds.), *Yoruba Muslim-Christian in Nigeria*, Lagos: Eternal Communications Ltd, 2001, pp. 52-58.

_____, "Aladura Churches and the Phenomenon of Spirit Possession," in Wellington, O. Weneka (ed.), *Religion and Spirituality*, Port Harcourt: Emhai Printing and Publications Co., 2001, pp. 156-164

Fatokun, S. A., "The Apostolic Church Nigeria: The 'Metamorphosis' of an African Indigenous Prophetic-Healing Movement into a Classical Pentecostal Denomination," *ORITA*, Vol. XXXVII, 2006, pp. 49-70.

Hackett, Rosalind, "Thirty Years of Growth and Change in a West African Independent Church – a Sociological Perspective," *Journal of Religion in Africa*, Xi: 3, 1980, pp. 212-224.

_____, "Nigeria's Aladura Churches-Gateways or Barriers to Social Development," *Africana Marburgensia*, Vol. XIVI, 1981, pp. 60-72

235

Hocken, Peter, "Pentecostals," in Nicholas Lossky, et al. (eds.), *Dictionary of the Ecumenical Movement*, Geneva: WCC Publications, 2002, pp. 900-902

Hollenweger, W. J., "The Theological Challenge of Indigenous Churches," in A. F. Walls and W. R. Shenk, (eds.), *Exploring New Religious Movements. Essays in Honour of Harold W. Turner,* Elkhart: Mission Focus Publications, 1990, pp. 163-168

Idamarhare, A. O., "Therapeutic Technique in the Acts of the Apostle in the Context of Healing in Selected Pentecostal churches in Nigeria," *NABIS*, 2004, pp. 236-247

Kalu, O. (ed.), *Christianity in West Africa: The Nigerian Story*, Ibadan: Daystar Press, 1978, p. 333-342

Labeodan, Helen Adekunle "Moral Responsibility and Punishment in the Yoruba Society," *ORITA*, XXX VI/1-2, 2004, pp. 31-42

Macchia, Frank. "Pentecost", in Nicholas Lossky, Jose Mignez Buonino, John Pobee, etal (eds.), *Dictionary of the Ecumenical Movement,* Geneva: WCC Publications, 2002, pp. 897-899

Marshall, R., "Pentecostalism in Southern Nigeria: an Overview," in P. Gifford (ed.), *New Dimensions in African Christianity,* Nairobi: AACC No 3, 1992, pp. 8-35

Nkwoka, A. O., "Healing: The Biblical Perspective," *NABIS,* Vol. VII, No.1, 1992, pp. 20-34

_____, "Interrogating the Form and the Spirit: Pentecostalism and the Anglican Communion in Nigeria," in Ogungbile, David and Akintunde Akinade (eds.), *Creativity and Change in Nigerian Christianity*, Lagos: Malthouse Press Limited, 2010, pp. 79-94.

Obi, Chris, "The Sign of Character of Speaking in Tongues in Pentecostal Spirituality: A Critique," in Wellington D. Wotogbe-Weneka (ed.), *Religion and Spirituality,* Port Harcourt: Emhai Printing & Publishing Co., 2001. pp. 135-155

Offiong, E. A., "Varieties of Christian Spirituality in Nigeria," in Wellington D. Wotogbe –Weneka (ed.), *Religion and Spirituality*, Port Harcourt, Emhai Printing and publishing Company, 2001. pp. 183-190

Ogungbile, David O., "Meeting Point of Culture and Health: the Case of the Aladura in Nigeria," *Nordic Journal of African Studies*, Vol. 6,

No. 1, 1997, pp. 98-111

_____, "Prognostication, Explanation and Control: The Interaction of Ifa Divination Process and the Aladura Churches," in Adewole, Lawrence Olufemi (ed.), *Ifa and Related Genres,* Casas Book Series, No 13, Cape Town: 2001, pp. 84-95

_____, "Cultural Revolution and African Spirituality: the Case of Ijo Orile- Ede Adulawo Ti Kristi, Nigeria," *Journal of Inter-Religious Federation for World- Peace,* Vol. 18, No. 2, 2005, pp. 11-25

_____, "Faith without Borders: Culture, Identity and Nigerian immigrant Churches in Multicultural American Community," in David O. Ogungbile and Akintunde Akinade (eds.), *Creativity and Change in Nigerian Christianity,* Lagos: Malthouse Press Limited, 2010. pp. 311-331.

_____, "Creativity and Change in Nigerian Christianity: Issues and Perspectives," in David O. Ogungbile and Akintunde Akinade (eds.), *Creativity and Change in Nigerian Christianity,* Lagos: Malthouse Press Limited, 2010. pp. 1-18

Ogunrinade, Adeware, "Predilection for African Indigenous Practices in the Pentecostal Tradition of African Indigenous Churches with References to Christ Apostolic Church, Agbala-Itura," in *Cyber-Journal for Pentecostal Charismatic Research,* 2009, pp. 1-13.

Ojo, Matthews, "The Contextual Significance of the Charismatic Movements in Independent Nigeria," *Africa,* Vol. 58, No.2, 1988, pp. 175-192.

_____, "Deeper Life Bible Church of Nigeria," in P. Gifford (ed.), *New Dimensions in African Christianity,* Nairobi: AACC, No 3, 1992, pp. 161-183.

Okome, Mojubaolu Olufunke, "African Immigrant Churches and the New Christian Right," in J. K. Olupona and R. Gemignani (eds.), *African Immigrant Religions in America,* New York and London: New York University Press, 2007, pp. 279-305

Olayiwola, D. O., "The Aladura: Its Strategies for Muslim and Conversion in Yoruba land, Nigeria," *ORITA,* XIX, 1987, pp. 40-56.

_____, "Hermeneutical-Phenomenological Study of the Aladura Spirituality in Ijesa Social History," *Asia Journal of Theology,*

Vol.6, No.2, 1991, pp. 253-263.

_____, "Ilesha as a Centre of Revivalism: The Babalola and Obadare Movements Compared," *Journal of Ecumenical Association of the Third World*, Vol. 2, 1993, pp. 84-92.

Olupona, Jacob, "Contemporary Religious Terrain," in Jacob K. O. Olupona and Toyin Falola (eds.), *Religion and Society in Nigeria, Historical and Sociological Perspectives*, Ijebu Ife: Adeyemi Press Limited, 1991, pp. 31-41.

_____, "The Celestial Church of Christ in Ondo: a Phenomenological Perspective," in Rosalind, I.J, Hackett (ed.), *New Religious Movement*, New York: Edwin Mellen Press, 1987, pp. 45-73.

Olupona, Jacob and Regina Gemignani, "Introduction," in J. K. Olupona and R. Gemignani (eds.), *African Immigrant Religions in America*, New York and London: New York University Press, 2007, pp. 1-24.

Omoju, Olu, "CAC at 70", *Christ Apostolic Church Publications,* Vol.33, No 2, 2000, pp. 6-7.

Omotoye, Rotimi, "Women Spirituality in an African Independent Church: A Case Study of Captain Abiodun Akinsowon of the Cherubim and Seraphim Church," in Wellington O. Wotogbe-Weneka (ed.), *Religion and Spirituality,* Port Harcourt: Emhai Books, 2001, pp. 111-124.

Oshun, C. O., "Nigeria's Pentecostalism, Dynamics and Adaptability," *Journal of the Nigerian Association for the Study of Religions*, Vol. 8, 1983, pp. 47-49

_____, "The Pentecostal Perspective of the Christ Apostolic Church," *ORITA,* Vol. 15, 1983, pp. 105-114.

_____, "Aladura Presence in Nigeria: A Pentecostal Re-Awakening," in S. O. Abogunrin, et al. (eds.), *Christian Presence in West African Response Through the Years*, Ibadan: WAATI Publications, 1984, pp. 217-226.

_____, "The Aladura Movement and Its Impact on the Nigerian Society," Ikenga-Metuh, E. (ed.), *The Gods in Retreat: Continuity and Change in African Religion*, Enugu: Fourth Dimension Publishers, 1986, pp. 195-218.

_____, "Ministerial Preparations in an Aladura Church," Journal of Arabic and Religious Studies, Vol. 4, 1987, pp. 75-82.

_____, "Aladura Presence and Revivals in a Colonial Situation: A Conflict Model in Mission," in O. Kalu, (ed.), African Church Historiography: An Ecumenical Perspective, Leiter: Lukas Vischer, 1988, pp. 197-219.

_____, "The Experience of Christ Apostolic Church," in Ademola Ishola and Deji Ayegboyin (eds.), Rediscovering and Fostering Unity in the Body of Christ: The Nigerian Experience, Lagos: ATF Publications, 2000, pp. 150-173

Owoeye, S. A. "The Place of Music in Healing Processes among Contemporary Christian Prophet-healers in Yoruba land," Nigerian Music Review, No.3, 2003, pp. 33-46.

_____., "Charismatic Prophet—Healer and Their Healing Activities in Yoruba land," in D. O. Ogungbile and A. E. Akinade (eds.), Creativity and Change in Nigerian Christianity, Lagos: Malthouse Press Limited, 2010. pp 171-191

Oyalana, A. S., "Spiritual Healing: A Challenge to Mainline Churches in Contemporary Nigeria," in Wellington O. Wotogbe-Weneka (ed.), Religion and Spirituality, Port Harcourt: Emhai Books, 2001, pp. 125-134

Trembath, Kern Robert, "Revelations," in Nicholas Lossky, Jose Mignez Bonino, et al. (eds.) Dictionary of the Ecumenical Movement, Geneva: WCC Publications, 2002, pp. 983-987

Welsh, Robert, "The Wesleyan Church, the Christ Apostolic Church and Mennonites," in Welsh Robert (ed.) Faith and Order, Vol. 79, Geneva: WCC Publications, 1976, pp. 411- 420.

Conference Papers

Adedeji, S. O. "The Theology, Practice and Evolution of Indigenous Music of Christ Apostolic Church in Nigeria and the Diaspora: Issues in Christian Transformative Musicality," a paper presented at the first International Conference on the Origin of Christ Apostolic Church, the First Pentecostal Churches in Nigeria and Ghana, held on 6th-8th August, 2012 at Joseph Ayo Babalola University, Ikeji Arakeji, Osun State.

Gaiya, M. A., "The Pentecostal Revolution in Nigeria," an unpublished paper Conference presentation at the Center of African Studies, University of Copenhagen, International African Institute, 2002, pp. 5-10.

Igenoza, A. O., "Medicine and Healing in Nigerian Christianity: A Biblical Critique." A paper presented at the First Annual Religious Studies Conference of the Department of Religious Studies, University of Ife (OAU), 1986, pp. 11-17

Ojo, M. A., "Definitions of Health and Illness within Nigerian Charismatic Movements," a paper presented at the Conference of the African Association for the Study of Religions (AASR), 4th International Conference in Religion, Environment and Sustainable Development in Africa, 2010, at Obafemi Awolowo University, Ile Ife.

Omoyajowo, Akinyele, "The Phenomenon of the Cherubim and Seraphim in West Africa." A seminar paper presented at University of Ibadan, Nigeria, May 20th, 1971.

Oshun, C. O., "Spirituality and Healing in a Depressed Economy: The Case of Nigeria." A Paper presented at the International Association for Mission Studies (IAMS) Conference, Buenos Aires, Argentina, 10-17 April 1996, now published in *Mission Studies*,15-1 (29), 1998:32-35.

Dictionaries/Encyclopedias

Boyd, J., *Boyd Bible Dictionary,* New York: Holman Bible Publishers, 1980,

Brown, Colin, *Dictionary of New Testament Theology,* London: Paternoster Press, Vol.3, 1976.

Hanks, P. Collins (ed.), *Dictionary of the English Language,* Glasgow: Wlliam Collins Press, 1979.

Harrison, R. K., *The Interpreter's Dictionary of the Bible,* Abingdon Press, 1976

Lossky Nicholas, Bonino Jose Miguez, et al. (eds.), *Dictionary of the Ecumenical Movement*, Geneva: WCC Publications 2002.

C. Long Essays

Adeniran, F. O. "A Brief History of the Origin and Growth of Christ Apostolic Church in Ibadan (1930-1980)," B. A. Long Essay, Department of Religious Studies, University of Ibadan, 1984

Odufowote, G. O., "The Adoption Church as a Denominational Name in Nigeria," B. A. Long Essay, Dept. of Religious Studies, University of Ibadan, 1984.

D.   Theses/ Dissertation

Fatokun, S. A., "Pentecostal in South Western Nigeria with Emphasis on The Apostolic Church, 1931 – 2001", PhD Thesis submitted to the Department of Religious Studies, University of Ibadan, 2005.

Olayiwola, D.O., "The Aladura Movements in Ijesaland, 1930-1980", an unpublished Doctoral Thesis submitted to University of Ife now Obafemi Awolowo University, Ile-Ife, 1987.

Oludare, S. E. A., "The Trio of Christ Apostolic Church Fathers: Odubanjo, Akinyele and Babalola," an unpublished Master's Thesis, University of Ibadan, 1999.

Oshun, C. O., "Christ Apostolic Church of Nigeria: A Suggested Pentecostal Consideration of its Historical, Organizational and Theological Developments, 1918-1975", an unpublished Doctoral Thesis submitted to University of Exeter, 1981.

Owoeye, S. A., "African Healer Prophets in Selected Independent Churches in Yoruba land, 1963-1998"; an unpublished Doctoral Thesis submitted to the Faculty of Arts, Department of Religious Studies, Obafemi Awolowo University, Ile-Ife, 2000.

E.   Internet Sources

Akinwumi, E.O., "Eternal Sacred Order of Cherubim and Seraphim," http://en.wikipedia.org/wiki/ Updated on the 27th April 2010, accessed 5/5/2010

Ayegboyin, Deji "Christ Apostolic Church," http://thechrist apostolic church.org/. Updated in 30th March, 2010, accessed 10/5/2010

BBC   News,   26   February,   2004, http://news.bbc,co.uk/2/hi/programmes/wtwtgod/34094 90 Accessed 24/6/2010

Gary, B. McGee – http://talkingpentecostalism.blogsport.com/2006/10/what-is-pentecostalism.html. pp. 1-4. Accessed 12/6/2011

Glen, Harris, "Revelation in Christian Theology,"

www.churchsociety.org ,pp. 9-12. Accessed 24/8/2012

Harvey Cox – http://talkingpentecostal.blogspot.com/2006/10/what-is-pentecostalism.html. pp. 374. Accessed 14/6/2011

http://en.wikipedia.org.wiki/revelations. Cited on 1/4/2002. Accessed 14/6/2011

http://www.dacb.org/stories/nigeria/orimolade_moses.html. Accessed 14/6/2011

http://www.mechon-mamre.org/p/pt/pt09a22htm. Accessed 14/6/2011

http://www.opensourse theology.net/node/1368. Accessed on 1/4/2002.

APPENDIX I

National Archive Reports (FILE 662)- Series of Allegations Against the CAC Revivalists Particularly Joseph Ayo Babalola from1930 Upwards

Source: National Archives, Ibadan.

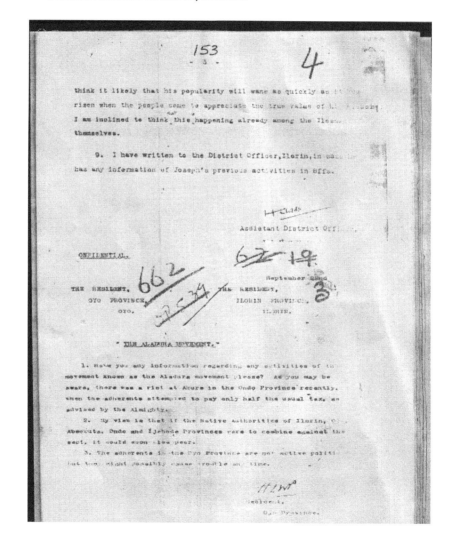

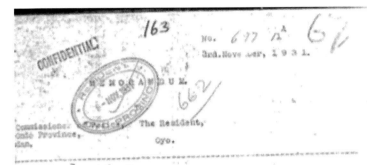

No. 677 /1^A

3rd.November, 1931.

CONFIDENTIAL

MEMORANDUM.

Commissioner,
Oyo Province,
Oyo.

The Resident,
Oyo.

Aladura Movement.

With reference to my memorandum No./1^A of 29th ulto.,
I have to report that the two Williams brothers and Turnbull
left for Lagos by train this morning at 9 a.m.

2. After arriving in Ibadan they did not leave the
town but had a series of meetings with the heads of the
various churches and sects including Babalola and Babaj16.

3. The proposal is to absorb Babalola and his followers
in the Apostolic Church and to establish Churches in Ibadan,
Ilesha and elsewhere under European Pastors.

4. I had an interview with the Williams and Turnbull
on 2nd inst. when they informed me of their intention of
placing their proposals before the Chief Secretary in Lagos
and to obtain permission to send out Missionaries.

5. In my opinion every effort should be made to oppose
the proposition. The tenets of the Apostolic Church are
most narrow although in no way as far as I can anti Government. The three pastors I have seen are narrow minded
and cannot be said to be educated to the standard one would
expect of ordained Ministers.

6. The idea has got about that these three pastors are
actually Prophets and faith-healers and that in Lagos they
cured a lame boy.

7. If these people are allowed to establish Churches
in Ibadan and Ilesha they will form the thin end of the
wedge. As you are aware a little injudicious preaching to

244

164

68

2.

masses of natives by ~~one~~ zealous religious cranks can
cause a lot of trouble and in view of present efforts
to re-establish trade in the country we cannot afford
to be embarassed by having the people upset by so called
prophets. X

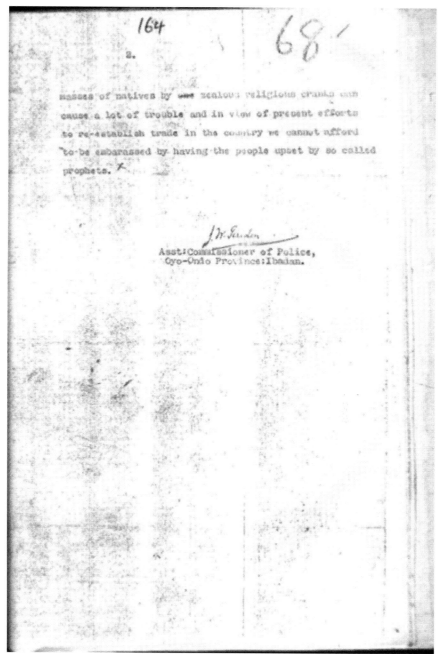

Asst:Commissioner of Police,
Oyo-Ondo Province:Ibadan.

APPENDIX II

Babalola as a Leader and Actor in the Faith Tabernacle Congregation in Nigeria

(Source: National Archives, Ibadan)

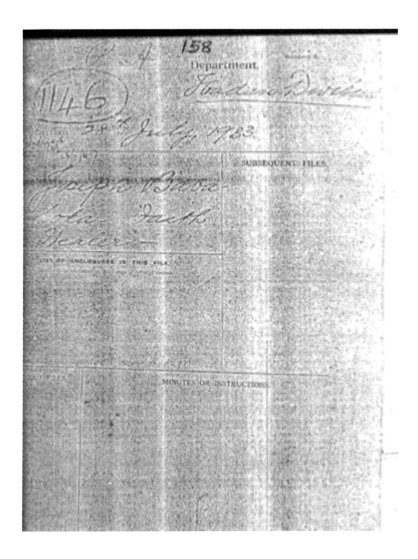

159

Confidential.

General No.

MEMORANDUM

No. CP. 408/16.

July 18th, 19[illegible].

From [illegible] Commissioner of Police. [illegible] Province. [illegible].

To The Divisional Officer. Ibadan.

Joseph Babalola, Faith Healer.

I shall be obliged if you will forward all [illegible]ble information regarding the above person. I understand that [illegible] some years he has been connected with the Aladura and Faith [illegible]acle Movements in your Area and in 1931 was charged with an [illegible] but discharged. He is now residing in Calabar and preaching [illegible] the Apostolic Church, being known as the Evangelist of this Mission.

[illegible]

Ag. Commissioner of Police.

[illegible] Chief.

You have expert knowledge of Joseph. Can you give some information re the Apostolic Church. Please [illegible] the [illegible] on his [illegible] activities

[illegible] 26/7

[illegible] JUL 193[illegible] DIVIS[illegible]

1140/8

29th July   33

atrict Officer,   The A..Commissioner of Police,

Ibadan.   Calabar Province,

Calabar.

JOSEPH BABALOLA - FAITH HEALER:

Your Memorandum No. CP. 489/18 of 19th July, 1933.

Joseph Babalola was a native of Offa in the Ilorin
Province. For a time, he was employed by the Public Works
Department as a Steam Roller driver.

2. In 1930, he had a hallucination and for the
next two years, he posed as a Faith-Healer holding meetings
at Ilesha, Ibadan, Offa and various centres in the Ondo
Province.

3. He enjoyed great notoriety and big crowds
attended his meetings at which the blessing of water was a
part of the ritual. So far as this Province was concerned,
the meetings were conducted in an orderly manner and he was
not charged with any offence. Your information on this point
may be derived from the Ondo Province where he seems to have
been continually in trouble. The Aladuras, it is understood,
were responsible for some agitation concerning taxation at
Akure.

4. He was closely associated with the Aladura and
Faith Tabernacle Movements and it was necessary to take steps
to check a campaign of misrepresentation which was begun with
the object of discrediting the established missions.

5. A West Indian, named Brown, took a prominent
part in these activities and especially in the dissemination
of various publications of American origin. While the contents
of these did not amount to libel or sedition, they were

nevertheless considered harmful in the hands of semi-
educated people, but Government policy in the matter
was not to interfere and to leave the people to discover for themselves, the speciousness of their propos
Mr. Brown controls what is called the International
Bible Union which has no connection with the Aladura
movement or with Babalola.

6. This policy has probably been justified
The Native Authorities were amused rather than concer
ed at the activities of the Aladura and there were no
wanting opportunities for making public the mercenary
motives of some of the promoters of the movement.

7. The Faith Tabernacle in Nigeria appeals
for help from the Apostolic Church in England, a sect
which believes in faith healing. Two missionaries -
Pastors Perfect and Vaughan - came to Nigeria and hav
visited Ibadan and Ilesha and the Faith Tabernacle ha
now become the Apostolic Church. Pastor Perfect, who
has his headquarters in Lagos, is a reasonable mission
and is anxious to work with peace and order. While he
dissassociates his mission from the Aladura movement,
he naturally does look then to increase his sect. In
Ilesha, he has started educational work. It is under
stood that Pastor Perfect interviewed Babalola in thi
Province, probably at Ilesha, but what transpired is
not known.

8. I hope this information is of some use.

APPENDIX III

SERIES OF HEALINGS AND TESTIMONIES
(Source: Oshun PhD. p.79)

IIIA -OBADARE'S REVIVAL

No.	NAME	SEX	PERSONAL TESTIMONIES
1	Felicia Adeyemi	F	Poisoned for ten years.
2.	Antony Olaniran	M	Ibadan graduate, partially mental due to accident in 1968.
3.	Abigail Owoyemi	F	Severe back pain for 13 months.
4.	Joseph Aseperi	M	Mental illness since 1958 (21 years) X
5.	Oladipo Fasakin	M	Sickle cell for 4 years. X
6.	Taiwo Ogunlade	F	9 year old, lame from birth.
7.	Ezekiel Talabi	M	Sleeplessness, blindness, stomach ache for 21 years.
8.	James Olowokere	M	Sleeplessness for 25 years.
9.	Mary Olaniyi	F	Lame for 3½ years.
10.	Funke Oke	F	3 yr. old, deaf, dumb, lame, blind, right arm paralysed.
11.	Jelili Sule	M	8 yr. old, lame from birth.

250

NO.	SEX	PERSONAL TESTIMONIES
12. Oladejo Oni	M	Lame for 13 years.
13. Yemisi Obadiya	F	Barren for 11 years.
14. Segun Akinola	M	Had joined 16 secret cults between 1967 and 1976.
15. Taibatu Adekoya	F	Former queen, emere (fairy) society.
16. Esther Joseph	F	Former member of 5 emere (fairy) society, claimed 14 powers in her eyes, 14 reincarnations, Dugbe Market inferno in Ibadan in December 1978 and a bus accident on the Lagos lagoon on 1st June 1979 caused by her group.
17. Folabomi Idowu	F	Former queen, emere (fairy) society.
18. Suratu Lasisi	F	Rheumatism for 1 year. X
19. Adeyemi	M	An old man, bed-ridden for 11 years. X
20. Florence Oredugba	F	Serious headache and hypertension. X
21. Jade Adegboyega	F	Experienced drowsiness from 1969. X
22. Abigail	F	Barren for 14 years. X
23. Yemisi	F	Former deputy head, emere (fairy) society claimed her group was behind Dugbe Market fire disaster of December, 1978. X
24. Alice Ogundeji	F	Member, emere (fairy) society involved in the Dugbe Market inferno. X
25. O. Oyelagbe	F	Member, emere (fairy) society, possessed demonic powers, witchcraft inclusive. X
26. V. Akinleye	F	Member, emere (fairy) society, possessed demonic powers. X
27. Mary Tayo	F	Member of 5 emere (fairy) societies, claimed to have exacted punitive measures on both her father and husband. X

(N.B. X = Healings accomplished on 21st June, 1979).

APPENDIX IV

COMPREHESIVE DEATH RECORDS OF TOP LEADERS IN CAC FROM 2000 -
2010, FROM THE CAC ARCHIVES

(SOURCE- CAC PASTORS CONFERENCE AND CONVENTIONS PAMPLETS)

DECEASED PASTORS FROM SEPTEMBER 2001 TO AUGUST 2002

1. Pastor Samuel Adeniran Afolabi	22. Pastor David A. Adeniji
2. Pastor Evang. J. P. Olawale (Rtd)	23. AGS Pastor J. A. Adesakin
3. AGS Pastor (Dr) D. A. Coker JP.	24. Pastor M.O. Balogun
4. Pastor Habila Gajih (Rtd)	25. Pastor Samuel A. Olorunmola
5. Pastor Yohanna Mafuli	26. Pastor D. O. Ariyo
6. Pastor J. A. Oyedele	27. Pastor J. A. Ayamolowo
7. Pastor Julius O. Emefe	28. AGS Pastor D. F. Adeyegbe
8. Pastor Silver V. Aruosighe	29. Pastor I. A. Olanibi
9. Pastor Samuila Fonibak	30. Pastor D. A. Obasanya
10. Pastor A. A. Adetayo	31. DGS Pastor S. A. Ekebafe
11. DS Pastor J. E. Idogbe	32. AGS Pastor P. F. Akinsanya
12. Pastor E. A. Olufowobi	33. DS Pastor J. S. Manannan
13. Pastor James Adewumi Olore	34. AGS Pastor S. A. Ogunlusi
14. AGS Pastor S. A. Babatunde	35. AGS Pastor G. O. Fanimokun (Rtd)
15. Supt. Pastor L. A. Emiade	36. AGE Pastor S. O. Folahan
16. Pastor J. Sunday Ojo	37. Pastor J. S. Onakoya
17. Pastor S.O. Adetiran (Rtd)	38. AGS Pastor I.D. Ibitoye
18. Pastor A. A. Abolade (Rtd)	39. Pastor J. O. Oni
19. Pastor Simeon Omotoso	40. Pastor I. O. Oluwabusola
20. Supt. Pastor S. O. Olubodun	41. AGE Pastor D. O. Olagbenjo
21. Pastor David O. Ogunlade	42. DGS Pastor J. A. Akinbileje

TRANSITION

1.	Pastor S.A. Adepoju	28/9/03
2.	Pastor I.K. Ojo	1/10/03
3.	Pastor E.O. Babalola	24/10/03
4.	Pastor J.O. Kayode	Sept. 2003
5.	Pastor G.O. Adeniyi	2/10/03
6.	" Christopher Anya	7/10/03
7.	" M.A. Oluwajuyigbe	18/01/04
8.	" P.O. Agbabiaka	24/01/04
9.	" I.A. Adebiyi	
10	" J.O. Ogunsola	
11.	" D.A. Adeleke	12/01/04
12.	" D.A. Ashaju	10/02/04
13.	" P.O. Omidiran	11/02/04
14.	" O.A. Okhitoya	13/01/04
15.	" S.N. Akansi	19/08/03
16.	" M.A. Adediran	06/02/04
17.	" J.O. Oluwadero	22/02/04
18.	" M.O. Omiyale	26/04/02
19.	" J.O. Olagunju	25/03/04
20.	" G.O. Kayode	28/10/03
21.	" S.D. Alabi	22/03/04
22.	" E.O. Elesho	26/04/04
23.	" S.O. Olorunnisomo	26/02/04
24.	" J.A. Adedini	04/05/04
25.	" S.O. Taiwo	10/05/04
26.	" D.A. Dada	30/04/04
27.	" S.O. Omotosho	05/05/04
28.	" W.O. Adepoju	01/06/04
29.	" E.O.O. Anjorin	21/05/04
30.	" T.A. Olowolaju	27/05/04
31.	" F.O. Akinbola	27/05/04
32.	" J.M. Akingbolu	24/05/04
33.	" B.I. Emerivem	10/06/04

30

TRANSITION

1.	Moses Sunday Dare	01-07-04
2.	Ezekiel Ajao Abimbola	14-05-04
3.	Akin Dada Jimoh	13-07-04
4.	John Adebayo Alabi	07-06-04
5.	Emmanuel O. Oluwajemilehin	09-08-04
6.	Blessing Bibi Ogundele	20-07-04
7.	Isaac Olabisi Olakunori	26-07-04
8.	James Oye Adegbenro	10-07-04
9.	Israel O. Feruke	09-11-03
10.	Joseph O. Idowu	06-06-04
11.	Moses Oladokun Olagunju	21-03-05
12.	Peter O. Umakha	13-07-04
13.	George Olusheye Shodiya	11-06-04
14.	Michael Gbadebo Oyejide	
15.	Isaac Ayorinde Olatunbosun	17-08-02
16.	Isaac Obasanjo Shoneye	26-08-04
17.	Timothy O. Olugbemi	06-10-04
18.	Ezekiel Kehinde Ige	30-09-04
19.	Reuben Masara Doy	19-09-04
20.	Ezekiel Omobamikole Akinjagunla	15-07-04
21.	George Oluwole Alonge	27-09-04
22.	Joshua Adeniyi Adesina	27-10-04
23.	Joseph Oyeyemi Bale Oladapo	23-10-04
24.	Johnson Olatunde Aduloju	04-10-04
25.	Timothy A. Eiyebiokin	25-10-04
26.	D Jr. Ekanem	21-05-04
27.	Daniel O. Adedoyin	09-10-04
28	Amos Aleshinloye Soyebi	19-10-04
29.	Jonathan Ajibade Bepo	13-05-04
30.	Joseph A. Adebowale	07-10-04
31.	A. A. Owomoyela	19-10-04

32.	Simeon Samuel Mabur	16-11-04
33.	Peter Oluwagbemi Osoku	27-06-04
34.	G. A. Kayode	20-10-04
35.	J.A. Gbade	20-09-04
36.	J. A. Ayelabola	29-11-04
37.	Samuel O. Ajibuwa	30-11-04
38.	Timothy Olufemi Ibitomi	12-12-04
39.	Timothy Ojo Onile	22-12-04
40.	Lawrence P. Odedele	26-12-04
41.	Joseph Kehinde Sanusi	20-01-01
42.	J. A. O. Ademibawa	22-12-04
43.	S. A. Adewale	Oct. 04
44.	J. A. Apata	29-12-04
45.	Gabriel Attafo	10-09-04
46.	Simeon A. Fajeminigba	13-11-04
47.	Michael Oluwarotimi Anjorin	27-01-05
48.	B. U. Etuk	12-12-04
49.	Isaac Ngene Njoku	
50.	James Agboola Olaseinde	24-02-05
51.	Daniel O. Oloriegbe	25-02-05
52.	S. A. B. Mobolade	
53.	Isaac N. Amaka	08-01-05
54.	Marion Bitrus Haruna	08-01-05
55.	Julius Abodunrin Taiwo	09-11-04
56.	Samuel Sunday A. Odeluyi	09-03-05
57.	Joshua Ola Olubiyi	29-03-05
58.	Ethien Tanimowo Isanbiyi	01-11-04
59.	Shadrack Efe Otobrise	02-05-05
60.	Daniel Ogbuodi Anyim	25-03-05
61.	Joseph O. Chima	08-06-05
62.	Matthew Abiodun Esuola	02-07-05
63.	David Ishola Ogunlolu	23-06-05

Transition

S/N	Name	Date
1.	Amos Sandi Edf	25-12-2005
2.	Stephen Shanu Ojo	20-7-2005
3.	John K. Abegunde	5-7-2005
4.	Daniel Oluwatoyin Oke	9-6-2005
5.	John Olatunde Olawuyi	4-8-2005
6.	Peter Sunday Eniwiolorun	4-8-2005
7.	Samuel Ibasoluyi Olowomeye	21-8-2005
8.	Joseph O. Faaji	20-8-2005
9.	Iyiola Kolawole Adigun	17-5-2005
10.	Joseph Bola Adeyemi	1-6-2005
11.	David A. Larayetan	24-8-2005
12.	Johnson Oluwatobi Oladele	7-9-2005
13.	James Olasunkanmi Adegbite	31-8-2005
14.	Lawrence Oladipupo Ayoola	15-6-2005
15.	Michael Abiodun Afolayin	21-7-2005
16.	Isabon Kabo Dipeolu	
17.	Titus Sunday Akpan	16-9-2005
18.	Isaac Olaoluwa Bakare	27-9-2005
19.	Abednego M. Akiling	30-9-2005
20.	Joshua Popoola Ogundipe	11-10-2005
21.	Albert Omo-Philip Aijiaboyo	-7-2005
22.	Peter Akanni Odusina	7-11-2005
23.	Joseph Oladosu Oke	1-11-2005
24.	Samuel Olatunji Olu Idowu	1-9-2005
25.	Benjamin Aodu Adejah	25-11-2005
26.	Nathaniel Olawoye Ayanfeoluwa	4-7-2005
27.	Samuel Samson Omopariola	23-11-2005
28.	Joseph Omotosho	-12-2005

29.	Emmanuel Adekunle Amudipe	17-12-2005
30.	George Babatunde Arije	17-12-2005
31.	Festus Babatunde Aiyedibe	21-12-2005
32.	Isaiah Ayinde Adeleye	6-1-2005
33.	Elijah O. Oyenekan	17-10-2005
34.	Ezekiah Ogunleye	16-3-2005
35.	Joseph Samiya	2-3-2004
36.	Emmanuel Oyelami Olayinka	28-9-2005
37.	David A. Akeredolu	12-2-2006
38.	Solomon Araromi Owoniyi	4-3-2004
39.	Ephraim Moses Kamrali	13-2-2006
40.	Solomon Adegoke Ogundeji	25-3-2006
41.	Ezekieli Adekunle Babarinde	29-3-2006
42.	Jacob D. Omokehinde	26-3-2006
43.	David Akande Oluwafemi	15-3-2006
44.	Moses Ojo Olanrewaju	15-2-2006
45.	Jacob Kayode Obisesan	4-3-2006
46.	Simeon Sijuade Oyeyemi	14-4-2006
47.	Josiah Ojo Adesuyi	29-4-2006
48.	Johnson Odunayo Akinyemi	22-4-2006
49.	Ezekiel Adebayo Adeyemo	22-4-2006
50.	J.A. Adedeji	22-5-2006
51.	Joseph Olatunji Owoeye	15-5-2006
52.	Elijah Ajiboye Oyedokun	24-4-2006
53.	Joseph Olusegun Asonibare	4-6-2006
54.	Deon Emmanuel Ademola	4-6-2006
55.	David Oduola Oyewo	3-6-2006
56.	P.A. Akintoye	
57.	Simeon Bauwaji Olusegun	20-4-2006
58.	Emmanuel Imonode Aikhionbare	25-6-2006

QUESTIONNAIRE
TITLE OF THESIS: THE PLACE OF REVELATIONS AND HEALINGS IN THE PRACTICES OF CHRIST APOSTOLIC CHURCH, NIGERIA, 1930 – 1994

Dear Respondent,

This questionnaire is sub-divided into three sections. The first section deals with your biodata while the remaining two sections deal with questions on the proposed research.

Also, the questionnaire aims at determining the place of Christ Apostolic Church on the religious practices of revelations and healing at the inception of the Church in comparison with the development in the ministerial and institutional changes that have taken place from 1980 – 1994.

The questionnaire also aims at understanding the oral tradition connected with the activities of leaders in the Church particularly in the areas of revelations and healing 1930 – 1994.

Lastly, the questionnaire aims at investigating the crises and schisms in the Christ Apostolic Church from 1990 – 1994, and their links with practices attributed to revelations and healings.

INSTRUCTION

Tick appropriate Box (Yes or No) and answer other questions as indicated in the questionnaire.

Please, your sincere answer to all questions will be appreciated and treated as confidential.

Thank you, Sir/Ma.

SECTION A

1. Name:_____

2. Age: 30-45 ☐ 45-55 ☐ 55-60 ☐ above 60 ☐

3. Marital Status: Married ☐ Widow/Widower ☐ Separated ☐

4. Professional Status _____

5. Ethnic Group: Yoruba ☐ Ibo ☐ Hausa ☐ Others ☐

6. Town:_____

7. Level of Education: Primary School ☐ Secondary School ☐

   Post Secondary ☐ University ☐ Others ☐

8. Religion:_____

9. Denomination: CAC ☐ Methodist ☐ Anglican ☐

   Celestial ☐ Any other denomination ☐

10. Title/Status in church: Bishop ☐ Chairman ☐ D/S ☐

    Pastor ☐ Evangelist ☐ Teacher ☐ Elder ☐
    Deacon ☐ Deaconess ☐ Others ☐

SECTION B

1. Have you ever heard about Christ Apostolic Church? Yes ☐ No ☐

2. If yes, when was Christ Apostolic Church established in your area?

258

3. How old were you then? _____

4. Are you a member of CAC? Yes ☐ No ☐

5. If you are a CAC member, when did you join the denomination? _____

6. Were you born and bred by a CAC Parent? _____

7. Were you once a CAC minister or member? Yes ☐ No ☐

8. If you were not originally a CAC member, how did you get converted to the Church? _____

9. Do you have special things that you prefer in CAC to other denomination?
Yes ☐ No ☐

10. If yes, list the things in order of importance

_____

11. Are you conversant with the Tenets and Practices of the Christ Apostolic Church?
Yes ☐ No ☐

12. Have you ever heard about the issue of divine healing in CAC? Yes ☐ No ☐

13. What is divine healing? _____

14. What do you understand about Revelation? _____

15. Do we classify Trance, Dreams, Prophecy, Speaking and Interpretation of tongue as part of revelation in the CAC? (Comments) _____

16. Do you believe that the CAC has its views about the use of revelation in the Church? Yes ☐ No ☐

17. Do you believe that CAC encourages the use of revelation to win converts only into the church? Yes ☐ No ☐

18. Do you believe that CAC Authority encourages leaders in the various assemblies to give sound teaching about the word of God and not just indoctrinating them with revelations? Yes ☐ No ☐

19. What is the relevance of revelation and healings in the growth of Christ Apostolic Church? _____

20. Do you agree that the religious practices of revelations and healing have contributed to the tremendous growth and divisions in the Church from 1930 1994?
Yes ☐ No ☐ Comment _____

21. Could the schisms and division in the CAC today be attributed to leadership problems? Yes ☐ No ☐ If Yes, Comment _____

22. What do General Executive Council and Supreme Council stand for in the Christ ApostolicChurch? _____

23. Do you agree that the CAC patriarchs had left the legacies in the building of revelations and healings? Yes ☐ No ☐ If Yes, how? _____

24. Do you agree that the CAC patriarchs did not support secession or operations of ministries within the Church? Yes ☐ No ☐ If Yes, make comments _____

25. What do you understand by the term, "Abuse of Gift"? _____

26. What are the efforts made by the leaders in your local assemblies to curb excesses in the use of spiritual gift by gifted leaders in the church? Discuss

_____
_____
_____

27. What is divination? How is it different from prophetic consultation?
_____

28. Do you have records of healings in your local assembly? Yes ☐ No ☐ If Yes,
Which assembly and when?
_____

29. Do you have records of when faith healings failed to work according to
expectations in your local assembly? Yes ☐   No ☐   If Yes, which
assembly and on what occasion?

_____

SECTION C

30. Do you agree that the practices of revelations and healings have contributed
immensely to crises that started in the Church between 1989 &1994? Yes ☐ No ☐
If Yes, comment
_____
_____

If No comment_____
_____

_____
31. As an observer or church member, what were the effects of crises on the
development and expansion of the Church?
_____

_____
32. Before the crises, can you give records of how many prophets in your assembly
particularly in 1989? (Mention the No of prophets and your assembly)
_____

_____
33. At the initial stage of the crises in 1990, how many prophets were in your
assembly? (Mention the no of prophets and your assembly)
_____
_____

34. At the climax of the crises between 1991 and 1992, how many prophets were in
your assembly? (Mention the no of prophets for 1991 and 1992 separately and your
assembly)
_____
_____

_____
35. What is your assessment? Do you think the crises have contributed to the
numerical strength in your assembly or not? Yes ☐ No ☐ If No, why?
_____
_____

_____
36. In spite of this division, the CAC continues to survive and also increase in
number. Do you agree with this view? Yes ☐   No ☐   If Yes, what is your
justification?

If No, support your view with evidences_____

Thanks.
From: Olusegun Alokan

Printed in Great Britain
by Amazon